TUCK IN!

TUCK IN!

A Feast of resource ideas for Christian Youth Workers and Young People

by
Michael Jebson

CHESTER HOUSE PUBLICATIONS
2 Chester House, Pages Lane
Muswell Hill, London N10 1PR

First Published June 1996
© Michael Jebson June 1996
ISBN 0 7150 0096 9

Design and illustrations by Twenty-Five Educational, London NW1 5JR
Printed by Clifford Frost Ltd., Wimbledon, London SW19 2SE

About the author

Michael Jebson's early career was in commerce and industry whilst having responsibility in his spare time for a large church youth group. He felt called by God to go into full-time youth work and trained for this at Westhill College, Birmingham. For twenty-seven years he served the Methodist Church as a youth officer, trainer and consultant in Liverpool, the north-east of England, Cumbria, London and the home counties. For seven of these years he was National Training Officer for the Methodist Association of Youth Clubs. Michael has always worked ecumenically and was involved from the beginning in the development of *Spectrum*, the unique and widely-used inter-church training scheme for youth workers.

This book, *Tuck In!*, is based on his wide experience of working with young people, youth workers, clergy and ministers in local churches and in colleges and at area, regional and national conferences, including large-scale Christian events such as Greenbelt and Easter People. He has also had experience of training youth workers in Zimbabwe, southern Africa.

Michael Jebson is currently a field-worker in north Wales and the north-west of England for the Training in World Mission Team of the United Society for the Propagation of the Gospel (USPG), a leading Anglican mission agency.

AUTHOR'S CONFESSION
– I hope I'm not in the soup!

Like many people who have been involved in working with young people and training youth workers, I have soaked up ideas from many sources, just like blotting paper. Now, after years of using games and exercises of many kinds which I have adapted to my own purposes and ways of working, I really don't know where some of them came from in the first place!

Where I know the original source of the material used I have mentioned it but, in most cases, the idea is expressed in my own words. If I have infringed any copyright please, this time round, forgive me trespassing on someone else's property, *it is not deliberate*, but please let me know for any future editions of this book. Thanks.

THIS BOOK IS DEDICATED WITH MY THANKS TO ...

... All my former colleagues at the Methodist Church Division of Education and Youth for their encouragement and assistance with this book

... Mrs Pat Parkins, my former secretary at MDEY, for her patience and help in preparing this book for publication

... all the Christian youth workers and young people who, down the years, have given me friendship, support, fun and inspiration

I pray that God will continue to bless you all in your work for his Kingdom.

Finally, this book is dedicated to my wife, Hilary, and our two daughters, Susan and Elaine and their families, with my love and thanks for all their love, understanding and help in so many ways.

Michael Jebson
June 1996

Deep peace of the running wave to you;
Deep peace of the flowing air to you;
Deep peace of the quiet earth to you;
Deep peace of the shining stars to you;
Deep peace of the Son of Peace to you.

A Celtic Blessing

by John Heath Stubbs (David Higham Associates)

CONTENTS

PART 1 – PREPARING FOR THE FEAST

Contents

PART 2 – WHAT'S ON THE MENU?

PART 3 – THE ICING ON THE CAKE

INTRODUCTION

Just about everyone enjoys a good meal. Eating in the company of good friends in comfortable surroundings can be one of life's greatest pleasures.

Think of a youth group as being like an invitation to a good meal! We want to be there. We're made to feel at home and welcome. We'll want to thank God together for all that he has provided and done for us. We know that great care will have gone into the preparation before we arrive to make sure that we have an enjoyable time. We anticipate that the surroundings will be comfortable and that we will come away satisfied. We will look forward to meeting friends, talking together and possibly making plans for the future.

Then, when it's all over, we will want to follow up new friends and contact those people who were unable to come along to tell them what they have missed. There may also be plans to be made for partying together again!

So this book gives you recipes for making every meeting of your youth group into a feast of good things. It's presented like a cook book for youth workers and young people (aged 13+) who meet together in Christian youth groups based in churches and homes. You will find here practical help for methods of involvement and programmes that cater for small and large youth groups.

The book is designed so that it can be used by youth workers and young people working together. It's certainly not an 'adults only' book.

So go on – Tuck In!

Keep on loving one another as Christian brothers (and sisters).
Remember to welcome strangers in your homes. There were
some who did that and welcomed angels without knowing it.

The letter to the Hebrews 13. 1 and 2.

COOK'S TOUR

Pointers to a purposeful programme

THE PROGRAMME IDEAS used by the youth group are most likely to be successful if youth workers keep asking the pointed questions summarized here.

START

OFF WE GO AGAIN!

Time to start another journey. The pattern of planning may be similar, but we'll do even better this time.

Phew! Let's sit down and talk about what's happened along the way. How could we have planned it better? What can we learn for next time? See Chapters 20 and 21.

1 Mile Stone

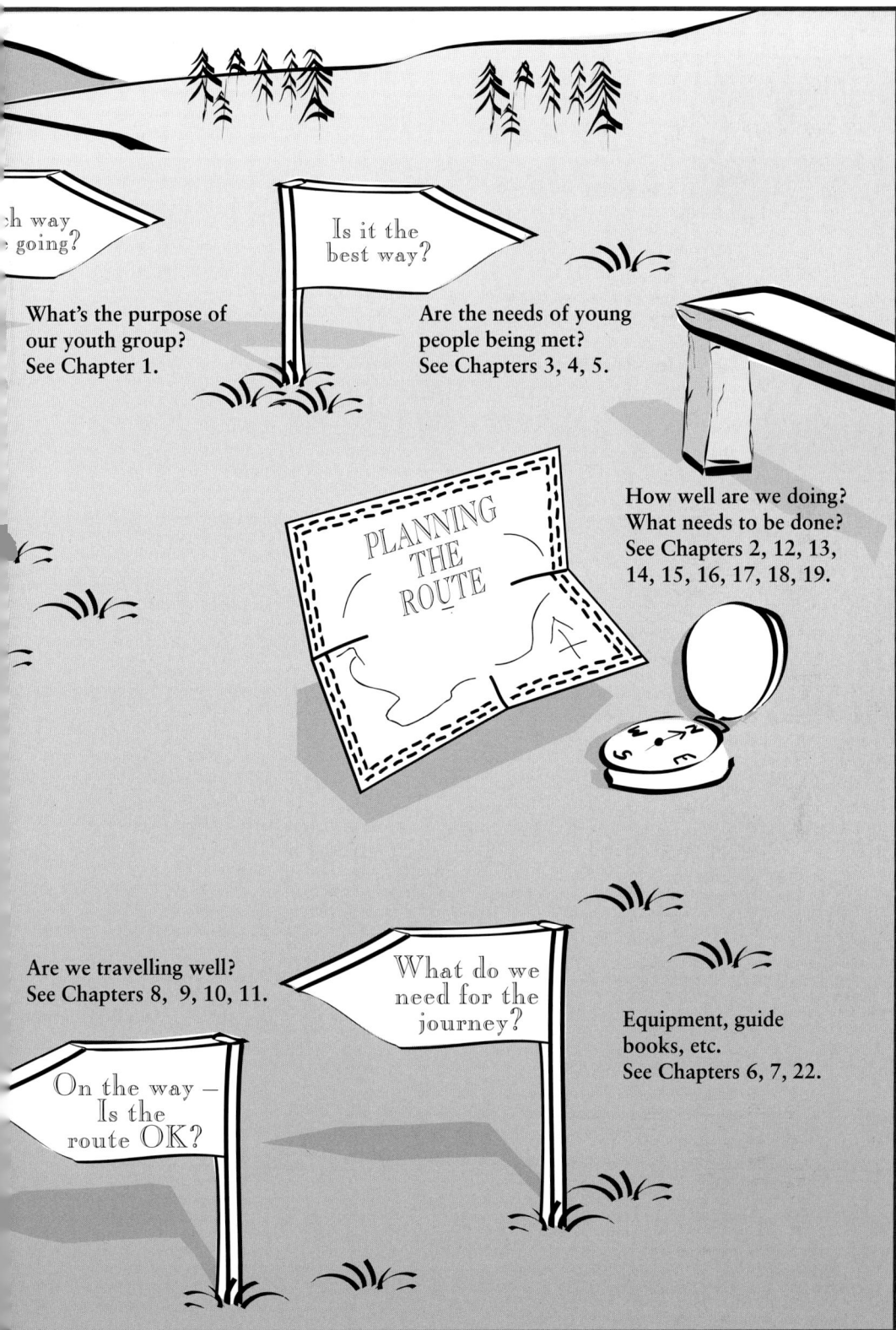

ch way
e going?

Is it the
best way?

What's the purpose of
our youth group?
See Chapter 1.

Are the needs of young
people being met?
See Chapters 3, 4, 5.

How well are we doing?
What needs to be done?
See Chapters 2, 12, 13,
14, 15, 16, 17, 18, 19.

PLANNING
THE
ROUTE

Are we travelling well?
See Chapters 8, 9, 10, 11.

What do we
need for the
journey?

On the way –
Is the
route OK?

Equipment, guide
books, etc.
See Chapters 6, 7, 22.

Recipe to make a Youth Group

Quantity:
This recipe is sufficient to feed a handful of young people or a big crowd.

Ingredients:
Young people who are looking for a place where they can be valued for what they are, who are looking for the friendship of other young people and adults and who want a balanced diet of faith, fellowship and fun.

Method:
Work with the Fruits of the Spirit: love, joy, peace, patience, kindness, goodness, faithfulness, gentleness and self control (Galatians 5. 22-23)

Add in imagination, excitement, trust and ways of involving, empowering and providing a listening ear.

Stir in action and concern for each other, the neighbourhood, the church and the world.

Do not beat – these are human beings! Handle with prayer.

Do not cook, especially under pressure. Instead offer warmth and allow time to mature. This may take several years but the end result is worth it.

Garnish with days out, weekends away, sport and all kinds of other goodies.

Method of serving:
Follow the Master. He always left people satisfied (see Matthew 15. 29-39), he taught people how to serve each other (see John 13. 2-17) and he said, 'I am the bread of life. He who comes to me will never go hungry, and he who believes in me will never be thirsty' (John 6. 35 NIV).

Part 1

Preparing for the Feast

Chapter 1

IS IT ANY EXCUSE FOR A PARTY?

What's the purpose of our youth group?

Maybe if your life-style is of the spontaneous kind you just decide at any time to have a party with whoever happens to be around at the time. Fine. Have fun!

There must be room for spontaneity in youth work, of course. Reacting correctly to the moment or the mood of the group is a precious youth work skill needing training and experience.

In this book we're thinking about making every youth group meeting a time to remember; a feast of good things. For this to happen week in week out, we need to be very clear about why we have a youth group anyway.

In business, industry and many other areas of society today there is an insistence on being clear about the purpose of the enterprise. What are we here to do? What are we aiming at? How can we measure success? Have we evaluated what we have done? Have we used the results of that evaluation to improve the way we work?

Many organizations now have a 'Mission Statement' or 'Statement of Purpose' which sets down in a few sentences their aims.

If you are just thinking of starting up a youth group you have a golden opportunity to pause and think about the purpose of the group. You will really find it helpful.

It is usually best to set up a small group to prepare the statement of purpose. This will need to include young people, representatives of the church and local community, other youth organizations and youth workers. In forming the group try to ensure that young people have at least an equal number of representatives to the adults invited to join. After all, the purpose of the group is to meet the needs of young people.

Get the group to consider questions such as:
- What is the purpose of this youth group?
- Why is it needed?
- Will it complement or compete with other existing youth work in the church and community?
- What is the long-term aim of the youth group?
- What are the objectives needed (or stages to go through) to meet the aim?
- Who manages the group? To whom are the youth workers responsible?

You will be able to think of other questions that need to be asked because of your own church situation, environment and needs.

Use the answers to these questions (and the questions in Chapter 5 – 'Invitations – who's coming?') to write a brief 'Statement of Purpose' for the youth group.

Use the statement to set up the practical things that have to be done to bring the youth group into being. And once you're in existence keep checking back on the statement to see if you are honouring it. Every year or so review the statement of purpose to see if it is still useful or if it needs modifying.

On the other hand, if there is already a youth group formed, even it if has been running for several years, you may still need to ask yourselves the questions given above. Like human beings, a youth group that wants to stay healthy, alert and useful, needs a health check every so often. Put yours through one using a monitoring group of the sort described.

HEALTH WARNING

Asking these questions just may produce a shock result. It could be that the answers to your questions add up to saying that, in the case of a new group, none is needed. With an existing group, big changes may be looked for. But, surely, this outcome is better than sinking slowly and painfully into decline because the original purpose has been served and no one can see that, sooner or later, death is inevitable.

> IF YOU DON'T KNOW WHERE YOU'RE GOING
> YOU MAY END UP WHERE YOU DON'T WANT TO BE
>
> *"In fourteen hundred and ninety-two*
> *When Columbus sailed the ocean blue..."*
> *It is said that when he set out –*
> *Christopher Columbus did not know where he was going.*
> *When he got to America he did not know where he was.*
> *When he left he didn't know where he'd been!*

Jesus set out very clearly at the beginning of his ministry his statement of purpose. He went to his own home town to do it. He spoke to the people who knew him best. Read about it in Luke 4. 16–21. (The verses up to number 30 tell of the consequences of his action.)

WHY DO WE DO WHAT WE DO?

A STATEMENT OF PURPOSE

The government, through the National Youth Agency, sponsored a series of 'Ministerial Conferences' attended by representatives of the statutory and voluntary Youth Service. From the November 1990 Conference came the following Statement of Purpose for the English Youth Service. There was a separate statement for Wales. How does your youth group measure up to this Statement?

> The purpose of youth work is to redress all forms of inequality and to ensure equality of opportunity for all young people to fulfil their potential as empowered individuals and members of groups and communities and to support young people during the transition to adulthood.
>
> Youth work offers young people opportunities which are:
>
> • educative – enabling young people to gain the skills, knowledge and attitudes needed to identify, advocate and pursue their rights and responsibilities as individuals and as members of groups and communities locally, nationally and internationally;
>
> continued over

3

- designed to promote equality of opportunity – through the challenging of oppressions such as racism and sexism and all those which spring from differences of culture, race, language, sexual identity, gender, disability, age, religion and class; and

– through the celebration of the diversity and strengths which arise from those differences;

- participative – through a voluntary relationship with young people in which young people are the partners in the learning process and the decision-making structures which affect their own and other young people's lives and their environment;

- empowering – supporting young people to understand and act on the personal, social and political issues which affect their lives, the lives of others and of the communities of which they are a part.

The government's Department for Education and Employment (DfEE) is urging the Youth Service (of which all youth groups are a part) to look carefully at its aims and purposes.

Many voluntary youth workers find the language used by some professional youth workers difficult and confusing. Through the words and statements though come some important questions for everyone engaged in youth work. Key questions about our programme, whatever form it takes:

- Why do we have a programme of activities for young people? (A sort of curriculum)
- Is it planned with a purpose in view? Do we expect young people to gain something from the activities? (Technically called learning outcomes)
- Can we measure results and see progress? (Professionally called Performance Indicators).

These are bread and butter questions for us all.

Do you see it all as pie in the sky or are you saying that everything in the youth group is in apple pie order?

The next chapter helps us look further at these questions.

TUCK IN!
'Cauliflower is nothing but cabbage with a college education'.
Mark Twain (1835–1910)

Chapter 2

FAMILY MEAL?

The youth group within the church community

'I just love it when we can all sit down together as a family. It's so rare these days. John gets in late most evenings and the kids dash in from school, grab something to eat, and off they go out again. So – it's a real treat when we can sit down and talk together with no hurry and bustle.'

People can be strangers in their own home, using it for little more than bed and breakfast. This can happen within the church family too.

It is natural and reasonable that people want to meet in groupings of their own choice – the womens' meeting, badminton club, the choir, Scouts, Guides, Boys' Brigade, Girls' Brigade, youth club and so on. But each of these organizations is only part of the whole. A part of Christ's church; his Body here on earth.

Of course a youth group can exist on its own within the church, but it will lack the sharing, caring, loving, teasing, fun and good wholesome food we look for in full family life. All of this and more will be found if young people are seen as part of the whole life and mission of the church. As in the average family, this relationship will have to be worked at. It will need patience and, at times, there may be disagreements and misunderstandings. These will have to be worked through with faith and hope so that people of all ages will grow closer together and be nearer the Kingdom of God.

In some Christian denominations, when a child is brought for baptism, the congregation, representing the local church, makes promises, in addition to the parents and godparents. In the Methodist Order of Service, for example, before the baby is baptised, the minister asks the congregation:

> 'Members of the Body of Christ, who are now in his name to receive this child, **will you so maintain the common life of worship and service** that s/he and all the children among you may grow in grace and in the knowledge and love of God and of his Son Jesus Christ our Lord.'

To which challenge the people are invited to respond:
> 'With God's help we will.' *

So in this form of baptism service the responsibility for nurturing children is shown to be the continual responsibility of the whole church. Youth workers and young people may, at times, need to remind other members of the church family of this obligation. Equally, they may need to remind themselves of their place within the full life of the church.

To many Christians the family meal is when they come together at the Lord's Table or Altar for Holy Communion or Eucharist (Greek for 'thanksgiving'). At this feast all are equal.

* *Extract from the* Methodist Service Book *(Methodist Publishing House 1975)*
Emphasis added by the author.

TUCK IN!

Come on,
Let us celebrate the supper of the Lord.
Let us make a huge loaf of bread
and let us bring abundant wine
like at the wedding at Cana.

Let the women not forget the salt.
Let the men bring along the yeast.
Let many guests come,
the lame, the blind, the crippled, the poor.

Come quickly.
Let us follow the recipe of the Lord.
All of us, let us knead the dough together
with our hands.
Let us see with joy
how the bread grows.

Because today
we celebrate
the meeting with the Lord.
Today we renew our commitment
to the Kingdom.
Nobody will stay hungry.

Elsa Tamez, Mexico

From *Bread for Tomorrow* – Praying with the
World's Poor. Edited by Janet Morley.
Published by SPCK/Christian Aid 1992.
Copyright sought from the author.

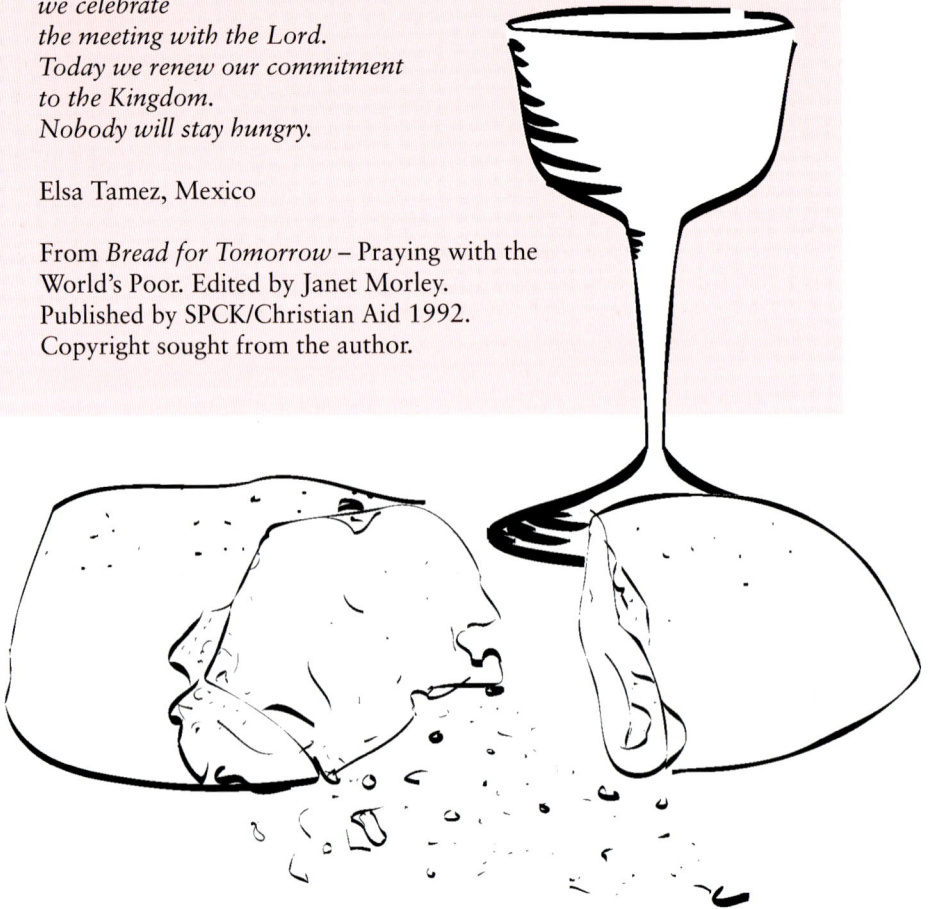

Chapter 3

MENU? WHAT MENU?

Meeting needs through the programme

'This is not a hotel you know! You'll have what I put in front of you. Take it or leave it!'

'Good day, madam. Good day, sir. Would you like to see the menu? And can I interest you in the Chef's Special?'

'Go and help yourself. You'll find something in the fridge.'

'Double beefburger, chips and beans, please. And where's the tomato sauce?'

Everyone to their own taste and life-style. It takes all sorts to make a world! And that creates a dilemma for youth groups. What should be on our menu? This book aims to give lots of ideas for the youth group programme. But what do we mean by 'our programme'?

Sometimes we mean a session at some point in the evening when we all do something together – have a discussion, a quiz, a simulation game. It could be one of a thousand ideas. And we usually limit this programme slot to about 30–45 minutes. Afterwards people return to playing table tennis, or chatting over a coke or meeting to plan for a future event.

On the other hand we can look at our whole time together in the youth group as 'programme' because, whatever we do, planned and unplanned, routine and special, should be there to meet the aims of the group and to meet individual needs.

When we are trying to achieve so many things in one session our programme needs to offer at least some of the following elements each time we meet:

- Somewhere safe to meet and talk (see 'Safe from Harm' below)
- A friendly, relaxed, welcoming, loving, accepting atmosphere
- Equality of opportunity for people with any kind of disability
- Help in spiritual growth
- Coping with sexual awareness
- A listening post where confidentiality is guaranteed
- New challenges through discussion, physical activity, involvement, trying new skills
- Fun
- Refreshments
- Ways of discovering and developing new talents
- Opportunities to take part in events outside the youth group – in the local church, community and beyond
- Meeting with adults as friends
- Experience of democratic ways of working with people and planning together.

See also the Statement of Purpose given in Chapter 1 'Is it any excuse for a party?'

HEALTHY EATING AND A BALANCED DIET

In the Western world where most people have enough to eat and to spare we have probably never been more aware of our diet. We are told that a balanced diet is good for us – and that probably gives us the licence to indulge in the occasional burger and chips!

Balance is what we are after in building up the programme of a youth group. It needs to be fun, tantalizing, relevant to the interests and needs of the group and purposeful so that it assists in the aim of the group (see Chapter 1 'Is it any excuse for a party?').

So although in a Christian group you will want to ensure that the programme includes a whole variety of ways of hearing about and experiencing what it is to be a Christian, there will also be sessions that will be purely for fun. Sport, parties, meals, silliness, holidays together all help to create a balanced programme that no one will want to miss. The pious people of his time criticized Jesus for partying. But Jesus shows us a fully rounded life, loving God and his neighbour first but still finding time to talk, rest, relax, get away from the crowds and have fun.

A number of psychologists have tried to list the basic needs of human beings. One psychologist named Maslow identified five levels of need. This diagram sets them out in a simple form.

**Does your youth group
programme meet these needs?**

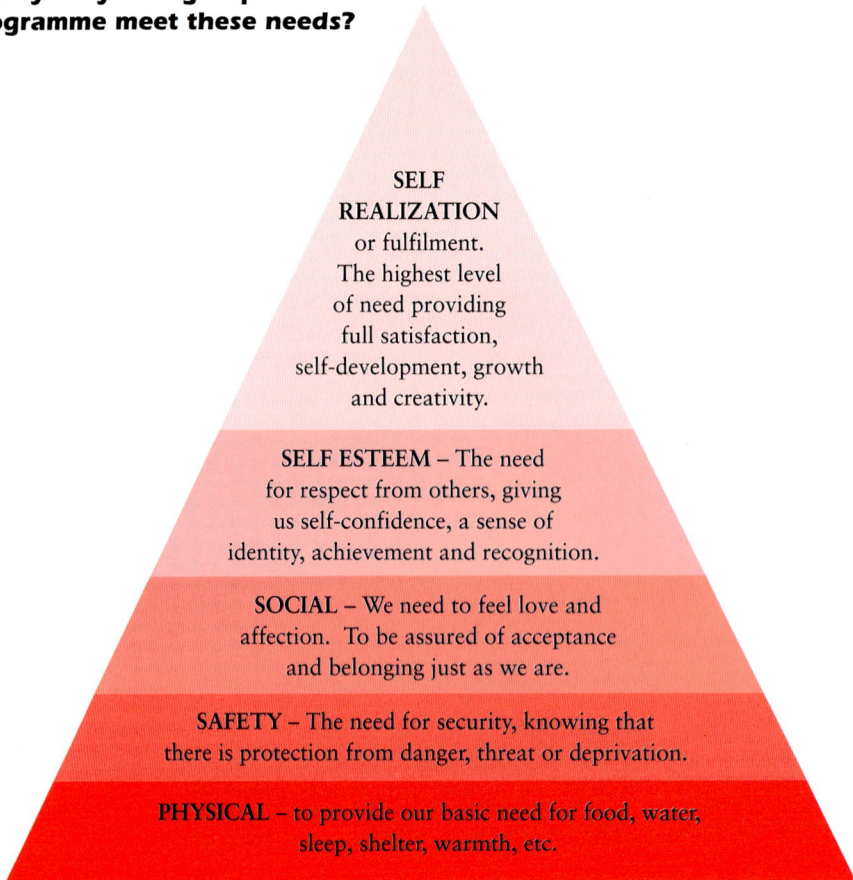

**SELF
REALIZATION**
or fulfilment.
The highest level
of need providing
full satisfaction,
self-development, growth
and creativity.

SELF ESTEEM – The need
for respect from others, giving
us self-confidence, a sense of
identity, achievement and recognition.

SOCIAL – We need to feel love and
affection. To be assured of acceptance
and belonging just as we are.

SAFETY – The need for security, knowing that
there is protection from danger, threat or deprivation.

PHYSICAL – to provide our basic need for food, water,
sleep, shelter, warmth, etc.

SAFE FROM HARM

This is the title of a Code of Practice for safeguarding the welfare of children and young people in voluntary organizations. It has been published by the Home Office.

It is a sad reflection on our times that it is necessary to produce such a Code of Practice but the issues it raises are too important for youth workers and their committees of management to ignore.

We are reproducing just the Summary of Recommendations from *Safe from Harm* and urge youth workers to obtain a copy of the full publication. It is suggested that youth organizations should consider the issues raised by each of the following statements of principle and then, if they wish to do so, take any action which they consider appropriate in the light of their circumstances and structure and the nature of their activities:

1   Adopt a policy statement on safeguarding the welfare of children. (Note: The Home Office uses the term children to include young people up to the age of 16 years)
2   Plan the work of the organization so as to minimize situations where the abuse of children may occur
3   Introduce a system whereby children may talk with an independent person
4   Apply procedures for protecting children to all paid staff and volunteers
5   Give all paid staff and volunteers a job description for any position involving contact with children
6   Use supervision as a means of protecting children
7   Treat all would-be paid staff and volunteers as job applicants for any position involving contact with children
8   Obtain at least one reference from a person who has experience of the applicant's paid work or volunteering with children
9   Explore all applicants' experience of working or contact with children in an interview before appointment
10   Find our whether an applicant has any conviction for criminal offences against children
11   Make paid and voluntary appointments conditional on the successful completion of a probationary period
12   Issue guidelines on how to deal with the disclosure or discovery of abuse
13   Train paid staff and volunteers, their line managers or supervisors, and policy-makers in the prevention of child abuse.

(From Safe from Harm *researched and written by David R Smith and published by the Home Office 1993) Crown copyright is reproduced with the permission of the controller of HMSO.*

Some youth organizations and Churches have produced their own publications to respond to the Home Office Code of Practice *Safe from Harm*. For example, *Safeguarding Children and Young People* contains guidelines for all who work with children and young people in voluntary organizations, including the church (published by the Methodist Church Division of Education and Youth, 2 Chester House, Pages Lane, Muswell Hill, London N10 1PR).

TUCK IN!

Lord, when I am hungry
Give me someone to feed
When I am thirsty
Give water for their thirst.
When I am sad
Someone to lift from sorrow,
When burdens weigh upon me
Lay upon my shoulders
The burden of my fellows.
Lord, when I stand
Greatly in need of tenderness,
Give me someone who yearns
For love. May your will
Be my bread; your grace
My strength; your love
My resting place.

Translated from the French –
Published by
Quaker Peace Service

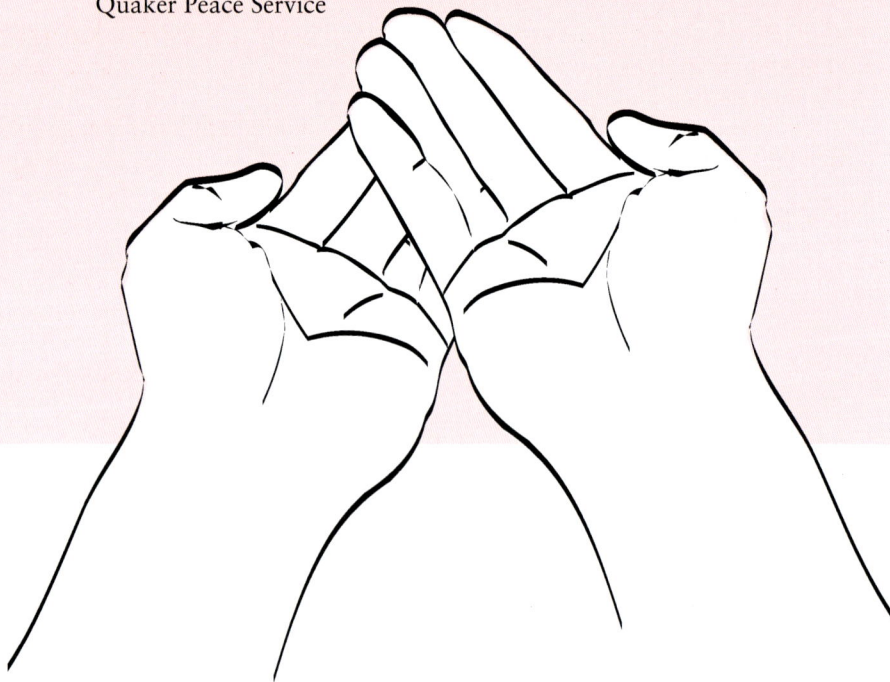

Chapter 4

DOES HE TAKE SUGAR?

Meeting special needs

This is the title of a BBC radio programme for disabled people. The attitude symbolized by the saying is, unfortunately, all too well known to people who are differently abled, especially those who use wheelchairs.

People often talk *about* rather than *to* those who have disabilities. It is as if they are young children. They will talk to the pusher of the wheelchair, whilst the person in it is probably perfectly capable of saying whether or not they like sugar in their tea.

We all have different needs and throughout the youth group programme there should be an awareness of these, especially where people have special needs.

How does the youth group score, then, on these two questions? Can you answer 'yes' to each of them? If not, how can things change so that everyone can feel welcome?

1   Are people with disabilities able to take part in all the activities of the group? Yes or no?

2   Are disabled people helped to feel they really belong? Yes or no?

If there are no disabled young people in the group then ask the question, why?

TUCK IN!
'*Real love begins where nothing is expected in return.*'
Antoine de St. Exupery

Chapter 5

INVITATIONS – WHO'S COMING?

Thinking about membership of the youth group

If we're planning a party we usually select our guests with care – 'They'd be good fun' or 'We can't ask John without inviting Sue' or 'Oh no, we're not having her again. Remember last time!'

With a youth group things aren't so manageable. So how do people know about your youth group? Do they just drift in? Come along with friends? Are you a secret society or is it always open house?

Here are some questions to help you establish a policy about who should form the membership of the youth group. Challenge your group to consider in their thinking the words of Jesus in Luke 14. 7–24 (see especially verses 12–14).

What is the purpose of the group? Who is the group aimed at? (See Chapter 1)

What should be the age range? Don't make it too wide. The year when young people change schools can be a good lower age bracket, but this should be flexible. Most 16- and 17-year olds look on 12-year olds as 'little kids', so consider your top age limit carefully. In the end, the decision you make about the age range will depend also on whether there is another group that people can move on to.

Having decided on an age range, stick to it fairly. The atmosphere and programme of the group can be dramatically affected by a membership that has allowed itself to grow too old or too young and has not encouraged young people to grow gracefully out of the group.

Gatecrashers are not usually welcome at a party. **Would you turn away someone who has arrived unannounced at your youth group?** How and why should you say no? Some clues to solving this problem are given later in this chapter – 'Invitations? What invitations?'

How do you decide upon the size of the group? Start this conversation by asking how many youth workers you have. You may want to decide on a youth worker to young people ratio such as for every eight young people there should be one youth worker. With a mixed group there should always be one male and one female youth worker.

How many can be coped with in the premises you use for the meeting? If you meet in a house, it can be great fun to be all squashed together in one room, but can you actually achieve anything? Can you hold worthwhile discussions or do any creative activities? Should you limit the numbers or perhaps divide the group and form a second one meeting with other youth workers in another home?

It will be different again if you meet in church rooms or halls. Have you got too much or too little space? Is the programme for the group difficult to manage because you have several rooms (perhaps some upstairs) and lots of doors in and out? Do you share the premises with an adult group who expect to be left in peace while they meet? Are there any official regulations determined by insurance, fire or accident prevention requirements that may limit your space or activities?

How is the entry and exit door (or doors) controlled? Remember, the youth worker who has been given responsibility by the church for the management of the group should know at all times who is on the premises when the group is meeting. If a fire breaks out the senior youth worker should know exactly who is there. Parents and guardians do, in effect, hand their children over to the youth workers for safe keeping for the period of time the group meets. (In the eyes of the law anyone under the age of 18 is a child or 'minor'.) Youth workers are said to be *in loco parentis*, a Latin term meaning 'in place of parents'. Parents or guardians have the right to assume that the person put in charge of youth work by the local church is responsible, law-abiding and trained. Even though they may be voluntary and unpaid, youth workers have at least a moral, if not legal, obligation to be responsible for the total welfare of the young people entrusted to them for a couple of hours or so each week (see Chapters 8 and 17 concerning responsibility on days out, residential events, etc.).

INVITATIONS? – WHAT INVITATIONS?

There could be at least two reactions to what has been written so far. 'What numbers? We struggle to get a handful of young people to come along. How can we get some to join?' Or maybe you're saying to yourself 'Everything's up and running for us. We can't take any more in and we're working at full stretch. Our problem is about keeping them away from the place!'

If your problem is an apparent shortage of young people try looking at it this way: numbers aren't everything. You can work with a small group and develop really close and worthwhile relationships on which you can build. Challenge the whole group to make the fellowship it offers irresistible to others! Be clear about why you're meeting, then go out and invite people in.

If you've got the 'House Full' signs up then you need to ask some of the questions about what happens when members of the group reach the upper age limit – is there somewhere else for them to move on to? Somewhere more appropriate to their age, maturity and interests? And, as young people move out of the group, what's happening to the lower end of the age range? Are you keeping up recruitment there? And are some of the older young people being invited to consider the challenge to train as youth workers? (see Chapter 21) These youth workers in training may join the team working with young people in the present group. Or they may be able to work in some other children's or youth work project in the church or local community.

GATECRASHERS WELCOME!
What then about young people who just turn up at the door and want to come in?

Do we look at them and assume they are gate-crashers and potential trouble-makers, or do we welcome them in?

Firstly, remember that for the sake of good management and safety we have the right to refuse entry, especially if the maximum number agreed for admittance to the group has been reached. If necessary this should be explained to the new young people standing at the door. After all, if we go to the cinema and the manager says it is full we can do nothing else but accept this and leave. But young people aren't generally so easily put off at the entrance to a youth club!

So, as we are there to help young people and not to turn them away, we should consider in advance a youth group policy for dealing with potential new members when we are in the position of having a 'full house'. Here are some options to think about:

- Have a waiting list. This would be linked to attendance and if a member has not been for, say, four meetings without giving a reason then their place is offered to someone on the waiting list. It is important that this policy is clearly explained to all members. Ideally it should be backed up by a personal and pastoral visit to the member's home to see why s/he has not attended recently. No one should just be 'struck off' without a good reason.
- Plan that there is space each week for a few 'guests' who are admitted on a one-off basis but are given the option of going on a waiting list to become full members.
- Some groups have a totally open 'no membership' approach where it's first-come-first-served. So there are no gate crashers, simply young people who want to enjoy being at the group for an evening. However, this radical policy demands careful handling with particular care about who's responsible for controlling entry to the group, making management decisions and dealing with matters concerning safety and security.

Chapter 6

GETTING THE ROOM READY

Practicalities, safety and welcoming

So much to do to get ready for the guests! Move the furniture around. Make sure there's enough room for everyone. And then someone turns up unexpectedly…

The hall or home we meet in for our youth work should have a welcoming air about it. People should feel at home because everything is ready for them. These preparations should be a team effort – a small advance party of youth workers and young people who arrive before the starting time to make things ready.

Here are some things to consider if you are using a church meeting room:

- Does it look like a meeting place for a Christian youth group? Could you put up some pictures and posters that say something about what we believe?
- If you have the use of a notice board, is it in a bright and uncluttered place? Is it up to date? Whose job is it to prepare notices and keep the board tidy?
- Can lighting be altered and chairs and tables be put in groups to make the room look more interesting? How about putting cloths and flowers on the tables?
- Are there things to do as soon as people arrive? Perhaps small table games, table tennis; good refreshments; books and magazines to read.
- Are fire exits clear? Is the location of fire extinguishers known? Are there extinguishers to deal with different kinds of fires – electrical, for example?
- Where is the nearest telephone in case of emergency? Does it require coins or a phone card to use it? Can someone bring their mobile phone?
- Where is the first aid kit and is it properly equipped?
- What is the phone number of the church official responsible for the property and of the priest or minister?

HOSTING AND WELCOMING

Those people who come to the youth group are looking for our friendship, our concern for their well being, our reassurance that they really are special and welcome.

We need to make sure that all the routine preparations for the meeting night have been got out of the way before the young people start to arrive. Then youth workers and young people will be free to greet and meet each other; to learn the names of new members and visitors; free to share views and news.

People coming for the first time will need special attention. They will need to know what the youth group is all about, what activities are on offer, any rules, the programme for the session – and so on. They will need introducing to other young people. Most people are shy to start with. We can't expect them to make friends straight away without some help and encouragement.

TUCK IN!

I saw a stranger today.
I put food for him in the eating-place,
And drink in the drinking place,
And music in the listening place.
In the Holy Name of the Trinity
He blessed myself and my house
My goods and my family.
And the lark said in her warble-
Often, often, often,
Goes Christ in the stranger's guise.
O, oft and oft and oft,
Goes Christ in the stranger's guise.

Celtic Traditional

Chapter 7

THE PLACE SETTING

What you need – equipment and resources

Of course you can eat food with any old knife or fork or even your fingers. But a good meal seems to taste better if care and imagination have been used in its presentation and you have the right knives, forks, spoons ... chop sticks!

Youth work needs its own special equipment. It does not need to be elaborate or expensive but it should be kept up to date, in good condition and be always available.

Here is a short list of resources for use in creative programmes. It is not in any order of priority and you will be able to think of other things you will need for special events:

Paper
You should not need to buy new paper and card. Collect old posters; ask for left over smooth wallpaper rolls. Ask printers and newspaper offices for offcuts and ends of rolls.

Pens
Non-toxic felt tipped pens/markers.

Paint
Poster paint (pots or powder). Water-based emulsion paint can be used (with care) on most paper. Ask for part-used tins that are no longer needed. From white emulsion you can make colours by adding poster paint.

Flip chart
A board on which you can clip paper and that will stand up in front of a group so that ideas can be recorded, questions written up, diagrams drawn and so on. Ask someone to make one for the group, preferably of a size to take A1 paper. This is the standard size of paper for flip charts.

String, scissors, elastic bands, sellotape, clay, plasticine, blu-tak, non-toxic glue, etc.
Essential for all kinds of creative activities.

Collection of pictures
Any picture that will be useful to represent an idea, stimulate imagination or provide a reference point (see Chapter 13 'Cooking Methods' – A-Z 'Pictures' for ways a picture collection can be used).

Clean junk!
Keep this in check or it will get out of hand, but a small collection of bits and pieces of card, wood, cloth, tin foil, card tubes, etc. can be very useful for helping to express ideas.

Hats, scarves, etc.

For role play and informal drama, people can often step into a character more easily if they can put on an appropriate hat or other accessory. Keep a small selection. (*See Chapter 14 'Giving Thanks – Worship in the Youth Group' for Worship and Bible Study Resources*).

OTHER MORE EXPENSIVE EQUIPMENT

It is very useful if you can have access to some items of audio/visual equipment. Some of these items are costly but it may be that you can borrow what you need from your church or the local education authority.

Overhead projector

A most useful and versatile way of displaying words and diagrams on a screen or wall in daylight. Every go-ahead church should have one so if yours has not perhaps a money raising effort could be initiated to buy one. (*Note: Printing the words of songs and hymns on to overhead projector acetates can infringe copyright. Check before you do it.*)

Slide projector

Still a useful piece of equipment especially if you keep a selection of colour slides handy which can be used to express ideas or provide a focus for meditation.

Record/cassette/CD player

Usually available in most homes. If you are wanting to present music or speech in a large hall or church try to ensure that the quality of reproduction is good. There is little more annoying or un-professional than using inadequate sound equipment for the purpose. Equally, of course, don't over-amplify and blast everyone's ear drums!

Back projection screen

(*See Chapter 13 'Cooking Methods' – A-Z 'Audio and Visual Aids' for details of how to make this.*)

Video player and monitor

Now available in many homes and in some churches.
CAUTION: Do not move this equipment from a house to a church, for example, without checking that it is insured for loss or damage away from its usual home. Be especially careful with rented models. These should not be moved from the premises to which they are on hire without the permission of the rental company.

Games equipment

Ask for people to donate: small games – Monopoly, chess, draughts, Trivial Pursuit, etc.
Depending upon the type of premises you use, build up a collection of indoor and outdoor games equipment or balls of different kinds (including soft balls), bats, rackets, nets, etc.

Musical instruments and music

Encourage people to participate by bringing instruments they play. Involve them in music-making for fun or with a purpose as frequently as possible. To increase the interest and participation build up a collection of percussion instruments that can be used by less skilled musicians – tambourines, shakers and small drums of different kinds. These are not just instruments for use by little children. Well used they can add a great deal to a performance. Start a library of hymn and song books.

Purchasing power

Many local authorities supplies departments run a central purchasing scheme in co-operation with Councils for Voluntary Youth Services offering attractive discounts to registered youth groups. You may be able to buy anything from a table tennis table to felt tipped pens. It could pay you to enquire if such a scheme operates in your area through the local youth officer. If you have difficulty finding the address of your local Council for Voluntary Youth Services, contact the National Council for Voluntary Youth Services, 11, St. Bride Street, London EC4A 4AS.

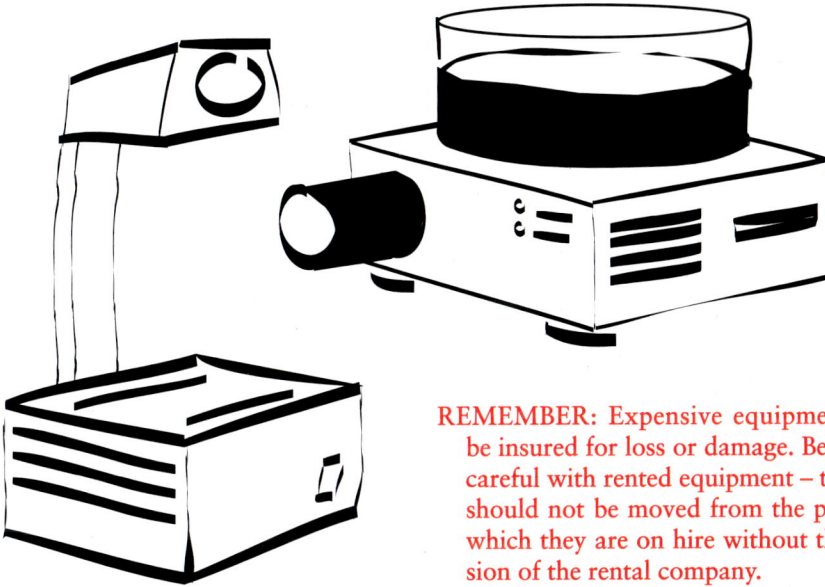

REMEMBER: Expensive equipment should be insured for loss or damage. Be especially careful with rented equipment – these items should not be moved from the premises to which they are on hire without the permission of the rental company.

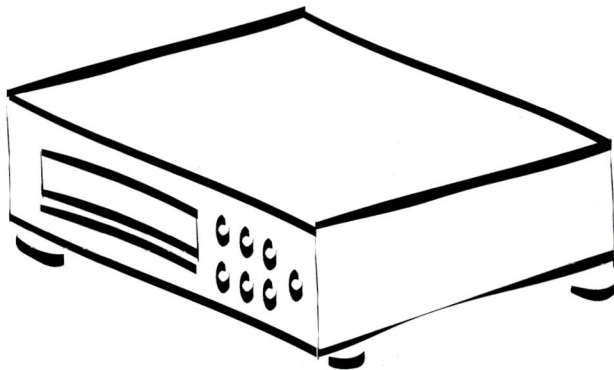

Chapter 8

TOO MANY COOKS?
WHO'S IN CHARGE?

Leader or worker? The skills required

'Look, if you want this meal on time get out from under my feet! I'm in charge here! I can't do with you hanging around all the time – and I can't even trust you to boil an egg properly!'

or

'Well, if we're going to eat this meal, who's going to help me with it?'

The good youth worker empowers young people. In an address he gave at a CAFOD (the Catholic relief and development agency) event, Father Joseph G. Donders, from the Catholic University of America, Washington, D.C. said:

> "Empowering people is the most important thing you can do. It means enabling them to discover what they can do, and who they are. You can feed people when they are hungry; you can quench their thirst when they are thirsty; you can equip them with appropriate technologies when they need those, but all this is nothing compared to enabling them to come into their own."

You have probably noticed already that in this book we use the term youth **worker** rather than youth **leader**.

Of course there is a place and a need for leadership, but it has to be offered with great care and sensitivity. Young people look to adults for guidance, for example, for a listening ear, for understanding, for acceptance, for resources and ways to do things.

Adults who see themselves as workers *with*, rather than leaders *of*, young people are most likely to be able to meet these needs. Working *with* is a demanding job. It is often easier to be a leader – to take charge; to be in control; to give out orders; to keep a tight hold on the reins. Of course we all need to understand the need for boundaries to what we do and to exercise self-discipline. The youth worker encourages and enables this attitude to life to happen and sees it grow because it is discussed, developed and experienced rather than demanded and imposed.

So the youth worker needs to develop very special skills and values – here's a short list to start you thinking:

- The ability to work with and alongside young people
- The ability to handle confidential matters shared by a young person with trust in a non-judgemental way.
- Understanding that real respect can only be earned and not demanded

- Realizing that in a youth group a young person usually chooses to come. The youth worker has no actual authority, other than that entrusted by the sponsoring church and the young people themselves
- Willingness to admit that they don't know everything and may sometimes be wrong but able to learn from mistakes
- Having a keen sense of humour
- Knowing how to share vision and enthusiasm
- To be adaptable and flexible and not be easily offended or moody
- To treat each young person as an individual
- Knowing how to delegate all kinds of tasks and responsibilities
- Having a firm and living Christian faith and know how to share it
- Being prepared to say no to someone who is doing something you consider unacceptable
- Being prepared to accept full responsibility when personal decisions have to be made at a time of crisis or emergency. Being willing to explain the action that was taken.

As stated right at the begining of this book, it is written for both adults and young people. So try to work out together what work can be delegated. Discover and use the talents that people have. When people take on a job make sure they fully understand what is involved and ensure that they are helped and supported to do the task. It might be an idea to set a time limit for people to do a job so that they can move on and try new skills and don't feel trapped into doing one thing for ever. Where it is possible delegate work to two people working together or to a small team so that they can support and encourage each other.

Monitor feelings, successes, problems and progress by having regular team meetings. Sort out problems and difficulties together and quickly. If someone is really struggling with a particular task see that extra help is offered. If necessary enable them to give up the task without feeling humiliated. Where it needs it, restore their confidence by moving them into a new job well within their capabilities and where they can see fairly quick results.

TUCK IN!

A leader is best
when people barely
know he exists, not
so good when people
obey and acclaim
him, worst when
they despise him.*

*But for a good leader,
who talks little,
when his work is done
his aim fulfilled,
they will all say
'We did it ourselves'.*

Chinese philosopher Lao-Tse.
*   For 'leader' read 'youth worker'. For 'him' read also 'her'!

YOUTH WORKERS' CHECKLIST

Use this to check out recent events and to plan for the future:

To achieve the aim of the session/event:
- Did we plan for it carefully as a group?
- Did we evaluate how it was going at all stages and take any action needed at the end?

To involve and motivate the group:
- Were responsibilities and tasks shared out?
- Were the resources of the group fully used?
- Was the co-ordination of the youth workers' team satisfactory?

To encourage and support each individual:
- Did the youth worker communicate effectively with all involved both facts and values (enthusiasm, for example)?
- Was the youth worker sensitive to each young person involved?
- Was each person involved helped to acquire and use new skills where necessary?
- Were the individuals involved encouraged and helped to take decisions and over-come any difficulties?

(Adapted from Face to Face with Young People *published by the Methodist Church Division of Education and Youth 1984.)*

START A TALENT BANK

Encourage every member of the youth group to disclose what they think are their talents and skills. Ask someone to make up a card index or computer data base that lists these talents so that they can be used. Remember the little gifts (good at remembering names; makes a great apple pie!) as well as the more recognized ones such as pianist, artist, gymnast, computer buff, etc. Prompt people about the talents they don't realize they have or forget about – 'You're really good at making new people feel at home' or 'You've got a really good singing voice. Could you help with...?'

LEGAL WARNING

With all this talk of sharing the work load it will still be necessary for someone to be seen as taking final responsibility for what happens in the youth group. This may be required by the church committee or officials who take responsibility for youth work policy. Parents and guardians will expect and assume that someone is 'in charge' (see Chapter 5 'Invitations – who's coming?' and the definition of *in loco parentis*). Similarly insurance companies and safety and fire officers will need to be assured that an adult is aware of risks and regulations and will take responsibility.

Discuss these legal responsibilities with the whole youth group so that they can see that, in some cases, the buck has to stop with an adult. This will help the understanding of everybody and enable them to help the adult youth worker to carry the extra responsibilities that are required of them. And having said this, to paraphrase US President, Harry S. Truman, if the adult can't stand the heat, they had better get out of the kitchen.

TUCK IN!

God's words to the Old Testament prophet, Joshua, and to us –

Remember that I have commanded you to be determined and confident! Don't be afraid or discouraged, for I, the Lord your God, am with you wherever you go.
Joshua 1. 9

Chapter 9

TABLE MANNERS

Making guidelines for behaviour

The restaurant was crowded. There was a pleasant buzz of conversation and occasional laughter. Suddenly the over-loud voice of a parent shattered the calm atmosphere, 'William, take your elbows off the table at once!' All over the restaurant adult elbows were guiltily removed from tables too.

Discipline is a word with a hard ring to it. It can suggest severity of manner, maintaining control, making rules, holding power, threatening punishment. Yet the word 'discipline' comes from the same Latin root as 'disciple' (learn) – a follower; someone under discipline, who accepts a code of behaviour, a way of life – but is hopefully always questioning, learning, growing and maturing.

Many youth groups do have a problem with maintaining order and with behaviour getting out of hand. And if people can get away with anything they will probably come away with nothing. So young people are sometimes 'banned' for some misdeed for one or more meetings or even for ever. Is this fair or right? The problem will probably only be pushed out of the way and not really be tackled.

A better way of dealing with discipline is to involve the whole youth group in deciding what is and what is not acceptable behaviour. Draw up guidelines rather than rules and review them at regular intervals to see if they are still helpful. Have the guidelines (or you could call them a code of conduct) available for all to see, perhaps on a membership card. Discuss them with newcomers so that they know what is expected of them.

When someone continually misbehaves in the eyes of the whole group try to discover the underlying cause of the behaviour. It may be a cry for help rather than a deliberate attempt to be disruptive. Love and concern may be what is needed rather than 'banning'. Love and concern are ways to make the person feel wanted and involved. Is there a real job they could be asked to do whilst being offered all the support needed to see it through? Is there a talent or interest they have that can be used for the enjoyment and good of the whole group? Is friendship hard for them and, if so, are they being helped to find and keep friends?

But what is to be done with the person who is a real pain, persistently annoying and determined to be different? Above all, try to keep calm! A lost temper doesn't help another's lost temper. Violent words or actions do not cure another's violence but may aggravate it. This calm, measured reaction does not rule out showing anger, firmness and pointing out that hurt has been caused, possibly to the whole youth group. But in a Christian organization there must always remain the opportunity for repentance and forgiveness – sometimes time after time (see Matthew 18 . 21–22).

In the end good behaviour is about what will help the group and each person in it to relate well, to grow and mature. We are not looking for a crowd of conformists, meek and mild wimps – how boring that would be!

Acceptable behaviour is mostly about trusting people and expecting the best of them, not the worst.

Walk cheerfully over the world, answering that of God in everyone.

George Fox (1624–1691) founder of the Religious Society of Friends (Quakers)

The Parable of the Eagle

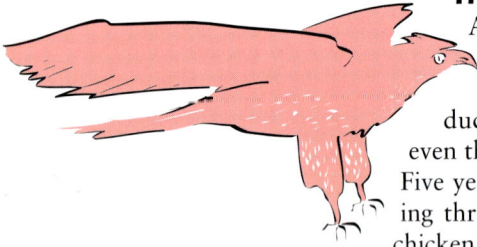

A certain man went through a forest seeking any bird of interest he might find. He caught a young eagle, brought it home and put it among his fowls and ducks and turkeys, and gave it chicken's food to eat even though it was an eagle, the king of birds.

Five years later a naturalist came to see him and, after passing through his garden, said: 'That bird is an eagle, not a chicken.'

'Yes,' said its owner, 'but I have trained it to be a chicken. It is no longer an eagle, it is a chicken, even though it measures fifteen feet from tip to tip of its wings.'

'No,' said the naturalist, it is an eagle still: it has the heart of an eagle, and I will make it soar high up to the heavens.'

'No,' said the owner, 'it is a chicken, and it will never fly.'

They agreed to test it. The naturalist picked up the eagle, held it up, and said with great intensity: 'Eagle, thou art an eagle; thou dost belong to the sky and not to this earth; stretch forth thy wings and fly.'

The eagle turned this way and that, and then, looking down, saw the chickens eating their food, and down he jumped.

Then the owner said: 'I told you it was a chicken.'

'No,' asserted the naturalist, 'it is an eagle, and it still has the heart of an eagle; only give it one more chance, and I will make it fly tomorrow.'

The next morning he rose early and took the eagle outside the city, away from the houses, to the foot of a high mountain. The sun was just rising, gilding the top of the mountain with gold, and every crag was glistening in the joy of that beautiful morning.

He picked up the eagle and said to it: 'Eagle, thou art an eagle; thou dost belong to the sky and not to this earth; stretch forth thy wings and fly!'

The eagle looked round and trembled as if new life were coming to it; but it did not fly. The naturalist then made it look straight at the sun. Suddenly it stretched out its wings and, with the screech of an eagle, it mounted higher and higher and never returned. It was an eagle, though it had been kept and tamed as a chicken!

James Aggrey wrote this parable* and concluded it with this comment –

'My people of Africa, we were created in the image of God, but men have made us think that we are chickens, and we still think we are; but we are eagles. Stretch forth your wings and fly! Don't be content with the food of chickens!'

* *The Parable of the Eagle is from* Aggrey of Africa *by Edwin W. Smith, published by SCM Press 1929.*

Chapter 10

DINNER WILL BE AT 6.30.PROMPT!

Timing the programme. How long is long enough?

For some years a woman had been away from the business world whilst she had worked full-time at home as a housewife and mother. She decided to apply for a managerial job she saw advertised and was called for interview. Because of her recent experience her managerial abilities were questioned by the interviewer. Had she got any? She explained how day after day, whilst keeping the children amused, she was expected to prepare meals for four people from the raw materials. This meal was usually of two or three courses, was invariably hot and was expected to be served in an attractive way, in the right order and on time. She got the job.

Timing is very important in youth work. A session, a programme or an event if the length is right and the interest held, can be a memorable success. If it drags on it may well flop. In preparing for any part of your youth groups programme go for a well prepared, high quality, snappy experience that leaves people wanting more rather than groaning with boredom.

So include in your preparations rehearsal and timing. Be prepared to be ruthless and cut material if it is too long. Make it clear at the beginning how long the programme is going to be. If more time is needed negotiate for this with the whole group. Study radio and TV programmes and consider how they have to work to very tight time limits. Knowing how and when to stop is as important as knowing how to start. Allow time, too, to talk about what has happened, to reflect on the experience that has been shared and, where necessary, to follow it up and take some action.

Take time to think—
it is the source of power.
Take time to read—
it is the foundation of wisdom.

Take time to play—
it is the secret of staying young.

Take time to be quiet —
it is the opportunity to seek God.

Take time to be aware—
it is the opportunity to help others.
Take time to love and be loved—
it is God's greatest gift.

Take time to laugh—
it is the music of the soul.
Take time to be friendly—
it is the road to happiness.

Take time to dream—
it is what the future is made of.
Take time to pray—
it is the greatest power on earth.
'There is a time for everything.'

(from *At All Times and in All Places* by Myra Blyth and Tony Jasper (Marshall Pickering) – based upon Ecclesiastes 3.)

Chapter 11

WHO PICKS UP THE BILL?

Making a budget

'The price of eating nowadays! Things just seem to go up and up. I tremble when I get to the supermarket checkout wondering what the trolley-load will cost. And as for eating out!'

It is said there is no such thing as a free lunch. Certainly everything has its price – you just can't go spending money that isn't there. If you do you will certainly have to pay for it, somehow, later.

Every youth group has some running costs. Sometimes these are quite small and can be found very easily, often through the generosity of the youth workers. But this isn't always possible. Some people would say it isn't even wise.

The local church needs to be aware of what its youth work costs and, where possible, support it. Individual generosity must not be assumed. The church should not always expect to get everything on the cheap.

So every youth group should make and work to a budget, however simple and small that might be. Special events will probably need to be costed separately and be additional to normal running costs.

All this can save a lot of heartache and embarrassment later on. It's little excuse after the event to say, 'But I'd no idea the extra lighting would cost so much.' It is particularly distressing when you are running an event in aid of a charity and end up making a loss because costs were not worked out properly beforehand.

As a reminder here is a simple list of items that can involve you in spending money:

EVERYDAY RUNNING COSTS OF A YOUTH GROUP
- Hire charge or donation for the use of premises
- Administration costs:
    Stationery
    Postage
    Telephone
- Membership fees to any organizations you belong to (Association of Youth Clubs, etc.)
- Expenses of invited guests/speakers (these should always be offered)
- Insurance cover (where it is not paid centrally by the church)
- Resources for sessions/programmes
- Paper
- Marker pens/paint, etc.
- Video hire, etc.
- A small reserve (contingency) fund.

FOR A SPECIAL EVENT

You may well have all the items given above to consider plus all kinds of extras depending upon what you are doing. Remember that if you are planning an outdoor event, especially one that involves 'adventurous activities', you may need extra insurance cover.

BUT WHERE DO WE GET THE MONEY FROM?

- A regular subscription from members (quietly helping those people who genuinely can't afford to pay). Check with other youth workers on the local 'going rate' for subs.
- Your church may be willing to give you an annual donation to support the youth group.
- Some Local Authorities provide some financial support to voluntary youth groups. Enquire at your local youth office or leisure services department.
- Running events that raise money, some of which may go to charity and some for the work of the youth group. If you are doing this, make it clear that the money will be divided and the purpose for which it is being raised.

TREASURE WHAT YOU HAVE

However small the finances of your youth group, keep the money in a bank or building society account in the name of the organization. Holding youth group money in a personal bank account can lead to difficulties and misunderstandings. In fact some churches (the Methodist Church, for example) have a regulation that no money that belongs to the church or one of its organizations is to be kept in a personal account. It is a good practice, therefore, to open an account in the name of the youth group (or relevant management committee) which will require the signature of two adults to withdraw money. It can be equally inefficient to keep youth group money in tins or jars on a kitchen shelf! What a temptation it can be to 'borrow' money or change and forget to pay it back.

But above all, it makes sense and is good stewardship to use an account where the money can be securely held – and earn a little interest (see the parable of the three servants, in Matthew 25. 14–30).

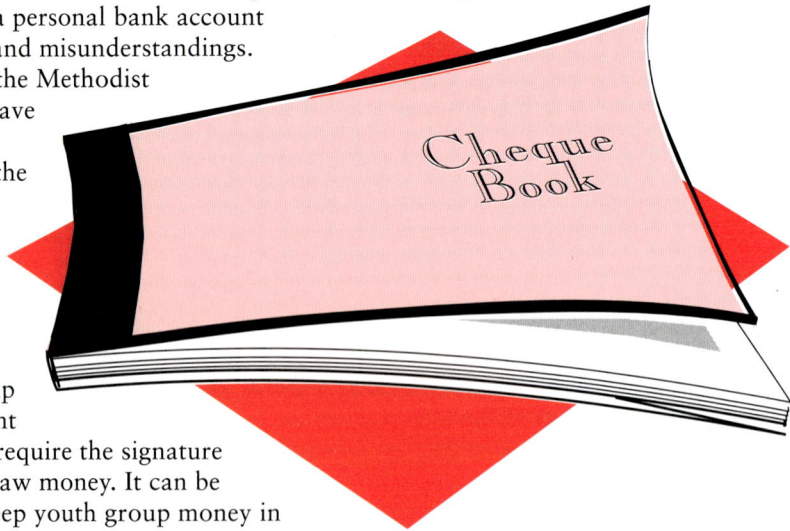

Chapter 12

INTERNATIONAL CUISINE

Taking a world view

Go down any high street and you're likely to be able to choose from a wide range of menus representing many parts of the world. Food from around the world is a delicious part of our way of life.

We should take as much pleasure in ensuring that our youth group has a world view. It is easy to live a cosy existence sheltered from what is happening beyond our own backyard. How much we miss of God's challenging and wonderful world if we allow this to happen. After all, as someone once said, 'Anyone who doesn't worry about the world situation these days needs to have their TV set examined!'

A few years ago, out of ignorance, we might have thought that individuals could make little difference to international issues. Environmental matters have woken us up to see that this is not true. Now we are constantly reminded that each one of us has a personal responsibility to conserve resources (fuel, water, timber, etc.), to promote recycling and act in many other practical ways to help save our ailing world.

As with environmental issues, so also with attitudes to many other world concerns. The youth group can be one place where we can learn to show tolerance and respect. We can enjoy and benefit from members of the group who come from backgrounds, cultures, religions and countries that are different from our own. We can ensure that differences of opinion and points of conflict are resolved sensibly and peacefully without turning to mistrust, bitterness, hate, and even violence.

The tiny 'world' of the youth group can be a place to confront prejudices, test out new ideas, increase knowledge of international affairs and become responsible world citizens. This will help us all to think and pray globally as we act locally.

Chapter 13

COOKING METHODS

An introduction to working with groups
and an A-Z of discussion and involvement methods

You can bake, boil, braise, fry, grill, micro-wave, poach, pressure cook, roast, simmer, steam, stew – to list some of the basic methods of preparing food. You may also need to whisk, stir, roll, garnish, melt, cut, decorate, grate and do many other things to make that favourite dish. Each method has its own purpose and each produces its own texture or flavour in the food. The good cook chooses from a variety of methods to produce the best results.

We need to be familiar with a wide range of group-work methods so that our youth group programme can be interesting, lively, thought-provoking and so that everyone can be involved.

The methods in this section are designed to help people to talk and express themselves – which does not always involve talking! They are given in alphabetical order so that you can quickly refer to the method when you see it mentioned in Part 2.

First some guidelines about helping people to talk in small and large groups:

- Aim to build trust and confidence in the members of the group so that they feel relaxed and able to share their point of view.
- It is important that people know each others names and use them. Use a game, if necessary, to help people learn names (see Chapter 15 'Starters'). Ensure that new people are properly introduced to the group.
- The size of the group should be no larger than eight people. Above this number, it becomes very difficult for everyone to take part in a discussion (see A-Z – Small Groups).
- At times even the group of eight may work more effectively if it is broken down into sub-groups or buzz groups. In these groups even the most shy person will be able to make a point which can then be taken back into the large group (see A-Z – Buzz Groups, Triads, Pairs, etc.).
- Make the meeting place for the group as comfortable as possible. So if, for example, you have to meet in a large hall, put the group or groups into a corner, seated in a circle. The two walls of the corner will give the impression of being in a smaller space and help conquer any problems with an echo.
- Encourage groups to sit in a tight circle so that everyone can be seen and heard.
- The group enabler should sit as part of the same circle and not outside it.
- Where it is possible to control heating and ventilation try to achieve a comfortably warm, but not stuffy or hot, atmosphere. People do not work well if they are either too hot or too cold. Similarly, where possible, control lighting so that it is easy on the eyes and neither too glaring nor too dark.

- Timing is important. Whether you are meeting in a group for a short discussion on just one question or all set for a major debate, make clear to the group the time available, for example, 'We have just ten minutes to talk about this.' Or, 'We have 45 minutes to decide what we are going to do and list up our ideas on this paper.' If more time is needed or the task is finished ahead of the time limit, re-negotiate timing with the whole group.
- Make sure that questions asked are debatable and are not likely to be answered with just a 'yes' or 'no' answer (see A-Z – Questions).
- If notes have to be taken or lists made for reporting back about the groups' discussion, it is generally best if someone other than the group enabler makes these notes. This leaves the enabler free to listen, without distraction, to all the groups' discussion.

THE GROUP ENABLER OR FACILITATOR

This person is not necessarily an expert on the topic or question being discussed. S/he is there, as part of the group, to carry out some or all of the following functions:

Initiating: giving people confidence at the beginning, asking questions within the range of people's experience.

Clarifying: making sure that the meanings of words used are understood by everyone. Clarifying the various stages of an argument.

Stimulating: suggesting new ideas, raising questions that push the discussion further.

Summarizing: drawing together related suggestions in an attempt to arrive at a consensus, decision or definition.

Fact-seeking: asking for pertinent facts.

Probing: asking questions that go below the surface of what is said.

Activating: thinking of ways of bringing others into the discussion, and using their particular experience or expertise.

Being group conscious:
prodding the group into better or faster action.

Valuing: thanking people for their contribution, especially those who say least.

Evaluating: at the end of the group discussion or as soon as possible afterwards, checking with the members of the group about how effective they feel the group has been. Learning from mistakes (see A-Z – Evaluation and Chapter 20 'Afters').

KEEPING DISCUSSION GOING*

Hopefully the discussion will be enjoyable and plenty of learning will come from it. However, any group of people is likely to hit upon problems – below are some of the common ones with some thoughts on how you might deal with them.

LONG AND DIFFICULT SILENCES:
Silence isn't always a bad thing! It can mean that some useful thought is going on. One constructive way of breaking the silence is simply to ask if the silence means that people are thinking, confused, or whatever – to ask if there is anything that needs to be done to get things going again. If the silence is caused by having a difficult task, it might help to break into pairs briefly to talk about it and then share ideas.

ONE PERSON DOING ALL THE TALKING
This needs to be tackled! If you don't then everyone else will lose interest in the group. Remind the person that there is only a limited time to cover each point and perhaps their particular ideas could be chatted over later. This could happen in a pair as well as in a larger group. Avoid being too blunt within the group. You may or may not upset the habitual 'rambler'; more worrying is the fact that you might stop others from speaking for fear of getting the same treatment. If you've got to be blunt, save it until outside the group.

TWO PEOPLE DOING ALL THE TALKING!
You may find it boring or upsetting if the whole session is dominated by two people having a private argument – especially if it is getting away from the point. You could suggest that the issue is saved up for a later session or that the two people could finish off their debate after the meeting time.

SOME PEOPLE NOT JOINING IN
Remember that people have a right not to join in if they don't want to and that some people learn well from listening to others. If someone's silence bothers you, you may want to chat to them about it informally outside of the meeting.

GETTING OFF THE SUBJECT
Don't jump in on this too soon, but in a convenient pause you could point out what is happening and suggest that maybe this is a topic for another session or that some of the group might talk about it elsewhere. If you don't do this you are likely to run out of time. Sometimes these 'red herrings' can be a way of avoiding something. Sometimes however a 'red herring' needs to be followed through if something very urgent has come up. As a guide, ask yourself, 'Is some practical action likely to come out of this?'– if your answer is 'Yes' it could well be worth sticking with it – if your answer is 'No', get back to the subject as soon as possible.

* *These notes taken from* Talking about Talking, *a do-it-yourself discussion pack. Published by Youth Clubs UK 1986.*

AN A–Z OF GROUP DISCUSSION AND INVOLVEMENT METHODS

AGENDA MAKING

This is a way of helping everyone to decide what they would like to talk about. The group make their own agenda which can be a list of things that interest people or different aspects of a topic. Firstly the enabler says that the group has, say, three minutes to list what they would like to discuss (see 'Brainstorming' overleaf). Have someone write ideas up as they are given so that they can be seen by all. As a group, decide how long you want to have for discussion and how many of the items listed you can deal with. Then if the list is too long, get a majority decision on which items should be dealt with now and whether you are going to talk about the others later. The enablers job is to keep the discussion on track and try to deal with the agreed Agenda within the time allowed and to see that if any action is to be taken on any matter, it is clear who is to do it. The method is democratic. The agenda is the work of the whole group and has not been imposed on them.

AUDIO AND VISUAL AIDS (see also Chapter 7 'The Place Setting – what you need')

The use of a piece of music, an excerpt from a video, a few slides or a single picture can all provoke discussion or, when the time is right, provide new information to take a conversation to a further stage. Here are some important guidelines in using audio and visual aids:

- If you need to use equipment, such as an overhead projector, make sure it is working and focused before you start your group discussion and that you have a spare projector lamp and know how to fit it.
- Ensure everyone can see the picture or screen and that any sound is at a comfortable level.
- Never use a video, slide set or film without reviewing it first. Check that it is really right for the purpose you have in mind. People tend to react better to a short section than a full presentation that may make all the arguments and leave little for the group to talk about.
  (See also A-Z – Using Video)
- Make sure that the audio or visual aid used does actually help the conversation and does not steer it in a direction that is not helpful or provide new information too early.

A simple back – and front – projection screen

This can be made inexpensively and to what ever size you require. Although rigid, the screen is virtually unbreakable.

The screen has been found to be ideal for small group use. It can be used in full daylight or in a fully lit room.

The picture is clearly visible on both sides of the screen – but remember if you are projecting text that it will be backwards on one side!

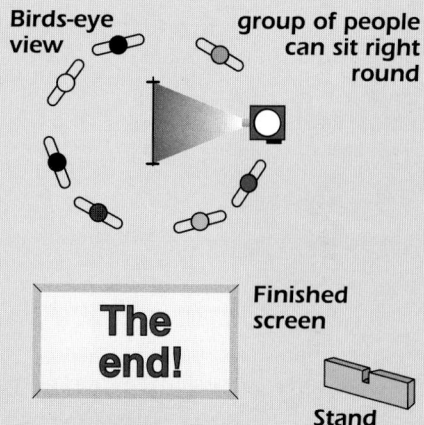

Birds-eye view

group of people can sit right round

The end!

Finished screen

Stand

How to make the screen

The screen is made like a sandwich – the 'bread' being two pieces of clear rigid plastic and the 'filling' a single piece of white translucent (semi-transparent) material.

Allow a small over-lap when cutting the inner sheet **B**. Stick this down to the edge of one piece of rigid plastic with sellotape so that it is taut. Then fasten all three pieces of the sandwich together with an edging of coloured sticky tape.

A & C – Clear, rigid plastic (polystyrene or acrylic) as sold for cheap double-glazing. The plastic can be bought to the size required or cut with a saw. It is obtainable by the sheet from DIY stores.

B – Sandwiched between the clear rigid plastic is a single piece of white translucent (semi-transparent) plastic* or a piece of good quality tracing paper. Even grease-proof kitchen paper gives a reasonable picture.

* *Plastic sheets sold by, for example, Boots the Chemist, for baby's cot or pram sheets (waterproof) give an excellent projected picture.*

Edge of B – secure with sticky tape to edge of plastic

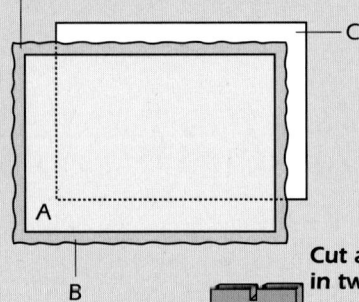

C

A

B

Cut a slot in two wood blocks to make a stand

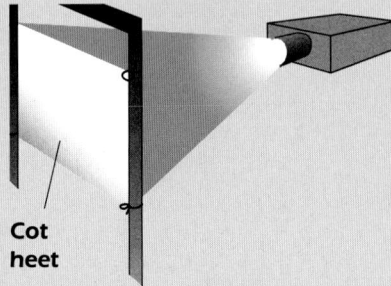

Cot heet

BRAINSTORMING

An effective and quick way of collecting a wide range of ideas and views (see also 'Agenda making' above). The group may be considering a topic, theme or looking for new ideas. The enabler encourages and accepts all suggestions, which are listed on paper for all to see. At this stage only questions of clarification should be allowed and the enabler should discourage discussion of particular points until the group decides that they have run out of ideas. Even so a maximum of five minutes is usually long enough for the exercise. When the list is complete, the group decides which ideas it wants to spend more time discussing and what further action is needed. To stimulate ideas, before brainstorming in a group, people can be asked to have a quick preliminary think in 'Buzz groups' (see following paragraph). This method almost always produces a quick and wide ranging response from a group.

BUZZ GROUPS

Sub groups of a small group. A buzz group is usually a short meeting of two or three people who then feed their discussion into the main group. The name comes from the sound of several groups all buzzing or talking together! This method is a great confidence builder. It enables the most timid person to voice their views in a safe way.

CASE STUDY or HISTORY

A case study gives the group either in written form or verbally, a brief description of a situation or 'case'. The more true to life the situation, the more likely it will be to create a reaction and discussion. The case study might be a newspaper report of an incident that leaves unanswered questions or raises moral dilemmas. The group having heard the details, acts like a jury considering what it has heard and passing an opinion on the facts. A case study can lead to Role Play or a Simulation Game (see below).

CREATIVE METHODS

Words! Words! Words! That seems to be how we expect people to express themselves – 'Why don't you say something!' or 'How can I know what you think unless you tell me!' But of course people have many ways of expressing themselves and words are not necessarily the best one. Many people find it better and more satisfactory to share their feelings by creative means, perhaps using their bodies and their hands instead of their mouth. At any time in a group programme or discussion it may be right and best to break off from talking and to encourage people to paint a picture or shape some clay and so answer questions or make comments in a different way (see Chapter 7 'The place setting –What you need').

A bonus in using creative methods can be to ask people in your church or community with practical skills to share these. However, this does mean that you will need to pre-plan and, out of courtesy to the person who has been asked to help, give them time to demonstrate their creative talent and encourage others to use it.

Remember to be careful when you are involved in some of the more messy creative methods and make sure that the floors and furniture are well protected with plastic sheets or newspaper.

Here's a reminder of some creative methods and materials:

Clay
> Get a small bag of it from an art shop. Stored properly it lasts a long time. Or you could use plasticine, but it is not as satisfying.

Paint, marker pens, etc.
> You might be able to come to some bulk buying arrangement with a local play group to get a supply of these. Make sure you use water-based markers.

Photography
> Ask people to bring cameras and use them with imagination to take a series of images or create a photo story (see also 'Knowing names' below).

Posters and pictures
> Ask around for a source of large paper (printers, newspapers offices, etc.) before you go out and buy (see Chapter 7).

Junk
> Cartons, tins, plastic – you name it, it can be used effectively to express an idea. You'll need glue, sellotape, string, etc., to fasten things together.

Strip cartoons
> Individuals draw their own to illustrate a point or tell a story. Or people can work

in a small group to produce a cartoon or even a whole group can work on a large piece of paper or on overhead projector acetates.

Collage
Use different materials to make a picture or poster. This can be an individual or group effort.

Montage
A similar technique to collage, only you use a collection of pictures, words from newspapers, etc.

Making a Newspaper
(see Chapter 18 'Ready-to-serve meals' – simulation games – 'Hold the front page!'). Use this idea or simply make a wall newspaper with everybody contributing different stories and pictures.

Radio or television programme
Put together a programme using a tape recorder or video camera. To do this will involve a whole range of people – script writers, actors, presenters, technical people, location managers, etc.

Drama
Informal or scripted drama; a brief sketch or a major production. Like radio and TV a wide range of skills can be used. Don't forget that dramatic action can also be presented using puppets and shadow plays on a screen.

Music
Expressing views or ideas through known music or songs or encouraging the group to create their own. Those who don't play instruments or compose may still be able to join in on home-made percussion instruments.

Poetry and prose
A writing workshop can be great fun if people work in small groups and are given real freedom of expression.

Multi media
This means mixing or integrating a variety of methods. So, for example, you could create a background for drama by preparing a montage or back projecting a slide on to a large screen. Or pictures and posters could be transferred to video to tell a story.

DE-BRIEFING AND AFFIRMING
(see also 'Role play' and 'Simulation games')
At the end of some exercises and games it is essential to allow time for people to talk about, and even talk out of their system, the experience they have been through. Don't treat this lightly. People can get very wrapped up and emotionally involved in the action of a role play. They may need help to snap out of their role and return to their own frame of mind and normal personality. Similarly, if, as part of a role play or simulation, someone has been seen as stupid or a 'baddy' and been verbally attacked, this person may need careful debriefing and affirming by the whole group.

A Z

EVALUATION

This is an essential part of any youth group programme. It means checking out with the whole group the value of what they have done and shared together. What challenged them the most? What didn't they like? What did they really enjoy? How can discussion/involvement be improved in future? (See Chapter 20 'Afters – Reporting back and evaluation')

EXHIBITIONS or DISPLAYS

Space for exhibiting news, notices, 'feed back' sheets, posters or messages is an important part of involving people in the youth group. If there is a notice board the group can call its own it should be someone's job to keep it tidy, interesting and up to date. Where no display space is available consider having a portable notice board that can be put away at the end of each group session. The illustrations show some other imaginative ways of attracting attention or exhibiting ideas.

▼ Paint cardboard boxes with emulsion paint to cover advertising wording. Stack them high as portable notice boards for special events.

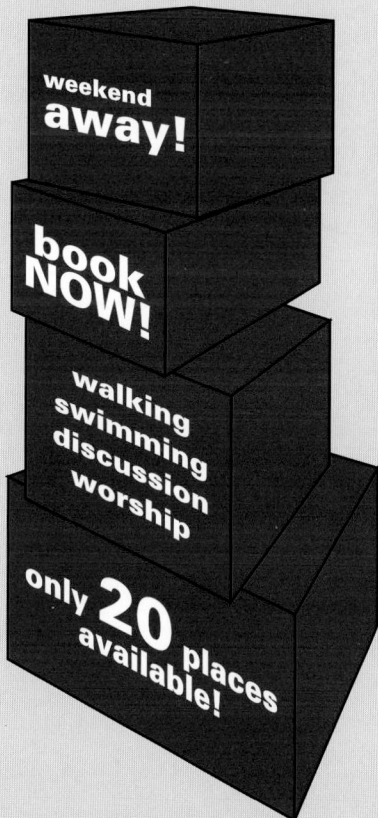

▼ Have someone take a sandwich board around made from two pieces of cardboard

▼ Peep hole box. Replace the top of the box with tracing paper to let light through. Cut keyhole spy hole in the front. Stick notice for the event inside the box on the side opposite the keyhole. Irresistible!

weekend **away!**

book NOW!

walking swimming discussion worship

only **20** places available!

d club **isco** next week!

Look! what's happening?

FEEDBACK or REPORTING BACK

When a group has discussed a question or concern they need to be able to share their conversation in a clear, effective and interesting way. The most common, but often least satisfactory way of getting feedback from a group is for someone to make a verbal report. This has to be very well done if it is not to be boring. Alternative and perhaps better ways of getting feedback from discussion are:

- Writing up, on large paper, headline statements of the main points made that can be displayed for all to see.
- Using one or more of the creative methods or materials outlined above. So, for example, the group could report back by presenting a brief drama that makes the point that they want to share.
- The enabler can ask questions of the group or interview a member of it to discover what they talked about.
- One person from each group can go into the group next to theirs and share what they discussed and hear what happened in the group being visited.
- By having a flip chart or large piece of paper on the wall with marker pens available points being made within a group can be written up by a designated 'scribe' as the group continues to talk. This enables groups to feed off each others ideas. Points made will almost certainly need clarifying by the enabler at the end.

FISH BOWL

See 'Role play'

GAMES

All kinds of games can be used to get people involved or even to make a point in discussion. Rather than talking first about topics such as communication, conflict, relationships, team work, competitiveness and so on, playing an appropriate game will spark off lively discussion (find some ideas in Chapter 15 'Starters' and Chapter 18 'Ready-to-serve meals').

INTERVIEWS

To make a change from asking someone to speak on a subject, ask instead if they are prepared to be interviewed. Two or three young people then go to meet the chosen person to discover what she or he has to say, what makes them tick, and decide on the main questions to be asked. At the same time they will all gain confidence in conducting the interview. When the person meets the full group and gives the interview, it is important that a time limit is decided on and kept to. Fifteen to twenty minutes should be long enough if the questions and answers are clear and to the point.

'IN' TRAY EXERCISES

A kind of simulation game (see Chapter 18 'Ready-to-serve meals'). This method focuses on reaching a priority order based on materials such as letters, messages, invoices, etc., left in an imaginary 'In' Tray in an office. As the example shows in Chapter 18 this can be a very creative and lively way in thinking about helping people decide what the real priorities are in a particular situation.

KNOWING NAMES

If we know each other's names it is much more likely we can get people involved. If someone calls us by our name first before they ask us a question or a request to do something, we are much more likely to take notice. As has been said earlier, make sure people know the names of the others who are in the same group. Take time to do this – it is time well spent. If necessary use a quick game to help the learning. Here are two ideas:

- Go round the group and ask everyone to say their name once and clearly. Then give a soft ball or bean bag to one person and ask them to throw it to someone else in the group at the same time saying the person's name. The receiver then does the same, but must throw it at a different person – and so on until the whole group has been named. Repeat if there are still some names not being remembered.
- Write on small bits of paper the names of all the people in the group. Put the name papers in the centre of the group face down. People go one at a time to pick up one paper, returning it if it is their own, and putting it at the feet of the person whose name appears on the paper. If they don't guess right the group helps them out.

(For many more games see Chapter 15 'Starters')

For the youth group as a whole you could have a photo album or display board containing everyone's named portrait. Appoint an official photographer whose job it is to get a picture of all the members of the group, adding new ones as they come along. To the pictures add a few details about age, school, work, interests, etc. Have respect for the fact that not everyone will want to have their photo taken. There could be a variety of reasons for this. But this doesn't rule out, if they'll allow it, their name appearing with the other biographical details.

MEASURING STRENGTH OF FEELING

This method helps people to share their feelings on a topic in a symbolic way and encourages them to talk about how they have come to their choice. Examples of this method are given in detail in Chapter 16 'Main Course' – see Consequences theme Session (c) and Choice theme Session (a). Briefly the method involves people answering questions with responses like yes, no or maybe, by putting a piece of paper with their name on it at a point on the floor that symbolizes these answers. So 'Yes' is in the centre of the room, 'No' at the edge, and 'Maybe' in between. Or a ladder is drawn on a large piece of paper and graded from 1 at the bottom to 10 at the top. People express their feelings about an issue by writing their name at points on the ladder that match their opinion. After answers have been demonstrated in this practical way discussion takes places on why they have voted as they have. After discussion you can go to another round asking the same question to see if opinions have been changed, and if so, why.

PAIRS

Even smaller than buzz groups! An enabler, when a question has been asked or a statement made, asks people to talk with their neighbour. Sharing in conversation with just one other person first will mean ideas can be tested out in private to help build the confidence to speak out in a bigger group.

PICTURES

Television bombards us with moving pictures. Frequently these pictures are fast moving, only giving us an impression or a glimpse of the whole image. Television directors can play on our thoughts and emotions with these constantly changing illustrations sometimes heightened by bold colours, strong music and clever graphics. Moods can be changed from solemn to joyful simply by photographic tricks and appropriate music. By contrast if we have for display and handling in the youth group 'still' pictures, people can study in detail the image that is offered and not feel manipulated by it. The message, meaning and purpose of the picture can be questioned and reflected upon. A collection of pictures can be a most valuable tool for group discussion and for other purposes. Try to build up a collection firstly by asking members and friends to bring along newspaper supplements and magazines. Have a session where people cut out any picture that interests them. Trim the picture and, if possible mount it on card of a handy size such as A4. Keep the picture collection growing and up to date. It should not take long, with the help of the church community, to get a collection of two to three hundred pictures so that there is real choice available. Here are some ways the pictures can be used:

Picture rummy

Give everyone in the group a random selection of, say, four pictures each. Any remaining pictures are put in a pile in the centre of the group. Ask the people firstly to select one picture that particularly interests them from the set in their hand. Next ask them to return the remaining three pictures to the centre pile. If in their first selection they really cannot find a picture that appeals they can return their set to the centre pile just once and take four more pictures. So now everyone should have just one picture in their hand. Pictures are shared and the pair are asked to decide which of the two they will keep, the second picture having to be returned to the centre pile. Lastly pairs join up to form a group of four which should now have just two pictures between them. Once again they have to choose which of the remaining two pictures they are going to keep and which return to the centre pile. When they have chosen the groups of four explain to each other why they have selected this one picture from all the ones they have looked at. Not only does this make a very interesting exercise but it can sometimes show the kind of topics and concerns that people in the group have which they may want to follow up with further conversation or projects.

Pictorial prayers

From all the pictures available ask people quietly to select just one picture that illustrates something they would like to pray about. With the pictures in the middle of the group so that everybody can see them and, in an atmosphere of meditation, encourage people if they wish to say a few words of prayer based on the theme of their picture. Alternatively you could have quiet music playing in the background while people simply reflect and pray silently about the illustrations before them.

Words in their mouth

Select from the collection pictures that have people in them. Have some bits of paper cut in the shape of speech bubbles. People are now asked to write on the speech bubbles what they think the people in the pictures may be saying. This exercise can cause great fun with funny and silly remarks being given to people in the pictures but it can also have moments of seriousness as the right words are chosen to put into the mouths of people who face starvation or tragedy or war.

News story

Write long captions or news stories based on what is in the selected picture. A game can be made out of this by removing the captions from the pictures, putting them in the centre of the room and asking people to decide which caption goes with which picture.

Revelation!

Choose two or three pictures without people seeing what they are. Cover the picture with a piece of paper. As the group concentrates on the picture gradually tear or cut away pieces of the covering paper so that the illustration is slowly revealed. Ask people to comment on what they think the picture is about as it slowly comes into view. Are they misled by some of the early glimpses? Does anybody guess very early on the format of the whole picture from a small visual cue? If so why?

Themes

Using an issue that is already being discussed or simply thinking of a title, use the whole collection to select appropriate pictures that illustrate and bring to life the theme.

Beyond the boundaries

Individually or in small groups people select a picture and place it in the centre of a much larger piece of paper. Now they use their imagination to draw on the paper the scene that lies beyond the edges of the picture in the centre. Groups should share their pictures with others and explain how they decided what lay beyond the boundaries.

Pictured psalm

Choose a psalm from the Bible that has plenty of detail in it and, using the picture selection, illustrate each verse with contemporary images. Set them out in order on the floor or 'blu tacked' on the wall and slowly read the psalm as people follow the order of the pictures selected. See also the Choice theme, Session (a) in Chapter 16 and use pictures instead of words.

PLENARY

The posh name meaning everyone meets together! So with a group of twenty-four people, you might first meet in three groups of eight to discuss something and then come together for a plenary session to share views, usually chaired by the enabler. Plenary sessions need to be handled with care so that they are not too long, keep to the point and, where appropriate, have a satisfactory conclusion including taking some action. As with all group work, make sure that people can still see and hear each other even though the group is much larger.

QUESTIONS

An excellent way to start and continue discussion. But questions have their dangers. The enabler should write key questions down in preparing for a session to ensure that they make sense and can be answered. To avoid the answer to a question being just 'yes' or 'no', start the question with 'who', 'what', 'where', 'why', or 'how'. This generally means that a fuller answer can be given. The broadcaster Rabbi Lionel Blue says that he is sometimes asked why Jews often seem to answer one question with another. To which he answers 'Why Not!' Come to think of it, Jesus often did the same and this is a skill that enablers will find it useful to practise (see Luke 10. 25–37).

QUESTIONNAIRES

Get the group to create their own to follow up on a topic they are researching. Then go out with the questionnaire into your church after Sunday services or into the street and ask for a response to the questions. Before going out, you may want to role play the experience of stopping and asking questions of strangers. This will help build confidence and effectiveness.

Some Do's
- Do carry some form of identity in the streets
- Do work in pairs and arrange for 'check points' to be staffed by adult supervisors
- Do share with people why you are seeking their views
- Do keep the list of questions short
- Do be polite
- Do make sure the questions can be answered unambiguously.

Afterwards compare answers, draw up a report, statistics and maybe recommendations arising from your research. (See also Chapter 16 Main Course 'Power' theme session (a))

QUIZZES

A fun way of putting information across can be to extract answers by means of a quiz. It doesn't always mean having teams. A whole group can be invited to join in. If there is unlikely to be much knowledge about the subject you can have available books and leaflets which contain the information to answer the questions. The group will enjoy hunting through them.

REPORTING BACK

See 'Feedback'.

RESEARCH PROJECT

This may arise from a discussion or may happen in its own right. It can involve a few people or many. It can take a couple of hours or a couple of months. However, if a research project is undertaken make sure that the information that is discovered and presented is valued and given a wide audience. Help researchers to know where they are most likely to obtain the information needed to follow up on a particular topic. A library will almost certainly be able to help, but also there may be people in the local churches and community who have specialized knowledge and who could be asked for advice. When the research has been completed it may well lead on to some people wanting to take action in some way as a result of what they have learned.

ROLE PLAY

This is usually an informal and spontaneous acting out of a situation by a few volunteers to portray a familiar human relationships problem. Role play is usually unscripted but those people taking part need careful briefing and, sometimes, debriefing. The method can be used in a wide variety of ways:

- The most common way is to take a situation (rather like a Case study – see reference) and have a few people act it out in front of the remainder of the group. For example, three volunteers take on the roles respectively of a mother, a father and their 17-year-old daughter. The 'plot' of the role play is that the daughter, who has been unemployed for a year, has at last got a job but it means moving away from home. In telling her parents the exciting news that she has found work, it emerges that her father is far from keen about her leaving home. The role players use their imagination to develop the story and the relationships between the characters (points to watch when using role play' see next page). The group who are observing the role play are encouraged to watch and listen carefully. It is a helpful idea to site the role players in the centre of a circle of observers, almost as if they are in a goldfish bowl. The audience can then see the characters from different angles, which will add to the interest. At the end of the role play, the enabler should first invite the observers to comment on what they heard and saw and discuss the various points made. Then the role players should have their turn but should speak 'out of role'. The enabler will want to encourage the players to say how they felt about their role; whether they could identify with the character they played. Were they surprised by any of the comments made by the other players or the observers?

- In a Simulation Game (see next page) all those taking part may be required to take on a role.

- The skills of making priorities and decision-making can be improved by a group role-playing a committee meeting. The group will need to have a realistic agenda and probably reports and other papers to make the meeting come to life. Roles are allocated to cover the chairperson, secretary, treasurer and other members of the committee who will take on a wide range of personalities and prejudices found in any age group. Once again it is important to allow plenty of time for an evaluation of what has happened once the role play is over. This is where the real learning takes place (see Chapter 18 'Ready to serve meals – Help! Pat's Ill').

- New insights into Bible stories can emerge through role play. Read the selected passage first then ask for volunteers to role play the central characters and perhaps some other people who could feature in the story. See if the role play can take the story on beyond the words in the Bible, remembering you are looking for new meaning and inspiration and not just trying to 'fictionalize'. Here are a few examples of scripture passages that lend themselves to role play:

    The Parable of the Prodigal Son (Luke 15. 11–32)
    Role play the elder son talking with his mother (who does not feature in the parable) the day after the welcome home party.

    The Rich Man (Luke 18. 18–23)
    Involve the rich, probably young, man in a conversation with two or three of his friends when he tells them about his encounter with Jesus.

    After the Resurrection (Luke 24. 1–11)
    Act out the reaction of the Apostles when the women return from the tomb.

An extra dimension can be added to role play by having 'character advisers'. We'll use the Prodigal Son story as an example. Having found volunteers to role play the elder son and his mother, give each character the opportunity to spend a few minutes with a group of two or three 'advisers'. They help the role player to build up his or her character – the attitude to take, the questions to ask, the emotions to display and so on. Once the role play has been proceeding for a few minutes the enabler can stop the action at a convenient point and allow the characters to seek the further views of the advisers.

Points to watch when using role play
- The enabler needs to set the scene carefully so that everyone, players and observers, understands the purpose of the role play.
- Watch timing. Do not allow the role play to drag on. The enabler must be prepared to step in and stop the action so that the points raised for discussion can be tackled.

A short 10–15 minute role play that is lively and interesting is likely to have much more effect than a longer one that starts to run out of steam.

- Try to avoid a role play becoming farcical and losing its point by ensuring the role players are well briefed.
- Allow ample time for debriefing the role players. People can become emotionally involved in the character they play and they may need time to talk themselves out of it. Get them to say their own name again and say 'I am no longer...' Similarly observers can continue to associate opinions shared by a character with that person when the role play is finished. Ensure that everyone knows the role play is over and everyone is back to being themselves (see 'Debriefing and affirming').
- Avoid people playing characters that are too close to a situation in which they have actually been or are working through.

A ROUND

A quick and effective way of getting a group to express feelings or brainstorm ideas. Sitting in a circle, the enabler invites the group members to add a brief comment to her/his opening statement. For example, the enabler says:

'The most important thing I have learnt in this discussion is...'

In turn, members of the group add their comments. If individuals don't wish to join in or have nothing to add they simply say 'pass' when their turn comes. A round can be used to measure the feelings of a group by asking some of these questions, perhaps part way through a discussion or after a break and before conversation is resumed:

'The best thing about this group is...'

'I don't like it in this group when...'

'Because of our discussion I now think we should...'

After all the views have been heard there will be the need for a few minutes discussion to comment on what has been said and to sort out any problems or difficulties that have been exposed.

SCRAP BOOK

Keep a youth group scrap book (see also Chapter 19 'Seasoning'). This is probably most easily done using a ring-binder into which you can insert A4 sheets and other items such as programmes from events, posters, etc. Appoint a keeper of the scrap book whose job it is to keep it up to date and interesting. Whenever the group meets the scrap book should be on show for browsing. Encourage people to write in favourite sayings, prepare reports on activities, paste in photographs, etc. The scrap book can be a lively and useful way of showing new members what the group gets up to.

SIMULATION GAMES

The well known game 'Monopoly' is a kind of simulation game. Players take on the role of the big spender and try to acquire as much property as they can. So a simulation is like an extended role play, often lasting for an hour or two and involving more people. An experience is lived out together, factors are introduced to give new challenges and twists and turns to the basic 'plot' of the game. A well planned and presented simulation game can be a thought-provoking and valuable learning exercise. But, be warned, a lot of preparation is usually needed, feelings and emotions can be highly charged and so it is essential to allow ample time for discussion and debriefing. In short, do not rush a simulation game. More harm than good may be the result.

Work with a team of enablers and evaluate the experience when the game and debriefing is complete. The use of simulation is particularly suited to day or residential events where people have time to relax together and there is time to do full justice to the aims and purposes of the simulation (see Chapter 18 'Ready-to-serve meals').

SMALL GROUPS

Serious discussion is most effectively carried out in small groups. In a group of up to eight people, it is possible for everyone to participate and for the enabler to work with the group in an informal but productive manner. Care may sometimes need to be taken in the membership of the small group. The enabler may want to encourage people to be in a different group from a brother or sister or a best friend to allow for a free and frank sharing of opinions (see guidelines in the introduction to this chapter).

A 'SNOWBALL' DISCUSSION

Yes, a talking snowball! This works on the same basis as a small snowball being rolled along and getting bigger and bigger as it collects more snow. Here is an interesting discussion method that starts with people studying on their own a brief Bible passage or an aspect of a subject. Ideally people work in groups that eventually total eight although you could use multiples of three. Here is an example of how a snowball discussion is started and progresses. The enabler needs to be alert to timing and offer to help any individual or grouping where they seem to have become stuck. It is best if all participants are provided with a sheet set out in a style similar to this example:

Getting his priorities right...

These incidents from the Bible show us something of the values Jesus had. Firstly, on your own, read the passage from the New Testament that has been marked on the list below:

1   Matthew 4. 1–11   – The Temptation of Jesus
2   Matthew 6. 24–27   – God and possessions (1)
3   Matthew 6. 28–34   – God and possessions (2)
4   Mark 6. 7 – 13   – Jesus sends out the 12 Disciples
5   Luke 9. 57 – 62   – The would-be followers of Jesus
6   Luke 12. 13–21   – The Parable of the Rich Fool
7   Luke 18. 18–23   – The Rich Man
8   Luke 19. 1–10   – Jesus and Zacchaeus

> **Note down anything you think the passage says about values and priorities.**
> After about five minutes share your reading and your thoughts with a partner. Your partner will have been reading a different passage.
> After about ten minutes join up with another partnership to make a group of four people. Share together now the main points that have emerged and list them on a piece of paper. (If you have time, please look up the four readings not covered by your group.)

You can stop the discussion rolling here or continue with a final group of **eight** people, drawing together the main points of all the readings. Non-biblical material can be handled in the same way by dividing information amongst eight participants. So, for example, if you were considering drug abuse, individuals could be given one of eight short extracts from leaflets about drugs which they study and then, progressively, in the manner described above, share their information and learn from others.

TAKE YOUR PLACE – Or the empty chair

Here is a slightly gimmicky but none the less effective involvement method for occasional use. It can be used for at least two purposes, first as a way of bringing a new dimension to a discussion group, and second, to bring new ideas and liveliness to a more formal committee meeting or planning group. In the first example, a group of, say, six or seven people are invited to discuss in front of everyone else a topic, let's say the problems of leaving home for the first time. This group sits in a circle but leaves one chair empty. Everyone else may only listen to and observe the discussion. They must not interrupt. However, if someone madly wants to add a point or comment on a view that has been expressed, they may do so by occupying the empty chair but only for long enough to make their point. They must then vacate the seat and leave it for someone else. Similarly, with a committee meeting, an empty chair is left, observers are invited who make their contributions to the meeting by occupying the empty chair. In this more formal meeting, it is important that the 'visitor' observes normal committee procedure and speaks only when invited to by the chairperson.

TALKS

Lectures or 'input'

Virtually all methods described in this A-Z are participative. This is deliberate as it enables young people to be fully involved and to gain confidence in sharing their views, learning tolerance and practising methods of gaining knowledge. But we must not rule out straight talk as a way of putting over information and opinions.

A well informed and experienced speaker who can be trusted to keep to a time limit can make a most valuable contribution to a programme and lead to lively discussion (see 'Interviews' in this section).

TRIADS

Nothing to do with oriental criminals but simply people meeting in groups of three for discussion. Break the usual mould of debate by asking three people to take one letter each – A, B, or C. A is first to talk about the topic being considered. B listens to what A is saying and, when s/he has finished reports, in his/her own words what has been said. C observes and, when B has finished, highlights any differences in interpretation and summarizes the main points made. If another topic is to be discussed, the members of the group take on new letters and new roles.

USING VIDEO

Hiring a video or using something recorded from the television is a very popular group activity. It may form a major part of a youth group meeting from time to time. But remember that it is largely a passive activity rarely provoking strong views. If, therefore, it is intended to use video material to stimulate discussion, it is usually better to use just a short clip and set it within a fuller session related to the topic being considered. And, of course, always check the video before you use it to make sure it really does provide the material or information that is wanted and does not take the conversation off at a tangent (see Chapter 7 'Video Player and Monitor' – caution note).

WARM UP GAMES or 'ICE BREAKERS' See Chapter 15 ' Starters'.

Part 2

What's on the Menu?

Chapter 14

GIVING THANKS

Worship in the youth group

'Jesus then took the loaves, gave thanks, and distributed to those who were seated, as much as they wanted. He did the same with the fish.'

This verse from John 6. describes Jesus saying grace before a remarkable picnic attended by well over 5,000 people!

Throughout this book we are likening the life of a youth group to a good meal – good company, a menu with a wide choice, informed but smooth running and fun. And the urge to come back again – soon.

Although sadly it's a dying practice, every meal should start by giving thanks to God: saying Grace. Simply offering a brief prayer:

> 'This happy meal will happier be,
> If we, O Lord, remember thee.'

And so it should be with a Christian youth group's programme. Prayer should be a part of all the preparations made for the group by adults and young people. It should spill over into the group's meetings and bubble up as natural and spontaneous worship that sends everyone out feeling challenged and blessed and with God's spirit empowering them to serve him.

In Chapter 16 'Main Course', suggestions are made for prayer and worship linked to the activities. Use these ideas creatively if they appeal to you. But work always towards lively, relevant worship that involves the body, mind and spirit of everyone.

Pray for and prepare worship that is:

- RELEVANT to the life and times of the group
- REVERENT, but not pious
- SIMPLE in style and language
- LIVELY and certainly not boring
- INCLUSIVE so that no one feels left out
- PARTICIPATIVE and not dependent on one person every time.

Someone has said that Christian worship should be like a party where God is the host and everyone is invited.

It can be helpful to use a basic structure to give the worship shape and purpose. Here is one format that could be used:
- *An invitation to worship*
  Start with a song or hymn or a Bible verse that invites people to worship.

- *A point of contact*
  A story, symbol, drama, audio or visual aid that is relevant to the particular youth group's programme, membership, mood and the moment in time when the worship is taking place.

- *A Bible passage...*
  ...that illuminates or comments on the theme of the worship. This should arise naturally from or be part of the Point of Contact.

- *What is our response?*
  In the Main Course sessions this may become part of the 'Follow-up' section. If not, it is important that people should be given the opportunity to consider how they respond to what God is saying to them through the worship. This response may be very brief with someone just making a comment, or saying a brief prayer of commitment. Another person may be inspired to sing a song or read another passage from the Bible that sheds light on something that had happened through the worship. Or the worship may touch someone's heart and mind so deeply that their response to God is life changing. After all isn't that what we are always praying for? – so we must have faith to expect it to happen.

RESOURCES FOR WORSHIP AND BIBLE STUDY

These are just as essential as all the paper, paint, games equipment and so on mentioned in Chapter 7 'The Place Setting – What You Need'. Once again some cost will be involved although you could find an appeal in the church magazine may get you useful books passed on that are no longer needed by the owners. If not, compile a list of the books the group needs and ask people to give them as a present to mark their birthday or some other happy occasion.

Build a collection to include:

- Hymn and song books (music and words editions) *
- Different translations of the Bible – but encourage everyone to bring their own copy. You may like to recommend a particular version so that everyone is following from the same translation. Other versions are helpful for comparison purposes
- Books of prayers
- Bible Encyclopedia or handbook
- Bible Concordance
- Bible Atlas
- Books with non-biblical readings for worship purposes.

** It is **illegal** to copy words and music without the written permission of the copyright owners. It is a good idea to obtain a copy of the Code of Fair Practice drawn up by user groups and publishers, available from Music Publishers' Association Ltd, 3rd Floor, Strandgate, 18/20 York Building, London WC2N 6JU. For information about the Hymn Lyrics Copyright Directory contact Stainer & Bell, P.O. Box 110, 23 Gruneisen Road, London N3 1DZ (send stamped, addressed envelope).*

TUCK IN!

'All of you are Christ's body, and each one is a part of it.'
1 Corinthians 12. 27.

Let's face it, a lot of young people don't like going to church! 'Worship's fine' they say 'when it's just us here together singing some choruses and so on. But the services at church are just so boring!' Many adults think the same, which is one reason why some churches are nearly empty.

Hopefully, the local church of which your group is a part is vibrant and it's a joy to worship there. (If not Main Course theme 'Change' session C – 'Their Church, Our Church' could help you to get discussion going about the present life, worship and witness of your church and lead towards some changes being made.)

In whatever situation you find yourself it is everyone's responsibility to see that the youth group remains part of the whole life of the church. The Church, 'Christ's body' (1 Corinthians 12. 27) is already broken enough without more injuries being caused by a youth group becoming a kind of alternative 'youth church' (see Chapter 2 'Family meal').

As a group, talk about how you can make sure that young people are actively involved in the whole life of the church; valued as people and members in their own right, with enthusiasm, skills and talents to share.

Young people are certainly not the church of tomorrow (it may never come). **They are very much the church of today.**

Chapter 15

STARTERS

'Warm-up' and 'ice-breaker' games

'Is it to be the soup (it's home-made vegetable), the prawn cocktail or fruit juice? – there's orange, grapefruit and pineapple. Madam? Sir? and for the young man? Thank you. And for your main course? What would you like?...'

A starter – an appetizing start to a nice meal, designed to get the taste-buds going before the main course comes along.

How we begin a session in a youth group can make all the difference to how it goes. Starters are important.

This section gives you lots of ideas for 'warm-up' games or 'ice-breakers'. Short games that help people relax and have fun together before moving into something more serious.

Even with a small group of people there can still be value in using an ice-breaker. Many of the ideas here can be used with groups of just eight or so people.

Pointers for Starters

- They don't need to have 'a point' other than bringing people together, having fun, helping people to relax.
- Some people don't like 'silly' games and some may be excluded by physical or mental games. Try to use starters that include everyone and are not always competitive (see 'New Games' below).
- Keep starters lively and short. Sometimes it may only take five minutes to warm people up before the main activity.
- Keep starters in proportion. They are not the main activity – just the appetizer.

'NEW GAMES' MOVEMENT

Games don't have to be competitive. Playing to win can be counter-productive to good youth work where we are trying to include everyone, build confidence and encourage co-operation. The New Games Movement sets out to help people see the fun and value there can be in non-competitive games. This does not mean that only 'wimps' will play new games. In fact many non-competitive games require a lot of skill, determination and energy. Try them and see.

The New Games Movement motto is:

Play hard – each playing as well as they can – for fun.
Play fair – players agree together the rules they want.
No-one hurt – it's easier to trust when we care about each other's safety.

READ AND PONDER...

...what Jesus said about feeling we are the best, the 'greatest', the 'winner'. Greatness, he suggests, comes from helping others, giving support and confidence to people who feel they are losers.

See Luke 9. 23–24 – 'he must deny himself...' and
Luke 9. 46–48 – 'who will be the greatest?'

PARACHUTE GAMES

– take Starter Games to new heights!

If you can borrow a parachute for games (at ground level!) you can be sure of great fun and lots of opportunity for co-operative games.

Parachutes are often available for loan from local Education Authority Youth Offices, from a 'New Games Movement' group or a leisure centre. Some play groups have them, although they are sometimes of smaller dimensions than the 'real thing'.

Games with a parachute can be played in a large hall, or better still, outside on a field or in a park, so long as it is not windy.

We will not attempt to describe here the many ways you can enjoy parachute games. It is best if you can borrow one locally and enquire if there is an enthusiast who can demonstrate the fun you can have. The group should not be fewer than twenty people to be able to sample the full range of parachute games.

QUALITY TESTED IN OUR OWN KITCHEN!

Here are more than forty starter games for you to choose from. Every game has been used by the author at some time with young people and frequently with a group with a wide age range. Most of the games need no more equipment than chairs to sit on. Where some preparation is needed or other items to make the game work, these are listed alongside the heading.

Games don't have to be led or run by adults. So the term 'game leader' is used for whoever is responsible for giving instructions and for keeping the game moving. Games work best if they're not too long. People soon get bored.

Codes used in the headings:

NC   Non-competitive or co-operative games where everyone's a winner.
YF   Standing for Youth Fellowship. Groups with this title often meet in houses or smallish rooms in churches. Games that can be played in a confined space bear this code.
NS   Need Space. Usually active games which need space for movement and would probably strike terror in the hearts of householder and neighbours if played in the average living room! Many of these games can also be played outside.
YF or NS
   Can be played in a confined space or a more open area.

SOURCE OF GAME WHERE IT IS KNOWN
(*see Reference Numbers*)

Ref 1   Methodist Church Division of Education and Youth, Children's Section leaflet.
Ref 2   Rev. Stewart Morris, formerly World Affairs Youth Secretary, Methodist Association of Youth Clubs.
Ref 3   Originally from Anton Baumohl, Director of Training, Scripture Union and quoted by Rev. Roger Walton, Methodist Church Division of Ministries magazine *React*.
Ref 4   Adapted from *Winners All* published by Pax Christie, London 1980.
Ref 5   Adapted from *Body Building Classes* by Graham Young, published by the Bible Society 1985.
Ref 6   Adapted from *Creative Crowd Breakers, Mixers and Games* published by Saint Mary's Press, Winova, Minnesota, USA, 1991.
Ref 7   Adapted from *The Pictorial Guide to Group Work Activities* published privately by the author, Geoff Sanders, 1991.

Note: Many of the publications listed are now out of print.

Introduction and name-learning games

1 Getting to know you (NC) (YF)

Stand in a circle with a ball – throw it to each other, but the thrower must call his/her own name and the name of the person to whom s/he is throwing the ball. If s/he gets the latter wrong s/he goes down on one knee; a second time down on two knees; a third wrong s/he catches with one hand.

The penalties are not for not catching the ball, but for not getting the names right.

2 New greetings (NC) (YF)

We shake hands; the Eskimos' rub noses; the French kiss on both cheeks. Invent a new way of greeting each other whenever you meet.

3 Guess who? (NC) (YF)

Everyone has a small card and the game leader asks them to write on it four or five factual things about themselves (I play football; I live in Sydney Road; I have been abroad; I hate pizzas; I am 14). They must not give their name or sex. All the cards are mixed up and redistributed. People have to guess whose card they have received.

4 Group rhythms (NC) (YF)

Sit in a circle and one person starts a rhythm by either clapping their hands or slapping their knees. Everyone follows suit. After a few seconds the rhythm can be changed or the group can stand up or start a fast rhythm and so on.

Add a new dimension by pointing at a person and their name is added to the beat, 'Karen, Karen, Karen, Karen'. Karen then points at Jim and his name is taken up.

5 Alphabetical adjectives (YF)

Sit in a circle with not more than ten people in it. Start up other circles if you have more than ten people. The game leader says that in saying their name people are to add a descriptive word (or adjective) before their name, but starting with the same letter. So the first person might say: 'I'm Mobile Mike', the second person says 'I'm Sensational Sarah and I'm sitting next to Mobile Mike'. The third person says 'I'm Pedalling Paula, sitting next to Sensational Sarah, who's next to Mobile Mike'. And so on round the circle. Help people who have genuine difficulty with remembering. It's meant to be fun. Be warned, the new names may stick – for a bit!

6 Human bingo (YF)

Everyone needs a sheet similar to the illustration opposite and a pencil. People move around introducing themselves and getting the signatures in the squares of people who match the statement. There can be three winners, one for the first person to get five signatures in a straight line, diagonally, vertically or horizontally. The second winner is the person who has the most signatures at the end of the allotted time. The third winner is everyone taking part because of the names and information they have learned.

Collect the signatures of someone who –

has blue eyes	plays sport regularly	was in church last Sunday	has two Christian names	has been on the London Underground
has a part-time job	plays a musical instrument	has a steady boy/girl friend	has a pet cat	has been abroad
has hair longer than twelve inches	is an only child	put your own signature here	helps regularly with chores at home	has a brother
has travelled by air	does voluntary work to help others	has a sister	leaves school within a year	is wearing something new
keeps a diary	has been to the cinema in the last seven days	knows the names of the first five books of the New Testament	collects something as a hobby	is new to the youth group

starter games

7 Ding and dong (YF) *(two objects to pass round required)*
Form a circle sitting on chairs. The game leader hands a small object, such as a pen or comb, to the person on his/her left. As this is done s/he says 'This is a Ding.' The person replies, 'A what?' The leader says again, 'This is a Ding'.

The person holding the 'Ding' now passes it to the person on their left and says, 'This is a Ding,' to which the reply 'A what?' is given. This answer only (not the object) is passed back down the circle to the game leader who started it off. S/he says 'This is a Ding' and the reply is passed back to the person holding the object. And so on round the circle. Next, to complicate the situation, a second object, different from the first, is started off by the game leader by passing it to the person on his or her right with the statement, 'This is a Dong.' The same reply is required, 'A what?'

Great fun when both Ding and Dong meet mid-circle!

8 'I feel blue today!' (NC) (YF) *Ref 4*
This game can be played either with people writing their reactions down or simply by answers being given verbally. The game leader asks the following, or similar questions:
   If you were a colour, what would it be?
   If you were a make of car, what would it be?
   If you were a flower, what would it be?
   If you were a character from history, who would it be?
   If you were a bird, which would it be? etc.

If speaking the answers aloud, ask people to share them first with one other person and to say why they have answered as they have. If people write down their answers, swap papers around so that people don't know whose they have got and ask for answers to be read out in turn.

9 Body language (NC) (NS) *Ref 2*
Singly, ask everyone to make their bodies represent the following letters: I, J, C, T. In pairs, ask people to make the following letters: E, F, H, A.

In the same pairs ask people to touch right hands, palms together in the air, on the count of one; to lift their left leg backwards on the count of two; to go on their right on tiptoes on the count of three.

In fours, ask people to do the same exercise as previously, holding palms together and get the groups of four to do it together in co-ordination.

When they have done this once or twice, ask people to spell out one phrase visually in letters and words as quickly as they can.

10 Lemons (NC) (YF) *Ref 4*
(or oranges, apples, horse chestnuts, stones or other natural object)
Distribute the lemons, one for each person if possible. Give a few minutes for everyone to become familiar with their lemon. Firstly they examine it with their eyes open, then for a minute or two, with their eyes closed. Now people go into pairs and introduce their lemons. Then move into groups of four to six people. Exchange and reclaim lemons. Lastly the lemons are passed round the whole group and people have to get their own one back. To add difficulty try the final exercise with eyes closed. Make lemonade or an apple pie at the end!

11 Birthday Sort (NC) (YF or NS)
Check that everyone can remember the date of their birthday! The game leader then identifies one side or corner of the room as being January. From that place s/he asks people to get themselves in the correct birthday date order, January to December. (Day and month only, not year!) There is to be no speaking whilst this is being done. Only non-verbal signals may be used. When everyone seems to have finished the game leader starts at January 1st and asks people to give their birthday date in turn to see how accurate the line-up is.

12 Get it together (YF or NS) (*Picture puzzles to be prepared*)
This is a game using pictures that are easily prepared. It can be used as an exercise to mix people up who don't know each other well. Few verbal or literacy skills are

required. To prepare the game, cut out from magazines about twenty pictures. Depending upon the size of the group and the room, you will need between eight and twelve sheets of paper or card (A4 size or larger). Cut each picture in two parts (not necessarily in half) and paste one part on one piece of paper and the other part on another. Scatter the pictures widely across all the sheets making sure that the two parts of each picture are always separated.

Now number all the picture parts. Make a note of the answers – for example parts 1 and 10 make one picture; parts 2 and 19 another, and so on. Put the separate sheets up around the room and provide people with paper and pencils for their answers. Working alone or in pairs, people now move around and by deduction decide which two parts make the whole picture. Vary the difficulty of the game by, in some cases, just snipping off the corner of a picture and doing the same to a similar picture so that there has to be a fair amount of to-ing and fro-ing to discover a correct match.

13 In a word (NC) (YF)
Small groups create a story together by just saying one word each in turn round the circle. Keep the game short and encourage the group to work towards a proper ending for each story.

14 The numbers game (YF or NS) (*Game area to be marked out*)
Mark out a pattern of 4 squares by 4 squares on the floor, 16 squares in total, with paper, carpet squares, etc. Invite fifteen people to occupy the squares and give them, out of sequence, a number 1–15. Tell them they are one of those sliding tile games and moving only into an empty square next to them in a straight line, never diagonally – they must rearrange themselves in numerical order.

15 Split personality (NC) (YF)
A similar idea to 'In a word' (number 13) is for people to work in pairs and, first, have a conversation by saying a word each in turn. The conversation usually flows most easily if a question is asked first or the game leader suggests a topic for them to talk about with each other. When people have got the idea of this kind of talking, ask one pair to hold a conversation with another pair. It can be very mind stretching!

16 Signs and symbols (NC) (YF) (*Symbols as illustrated*) Ref 3
Use Highway Code symbols (see examples overleaf) to get people to express their views about the youth group, or the church or any other topical or relevant issue. Allow people to think about the symbols on their own and then encourage open and honest discussion. So, for example, it might be said that 'I think our youth group is like the roundabout symbol. We just seem to go round and round in the same old way without getting anywhere.' Or, 'Our church is as old fashioned and slow as that horse and cart symbol.' Comments must be taken seriously and time taken to discuss what people are saying and how action can be taken, where necessary, to improve things.

17 This is a... (NC) (YF) (*Scarf or other object required*)
The game leader takes any object, say a scarf, into the circle. S/he, taking the scarf, says, 'This is not a scarf, it's a stinging nettle!' S/he passes it on, as though it were a stinging nettle, to the person next to her or him, who reacts to the handing over of the nettle. This person now invents a new identity for the scarf ('This is not a scarf, it's a jelly') and so on round the circle.

SIGNS AND SYMBOLS
(Game16)

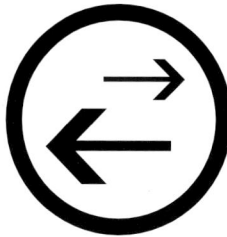

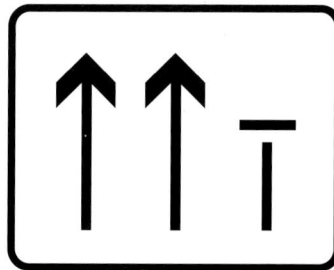

18 Non-stop musical chairs (NC) (NS) *(Music needed) Ref 5*
No dropping out in this session – so set a time limit. Apart from some background music ensure you're using strong chairs! Have the chairs in a circle, facing outward, or scattered around the room. When the music stops people sit on a chair. The variation on the original is that people are not 'out' if they can't find a seat. As the chairs are removed one by one when the music starts again, players remain in the game and if there is no chair for them they simply sit on someone's lap – or someone's lap who is already sitting on someone's lap!

19 Pandemonium (NS) *(Instructions to be prepared in advance)*
Each player is given a slip of paper bearing an instruction – 'Sing a song', 'Sing a nursery rhyme', 'Stop someone singing a song', 'Stop someone singing a nursery rhyme', 'Do a ballet dance', 'Take one shoe off the ballet dancer', 'Take all the chairs out of the room', 'Bring back into the room all the chairs', 'Go to the door and sing a carol', 'Gag the carol singer', and so on. One person, however, is told to sit still for five minutes, and then stop the game. Very lively! At the end ask people to guess the instructions other people had. They may even want to discuss the value of law and order!

20 Balloon moves (NC) (NS) *(Balloons needed)*
Stand together in groups of between five and seven. The game leader gives each group a balloon. The group decides together a course they will take around the space they are in (room or outside). Keeping close together they start to follow the course but must, at the same time, keep the balloon in the air using their knees or body but not their arms or hands. Conclude this game by a group squeeze to burst the balloons!

21 Come dancing (NC) (NS or YF)
Take a song, chorus or hymn and invent a dance to it.

22 The squeeze machine (YF)
Sit in a circle. The game leader nominates one person in the circle to be the generator who starts 'the message'. One or two people in the group are called 'Stations', who make a noise to signal the arrival of 'the message'. One or two people are called 'Generators', who can send the message either way round the circle. One or two people are 'Telephones', who make the appropriate noise whenever 'the message' reaches them.
   Having given out these key parts, the game leader asks the Generator to pass the message round the group by squeezing the hand on either her/his left or right. The squeeze is passed on round the circle with Stations, Generators and Telephones reacting accordingly to the receipt of the message. Do it like this, just for fun or put someone in the middle who has to try to interrupt the squeeze. Whoever is spotted squeezing has to change places with the interrupter.

23 Height Sort (YF or NS)
A similar game to Birthday Sort (number 11) but in this case people get into a line in order of height. The game leader states which part of the room is the low end and which the high. The handicap this time is that the sorting has to be done with eyes closed.

24 Quick on the draw (YF) *(Coins needed)*
Stand in pairs with one 10p piece for each couple. The game leader asks each pair to stand with their right hands, palm down, just touching at the finger tips. Place the coin on the join of the two hands. At the count of three part your hands and let the coin

drop. Each partner has to try to catch the coin before it hits the ground, using their right hand. Now do it in the same pairs using left hands. Now stand in close circles of pairs and try it again.

25 Mexican wave variations (NC) (NS)
With a large group have fun with the Mexican wave now popular at sporting events all over the world. The Wave starts by one section jumping up with their hands in the air and cheering. The Wave continues as everyone, in turn, follows suit. Think of variations, such as everyone lying on the floor and doing a Wave with their legs or their trunks. Try the Wave with eyes closed. Or number people one to three and the 'ones' start, followed after a count of three by the 'twos' so that the waves literally go up and down round the group.

26 Moving cards (NS) *(Playing cards needed)*
The group sits in a circle on chairs. Each member is given a playing card at random. The game leader stands outside the circle with the rest of the pack of cards.

The game leader calls the suit of the top card and all those with that suit move one place to the left. S/he then works through the pack calling the suits. As s/he calls them those holding the same suit move one place to the left – if no-one is sitting on them. They are not allowed to move if someone is on their lap, but must wait until they are on their own or on the top of a 'heap'!

The object is to get right round the circle.

Body contact games

27 Ever decreasing circles (NC) (NS)
Everyone holds hands in a circle and the game leader breaks the circle leading under-arms round and through. Everyone hangs on until the knot is too tight to go any further. Then try to untie the knot of people.

28 In touch (NC) (YF)
Having pushed all obstacles to one side, everyone is blindfolded. Stand the group at random in the room – the leader then gives commands – 'one pace left', 'turn round', 'sit', 'stand', etc.

This game and infinite variations on it give permission for body contact in a group, without embarrassment. It breaks down the fear in a new group where people do not know each other.

29 All in O'Grady (NC) (NS) *Ref 1*
The old game with a new co-operative twist. You will remember the rule is that the game leader must be obeyed when s/he says 'O'Grady says ...', and an action is suggested and performed. For example, with people standing, the leader says 'O'Grady says raise your arms above your head!' Everyone playing does this. 'O'Grady says wave your arms about'. If the leader says just 'Wave your arms about' and misses out the 'O'Grady says' and people do the action a 'life' is lost. Players can have about three lives to start with. In this 'all in' version, start in the usual way with the group together. When the first player is eliminated, having lost all three lives, s/he goes off to start a new group. Those eliminated from Group 2 start Group 3 until you have several groups going and players eventually return to the original group. Set a time limit for play to end!

30 Huff and puff blow ball (NC) (YF) *(Table tennis balls needed) Ref 1*
Get the members to kneel or crouch around a table; a table tennis table is ideal. Start by placing a table tennis ball on the table. By blowing keep the ball on the move from side to side and up and down the table. You can add more balls to make it more hectic. If there are more members than will go around the table, some can stand around the table and take the place of exhausted players who can then rejoin when refreshed.

31 All change (NC) (NS) *Ref 1*
When playing team games such as handball, five-a-side and the like, give each player a number. While the game is in progress, call out one of the numbers. The players in each team with that number then change teams. Keep doing this during the game.

32 Circle sitting (NC) (NS) *(This game needs care and supervision)*
A real game of team co-operation and mutual trust. Can be tackled by any group of people from about fifteen in number upwards. People stand in a circle all facing in one direction and touching back and front. Where there is a marked difference in height, it will be best if people are next to people who are roughly their own size. When the circle is formed, the game leader asks everyone to put their hands on the waist of the person in front of them. Then slowly and carefully everyone sits down on the lap of the person behind. Warn people that if they feel they are going to fall over they should let go of the person in front so that people are not dragged over and hurt themselves in falling.
   Variations on this activity are to form a spiral or interlocking circles.

33 Group 'Twister' (NC or not as required) (NS)
'Twister' is a popular family game demanding a fair amount of agility by the players. Here is a group game based on 'Twister'. Break up into groups of between five and seven people. Groups can play the game just for fun or be in competition with each other. The game leader calls out an instruction and all the players in the group have to perform the action co-operatively involving all members of the group. So the instruction to the group(s) could be: 'Head to elbow'. Everyone has to get their head touching someone else's elbow. If in competition, the winners will be the first group to have all members of the group correctly in touch.
   Other instructions: Knee to shoulder; Hand to toes; Elbow to knee; Bottom to right foot; Head to waist, etc. etc. Keep the game fast and furious!

34 Heads and tails (NS) *Ref 1*
Divide into groups of not fewer than five. Each group then gets into a line holding the waist of the person in front, making a 'snake'. Detach the end player in each group who then must try to join on to the end of any of the other snakes while the snakes race round. As soon as each snake gets a new tail the head must leave and go and try to get attached as a tail to another snake. As an alternative, make one long snake. The tail while keeping hold then tries to touch the head while the snake moves around to prevent it. If the tail succeeds s/he becomes the head and the game goes on.

35 Blanket ball (NC) (NS) *(One or more old blankets needed) Ref 1*
For this game you need a strong piece of blanket or material. The players get round its edge in the same way as do fireman when catching someone. A large ball is placed on the blanket. A rope is stretched across the room or outside between trees, about five feet from the ground, and the groups stand at one side and toss the ball into the air over the rope

and then dash underneath to try and catch it at the other side, keeping the ball going for as long as they can. If there is a large number of players you can have several groups. This idea can be extended in a number of ways – get the players to make suggestions.

36 Slaughter into laughter (NC) (NS) *(Music needed) Ref 1*
In the game known to some as 'Slaughter' the idea is to remove everyone else from a marked out area or agility mat, the winner being the last player left in the area.

Now let us change the rules and the aim and make Slaughter into Laughter. The idea of Laughter is to get as many people as you can on to a small marked out area or areas. Start with everyone running around outside the area(s) to music. When the music stops the players co-operate together in order to get everybody into the area. You can start with quite large areas and reduce them in size until you discover the smallest area into which everyone can fit.

37 Get knotted (NC) (NS)
Stand in circles small enough so that everyone, with raised hands, can touch in the middle. Now the game leader asks everyone to lower their arms and close their eyes. Then the instruction is given to raise hands again but this time everyone slowly finds two other hands to clasp. Now holding hands, and with eyes open again, the group tries to untangle itself and form an open circle. The game leader may allow 'breaks' if the untangling becomes impossible and it helps to achieve the task.

38 Games requiring trust (NC) (NS) *All these games need care and supervision*
Start in twos. One person stands two to three feet away from her/his partner (who should be of roughly the same height), and turns his/her back on the partner. With eyes shut s/he falls back on the partner, keeping feet together, and the partner behind catches her/him and restores to vertical position.

This game should be done in complete silence. After a while, change round and repeat actions.

Secondly in pairs sit back to back and link arms at the elbows. Now pushing with the feet (ensuring shoe soles have a good grip) and pressing against each other's backs, stand upright. Then do the exercise in reverse and sit down – slowly!

A third stage is to get the whole group to stand in a circle with one person in the middle. This person stands rigidly with hands to her/his sides. S/he falls towards one person in the circle who catches the 'log' gently by the shoulders or waist. The person is then carefully moved and passed round the circle. To add to the trusting element, blindfold the 'log' person.

The fourth stage is to 'lift the log'. One person in the group lies on the ground with eyes shut and hands crossed on chest. The other members of the group station themselves around the body, one at the head and one at the feet and others down the sides. In silence, they stoop and start to cradle the body, keeping it straight, from side to side. **Gradually,** they lift the body, keeping it straight, high into the air until the body lies above their heads on their outstretched hands. Keep there for a moment and then slowly bring the body down, starting the cradling motion as it nears the ground. Continue cradling for a few moments and then change round, a second person taking his/her place on the floor.

Quick evaluations at the end of each of the stages are useful in gauging how people felt. Did they feel distrust or confidence in each other? Did their trust grow? How did their feelings change from beginning to end?

Construction and building games

39 Co-operative building programmes (NC) (YF) *(Playing cards, empty milk bottle, matches and dominoes needed)*
Variations on a theme:
- Taking it in turns each member of the group has to place two playing cards, on edge, on a card tower – woe betides the one who giggles and knocks the whole structure down.
- Each member of the group has to place a matchstick on the top of an empty milk bottle. Each one can have several turns.
- Build a tower of dominoes with each member of the group adding one at a time. (See also number 41.)

40 Body building (NC) (NS)
Build a human structure using all the group members. Try to get as few parts of the body as possible touching the ground. The game leader should point out the potential dangers of this game – as well as its fun!

41 The ultimate co-operative ice breaker game (YF) *(Ice cubes needed)*
Have a bowl of ice cubes and people take it in turn to place one cube on top of the other to build a tower!

42 Team tower building (YF or NS) *(Materials needed – see list)*
This exercise can be either competitive or non-competitive. It can be used with a small group or with large numbers of people.
　　Divide up into teams with no more than five people in each. (If the exercise is to be competitive, the teams will have to be of equal size.)
　　Supply each team with identical equipment:
- Pair of scissors
- Equal number of sheets of newspaper of the same size
- One role of Sellotape.
(An optional extra is to give each team a piece of string, say, 10 metres long)

All the teams are briefed together and time is allowed before the exercise starts for questions to be asked and for equipment to be checked.
　　The aim of the exercise is to build a tower from the simple materials supplied that is **free standing** – it must not be attached in any way to the floor, ceiling or any other kind of support. At the end of an agreed time limit (probably about twenty-five minutes) all the team members must stand away from the tower they have built and it must remain self-supporting for five seconds. It is best if a target height is set for the team to try and reach. This could be the ceiling of the room or a string hung across the room. Or, if working outside, (in windless conditions!) the branch of a tree.
　　Once the instructions have been given and a time limit announced there are several alternatives to how the activity can proceed:
a) Let the activity be a competitive one between teams. The winning team will be the one that has reached the target height first and met the free-standing time limit.
b) At the moment of telling the teams to start, inform them that the construction is to take place in silence. There must be no verbal communication of any kind between team members.
c) If using the silent method (b) you can decide to allow speaking for the last five minutes of the allotted time.

d) An observer can be appointed to each team to note down how the team works together. Does a natural leader emerge? Did they plan their tower first before beginning to build? Did they copy ideas from other teams? Were they panicked by the approaching time limit? How well did they co-operate as a team? If method (b) and (c) were used, did the breaking of the silence alter the way the team worked? And so on.

This exercise is fun and creative but also gives lots of opportunity for valuable discussion after it is finished, about working as a team; leadership and management skills; the use of time; frustration; aims and objectives.

This exercise is obviously longer than most of the other ones in this section, but it does make an excellent starter, perhaps at a residential weekend.

43 Chariots of fire (NC or competitive as required) *(see list of materials below) Ref 7*
People are in teams of three or four people and each team has an identical collection of 'junk' material, for example:
- Plastic pop bottles
- Cereal cartons
- Egg trays.

Each team also has a role of sellotape, a few metres of string and a safe candle, such as a night light. The aim of the exercise is to move the candle (which will be lit by the game leader) over a smooth pre-determined course in a vehicle constructed from as much of the junk as is necessary. The candle must not go out as it is being transported.

Team/group making games

44 Happy McFamilies (NS or YF)
A different way of forming teams or groups. Prepare small pieces of paper bearing the names of imaginary people who all have similar Scottish-sounding surnames. For example, to make a team of six people:

> Jim McKernon
> Joe McKernon
> Jill McKernon
> Jane McKernon
> John McKernon
> Janice McKernon

Have other sets of papers with the same Christian names but followed by a surname such as:

> Mackervoy
> Mackey
> McKibbans
> McKie
> McKiernan

Mix up the papers and give one to each person. At a signal everyone goes round calling out their name until they have met up with the other members of their 'family'. Adjust the sign of the families to what ever size group is required.

45 Body search (YF) *Ref 5*

This game enables you to make up to five groups or teams with up to eight people in each. Each team takes on the name of a part of the body. (See references below.) For this version of the game Good News Bibles will be needed so that you have at least one Bible for every four or five people. (Other versions of the Bible can be used, but check the references to ensure that the word required is still there.) Prepare for the game by putting on slips of paper just one Bible reference for each team member needed. So to create a 'feet' team of seven people you need seven slips from the Bible references below, one on each of seven slips of paper. The papers are given out so that everyone has one. They are asked to look up their reference and write out the verse on the paper underlining the part of the body mentioned. If it is feet or foot they then go round to form a team of all the other people with feet references.

HANDS

Deuteronomy 4. 28	Matthew 15. 20
2 Chronicles 6. 29	Luke 4. 40
Psalm 16. 5	Acts 20. 34
Ezekiel 25. 6	1 Timothy 2. 8

FEET

2 Samuel 9. 13	Luke 7. 45
Nehemiah 9. 21	John 13. 5
Daniel 8. 18	Acts 13. 25
Matthew 10. 14	Revelation 19. 10

EYES

Genesis 29. 17	Psalm 119. 18
Deuteronomy 6. 22	Matthew 9. 29
1 Samuel 16. 12	Luke 2. 30
Job 16. 20	2 Peter 1. 16

EARS

Psalm 40. 6	Isaiah 42. 20
Psalm 44. 1	Jeremiah 26. 11
Psalm 58. 4	Matthew 11. 15
Job 15. 21	Revelation 2. 7

MOUTH

Job 20. 12	Matthew 15. 11
Job 37. 2	Mark 9. 20
Psalm 81. 10	Acts 23. 2
Daniel 4. 31	Revelation 3. 16

TUCK IN!

O Lord, grant that we may not be like porridge,
Stiff, stodgy and hard to stir,
But like cornflakes,
Crisp, fresh and ready to serve.

Possibly the best and most popular 'Starter' for any group is eating together! Food and drink bring people together in so many situations. Use refreshments creatively in the youth group as an 'ice-breaker'.

- Always serve refreshments attractively so that people are made to feel relaxed and at ease and able to talk with each other.
- Have hot and cold drinks available at the start of a session, served with a piece of home-made cake. Youth group members can take it in turn to provide this. Put small flags on the pieces of cake, make with cocktail sticks. On the flag is the name of a group member. People take a name other than their own and start by talking to that person for a few minutes. Have some blank flags ready to put on the names of visitors or new members.
- Start a non-alcoholic drinks bar. This can be an interesting venture and a preparatory session experimenting with recipes is fun. It can also lead to discussion about the responsible use of alcohol or the right not to drink it at all. For advice on non-alcoholic bars consult: Hope UK, 25 (F), Copperfield Street, London SE1 OEN. Tel: 0171 928 0848.
- Get into the tradition of having a birthday party for the youth group on the anniversary of its formation. It's a good excuse to invite friends and supporters of the group along as a thank you in addition to being an event for which everyone can have some part in the preparations.
- Set up a 'safari meal' when you take each part of the meal in different houses or churches – Sample menu:

House 1	Fruit juice or soup
House 2	Fish, chips and peas
House 3	Dessert
House 4	Cheese and biscuits
House 5	Tea and coffee and mints.

This walk-about meal can be turned into a charity fund-raising event with the mobile diners being sponsored for the distance they cover.

TUCK IN!

'So whether you eat or drink or whatever you do, do it all for the Glory of God.'

1 Corinthians 10. 31.

Chapter 16

MAIN COURSE

Programme ideas arranged under theme titles

(Thinks!)... 'Ah!, now we're getting down to some serious eating at long last. None of those fancy, fiddly starters. Here's the real stuff – meat and two veg, with all the trimmings. Time to tuck in!'

Here is a wide range of themes and programme ideas. All have been used with young people, mostly in the age range thirteen to twenty-one, in different settings and in various parts of the country.

The ideas are collected together under broad themes, so that they can be followed through as a short series. However, in most instances, they can also be used as 'one-off' sessions.

Although each session has been set out so that it makes a complete programme, the material is intended to be used flexibly – adapted and added to, to suit your youth group.

BASIC RECIPE FOR EACH SESSION

Title
Gives a hint of what's to come, within the theme or as a one-off session.

Timing
Very approximate, but to give an idea of the minimum time you allow for a session.

'SSG'
A code put against some sessions meaning it is suitable for use by small groups. If your youth groups numbers are between eight and twelve people you should be able to use the ideas suggested. In some cases even smaller groups will be able to use the central idea.

Preparation/equipment needed
Tells you the advance preparation that is required and any equipment that is needed, although this has been kept as simple as possible with a few exceptions such as the Consequences Special – 'All back to front' and the Building theme session 'Shelter'.
* IMPORTANT * All the sessions assume that some basic equipment and materials are always available, such as paper, pens or pencils, marker pens and Bibles. (See Chapter 7 'The Place Setting – what you need'.)

Meat of the Sessions
(This is metaphorical – ideas still suitable for vegetarians!)
Note that Starter Games/Ice Breakers have not been included. But remember they can be important to help a session start off with a good atmosphere. Make your own choice from the wide menu given in the 'Starters' in Chapter 15.

This section gives you step by step, the main material for each session.

The leader for each session is described as the enabler – the person who enables, or helps each session to happen. It is probable that this will be an adult youth worker, but this need not be the case all the time. As is stated at the beginning of this book, it is not for adults only. Young people will be able to try out and improve their youth work skills by being fully involved in programme planning and presentation.

With one exception (Theme: Choice – 'May Day! May Day!') audio and visual aids are not suggested as essential as some youth groups will not have the necessary equipment available nor the funds to purchase or hire videos and sound-strips. But many sessions will benefit from the careful use of audio and visual presentations so keep informed about what is available and, where you can, spice up some of the sessions with this extra material (see Chapter 13 'Cooking Methods', 'A–Z: Audio and Visual Aids').

Bible study, Prayer, Praise

Most sessions make suggestions for Bible study and worship. This assumes that current translations of the Bible are always to hand, preferably with some books to help further research, such as a concordance, Bible dictionary and atlas. If you haven't already got them, save up and buy easy to use editions together with a set of hymn/song books (see Chapter 14 'Giving thanks – Worship in the youth group').

Follow-up

When the session is over – now what? Can we put into practice what we have discussed and experienced? This section gives some ideas to show that the end of any youth group meeting could well (and should) be only the beginning!

PRAYER AND SERENDIPITY! – ESSENTIAL INGREDIENTS

Underpin and shed light on all your programme preparation, presentation and follow-up by offering up all that is done in prayer. Youth workers and young people should see this as an essential part of their working and growing together.

Serendipity? A musical sounding word that means having the gift of making happy and unexpected discoveries. Essential in youth work! Making the most of the moment; seizing the opportunity before it passes. Be serendipity conscious.

TUCK IN!

Dom Helder Camara from Brazil has written:
'*Accept surprises*
that upset your plans,
shatter your dreams,
give a completely different turn
to your day and – who knows? – to your life.
It is not chance.
Leave the Father free himself to weave
the pattern of your days'.

Taken from *A Thousand Reasons for Living*, by Dom Helder Camara. Published and copyright 1987 by Darton, Longman & Todd and used by permission of the publisher.

THEME – RELATIONSHIPS
Sessions looking at some of the issues
related to relationships with friends, family and God.

a) 'Just looking, thanks' (45–60 minutes) (SSG)

Preparation/equipment needed

Lots of pictures taken from magazines, etc., of people, preferably close-ups of faces. Some of these should be collected in advance of the session but Sunday supplements, newspapers and other picture sources could also be brought along for group members to look through with the request to tear out pictures of people, known and unknown. Have to hand at least one picture of Jesus.

Meat of the Session

i)   Divide into small groups. Give each group a roughly equal number of 'people' pictures, including one of Jesus in the set, if possible. The group is asked to sort the pictures into two sets in answering these questions:
  • Which of these people would you find it hard to get on with? Why?
  • Which of these people would you find it easy to get on with? Why?

ii)   The group enabler should ensure that extra questions arise from the discussions about:
  • Should we only judge people from their appearance?
  • How do we overcome stereotyping people – putting them into categories, such as 'old', 'coloured', 'traveller', 'disabled', etc?
  • Can the picture of Jesus be discussed in the same way as the other pictures?

iii) When there has been adequate time for discussion, encourage sharing across groups, highlighting pictures that have created particular interest.

Bible study

Work at some passages that show how people 'pigeon-holed' Jesus; for example:
  Luke 4. 22
  Luke 5. 29–30
  Luke 9. 7–9
There are many other references!

Prayer

For people we find it hard to like and for each other, especially if we are doing the Follow-up suggestion.

Follow-up

The challenge to each individual to work on healing or improving a personal relationship within a set period of time.

b) 'In Love' (45–60 minutes) (SSG)

Preparation/equipment needed

Optional: brief selection of songs and hymns which include the word 'love' (pre-recorded if possible, selecting the relevant lines. Keep brief – no more than three minutes). One large sheet of paper for each group. Ready prepared cards and some blanks – see 'Meat of the Session'. Marker pens for each group.

Meat of the Session

i) Brief introduction about the different meanings of the word 'love'. The Christian writer, C. S. Lewis, identified four types of love:
   - **Sentimental love** – a love of 'lower' things. 'But I love my old jacket – you can't send that to the jumble sale!'
   - **Sexual love** – the Greek word for it is 'Eros'
   - **Love of friends** – a special relationship neither sexual nor sentimental
   - **Christian love** – the Greek word for it is 'Agape'. The Latin word is *Caritas* (Charity).

   Ask for examples of how love is used in everyday language ('Hello, love'; 'I'd love an ice cream'; 'I love my dog'; 'I love you Mum'; 'Let's make love').

   Play song tape if one has been prepared.

ii) **What helps us to decide if we love someone or not?** Divide into small groups. Each group is given a set of cards and a large piece of paper (old wallpaper would be ideal) on which is drawn a ladder. Each card has on it one of the words given in the list below. Use as many as you think the groups can handle. The groups also receive some blank cards and a marker pen.

   The groups are asked to look at the words on the cards. These are some of the reasons people give for loving someone of the opposite sex. Using the ladder as a means of grading importance, with the highest rated at the top, the groups are asked to consider each reason and place it, according to their feelings, on the ladder. The blank cards are for adding extra words of the group's choice.

   I could love someone if s/he was:

Good looking	Exciting	Loving
Talented	Romantic	Reliable
Modern in outlook	Liked by my friends	Studious
Honest	Wealthy	Full of new ideas
Hard-working	Stylish	Ambitious
Adventurous	Considerate	

   When the group have had sufficient time to form their ladder of reasons for loving, ask groups to compare results.

iii) Now ensure that each group has about ten blank cards and ask them to use these cards and the ladder to give the most important reasons why people love God. Again allow time for the comparison of the lists from the different groups.

Prayer and Praise

Use one of the great hymns about love such as 'Love Divine, all love's excelling ...' or 'O love that will not let me go ...' Read and ponder the words before singing them. Ask one person to read slowly 1 Corinthians 13.

Follow-up

This is a huge subject and one of great interest to everyone. Ask if people would like to spend more time and another session on thinking about both love between humans and our love for God. Are there particular aspects of the subject people would like to discuss? Remember, not all the group may want to do this but some may be very keen to do so, in which case try to arrange an optional time to meet.

c) 'Just Good Friends' (45 minutes) (SSG)

Preparation/equipment needed

Blank cards and marker pens as in b). A flip chart, large paper, blackboard or over-head projector.

Meat of the Session

This is a similar idea to b), but the subject and method give it a new slant.

i) Unless the group is very large (in which case, break up into groups of about eight people) begin this exercise with everyone together.

ii) Tell the group we are going to think about friendship. First ask people to talk with one other person about what they look for in a friend and to come up, where possible, with single words that describe these qualities, e.g., loyalty, fun.

iii) Now using a flip chart or large piece of paper to brainstorm (see Chapter 13 'Cooking Methods') all the ideas that can be thought of. List the words up as quickly as possible.

iv) People are asked to go into small groups where they can see the brainstormed list. Each group has a supply of five blank cards and a marker pen. The groups are asked to discuss the list of friendship qualities and decide on their top five, writing one on each card and putting them in order of priority 1–5.

v) Now each group in turn is asked to send out one person with their number one word on friendship. Is there agreement or are there differences? Why? Carry on through the chosen words for each group down to number 5. Have a brief discussion at each stage. Now that all the words are out, can we make one priority list? Gradually eliminate words that do not have the backing of the majority and try to end up with just five key ideas.

Bible study

Look at the story of Lazarus, Mary and Martha, some of Jesus' best friends, in John 11. Apart from the miracle itself of bringing Lazarus back to life, what qualities of friendship does Jesus display in this passage?

Prayer

With groups used to praying together, suggest that good friends actually pray together and for each other, making sure that no one is left out. Where this is not appropriate, pray both for those who find it difficult to make friends and keep them, for people who have fallen out and for the gift of friendship.

Hymn

'What a friend we have in Jesus'.

Follow-up

Write or phone a friend we haven't been in touch with recently.

SPECIAL SESSION on or near St. Valentine's Day:

d) 'Love is…' (20–30 minutes) (SSG)

Preparation/equipment needed

Several blank pieces of paper or card and one larger than the rest. Marker pens.

Meat of the Session

A shop was selling Valentine cards that said 'You alone are my love'. They were available in economy packs of ten!

i)   Encourage light-hearted conversation about giving and receiving Valentine cards.

ii)   Who was St. Valentine? A great lover? No. It's a name associated with two Christian martyrs, one a Roman priest and one a bishop, both of whom died for their faith in the third century. How their names became linked with a festival for lovers is obscure, but there was probably a Roman fertility festival around this time in February – possibly when the two men met their death.

iii) Initiate a discussion on who needs our love at present. Use the blank cards to make Valentines to the forgotten people, the loveless, the neglected of this world. Split into small groups to do this if necessary.

Prayer and praise

Read the words of Jesus in Luke 6. 27–36. Use the big card to write down messages of praise, thanksgiving and love to God. Perhaps sing the song 'Let there be love shared among us …'

Follow-up

Write to, or arrange for one or two people to call on, someone who may feel lonely and neglected. Perhaps they were bereaved recently or have been made redundant. Consider carefully what would help the person most at this time. A bunch of flowers? An invitation to join a group going out somewhere? A card saying that the group has been thinking of them? The opportunity to join a family for Sunday lunch?

e) 'Home, sweet home' (45–60 minutes) (SSG)

Preparation/equipment needed

A large piece of paper squared up as for a 'Snakes and Ladders' board. Separate pieces of paper cut out to resemble snakes, but wide enough to be written on. Similarly, narrow strips of paper on which has been drawn a ladder, but with space for writing. For the second exercise, one paper for each of four groups with the questions given in *iv)* below.

Meat of the Session

i)   As this session is to be about home life, the enabler will need to be aware of and sensitive to any recent family problems within the group – redundancy, death, illness, break-up, etc. Some of the discussion that arises from the exercises suggested will, no doubt, be light-hearted but, in some cases, it may be painful. Distress should not be ignored or swept under the carpet but faced up to and talked about openly where it is appropriate and supportive to the person. Further private conversation may be necessary later between the person concerned and perhaps a youth worker.

ii) Divide people into small groups. Put the squared up paper in the centre of the room. Give to each group a small supply of the separate paper 'snakes' and 'ladders' and a pen or pencil. Ask the groups to talk about the 'ups and downs' of family life. What are the slippery snakes we should avoid? How can we build relationships and a happy home – ascend the ladders? Groups summarize their discussion with a few words on the snakes and ladders.

iii) Share the snakes and ladders, discussing each idea as it is placed on the board.

iv) Now re-form into four groups and, in this case, each group should be well separated from the others. Tell each group that they will be receiving five similar questions. At the top of their question paper it will say which member of a family they are as a group. They are to try and reach agreement on the answers as a group, thinking them through from the point of view of the person they collectively represent. At this stage do not let the groups know the identity of the members of the family they will play. Hand each group their paper and say they have about ten minutes to come up with the answers. They should be ready to give and defend their answers at the end of discussion time. The questions are similar but not identical:

a   *You are a 12 year old!*
Decide the answers, so far as you are concerned, to the following questions:
- How much money should you receive from your parents (assuming this is for entertainment)?
- What is the latest you should be in at night?
- Should you have complete freedom of choice in what you wear?
- Should there be any restrictions by your parents on your choice of friends?
- To what extent should you be expected to share household duties?

b   *You are the parents of a 12 year old!*
Decide the answers, so far as your child is concerned, to the following questions:
- How much money should s/he receive for entertainment purposes?

- What is the latest s/he should be in at night?
- What say should you have in your son/daughter's choice of clothes?
- What say should you have in your son/daughter's choice of friends?
- To what extent should your son/daughter share in household duties?

   c *You are a 17 year old!*
  Decide the answers, so far as you are concerned, to the following questions:
- From your £...* a week wage, how much should you hand to your parents?
- What is the latest you should be in at night?
- Should you have complete freedom of choice in what you wear?
- Should there be any restrictions by your parents on your choice of friends?
- To what extent should you be expected to share household duties?

   d *You are the parents of a 17 year old!*
  Decide the answers, so far as your child is concerned, to the following questions:
- From his/her £...* a week wage, how much should he/she hand over to you?
- What is the latest s/he should be in at night?
- What say should you have in your son/daughter's choice of clothes?
- What say should you have in your son/daughter's choice of friends?
- To what extent should your son/daughter share in household duties?

  * *Put in here what seems to be the 'going-rate' for a 17 year old employed person in your area.*

v)   When the time limit has elapsed and the questions have been answered, ask each group to appoint a spokesperson to give their answers.

vi)   Now introduce the groups to each other – 'twelve-year-old, these are your parents!' 'Parents of the seventeen-year-old, here is your child!' Next take each question and stimulate conversation (probably argument) between the different members of the family. Be firm about why they have answered as they have. Are the parents being reasonable? Are the children being considerate?

Prayer
For our families. For any situations known to us needing special prayer. For organizations that help children and parents.

Follow-up
Personally where necessary as outlined in i) above. Find out more about the work of charities such as NCH Action for Children and Barnardos who care for children affected by death, illness and division in families. Is there a local unit needing any kind of help?

f) 'Those whom God has joined...' (45 minutes) (SSG)

This is a different kind of session that could be helpful in a series on relationships. Consider inviting two married couples to meet with the youth group. One recently married and one married for many years. If possible, arrange for one or two young people to meet the couples in advance of the sessions and to prepare some questions based on what they learn about the experiences of the people. At the session set up a panel of the couples and interviewers. Talk about how they met; was it 'Love at first sight'? What did the marriage ceremony mean to them? (Have some copies of it available.) What are the joys and problems of a life-long commitment?

Make sure there is ample opportunity for everyone who wants to join in the conversation. Be prepared to face up to questions about living together before marriage and living together as an alternative to marriage.

Follow-up

Plan for small groups to attend wedding ceremonies in the churches of different denominations and, if possible, of different faiths. Go to a civil ceremony in a Register Office. Compare notes. Discuss symbolism. Talk with a Christian couple who live together. Invite a counsellor from Relate (marriage guidance) to talk with the group.

<hr>

g) Series evaluation

If several of these sessions are used it may be helpful, after a period of time, to make time for some kind of personal evaluation. Is the series making any difference to our personal relationships?

A simple measuring/checking method can be tried out. On their own, each person marks out a scale and lists against it the names of family and friends. For example:

```
        0                                                        100
        [_____]

Mum                                                             ×
Dad                                   ×
Brother                                       ×
Sister                                              ×
Friend                                           ×
Name (a)                        ×
Name (b)                                          ×
  etc.
```

Mark on the scale where the relationship stands, very good being '100'.

Which way is the relationship going, up or down? For example:

```
              0                                            100
Mum           [ _____> – × _____ ]
```

What action needs to be taken to improve the relationship?
Prepare a similar scale to gauge our relationship with God. Ask the same questions.

Bible reading

Read 1 John 4. 7–10 and 19–21.

THEME – POWER
**Sessions designed to help explorations of the use
and abuse of power in different situations and
to recognize the power available to us through the Holy Spirit.**

a) Switch on (1) (45–60 minutes) (SSG)

Preparation/equipment needed

It is suggested this session is handled in two parts. The first part is planned so that those taking part prepare and take a questionnaire out to people and look for their opinions. This could be with the local church community, perhaps at the end of a service of worship. Or, with more care and supervision, into a shopping area, a late shopping evening, or on a Saturday. The first session needs pictures, slides or video shots of different aspects of power – water, electricity, natural wonders such as volcanos, wind, etc. A collection of pictures is also needed (from newspapers, magazines, etc.) of famous people.

Meat of the Session

i) Introductions to the theme of power, preferably with a display of pictures from magazines or using slides or videos – or a mixture of these media. Encourage conversation about the powers shown as they are displayed. Which are frightening, awe-inspiring, useful, beautiful, etc? What other sources of power could have been shown?

ii) What powers are at work in this room? (Electricity, gravity, sound, muscles, etc.)

iii) That's one use of the word power. Power that provides us with strength, force, control – for good and evil. This kind of power can build or destroy.

iv) It is said that some people have power. (Show pictures of famous people – try to include royalty and politicians as well as actors, pop stars, etc.) What kind of power do these people have? Do some have more power than others? Of all the people alive at present, who has the most power in the world?

v) Introduce the idea of the questionnaire which will lead into the second session. (Depending upon when the group is meeting, it could be possible for the group to go out and canvass opinions straight away or before the second session begins. But make sure preparation is adequate.)

The object of the survey is to collect people's answers to questions such as:
- Where does the power lie in our country today?
- Do you feel you have power as an individual to influence decisions –
  - in this community (town/city)?
  - in the nation?
  - in Europe?
- Does the church (local and national) have any power?

Please, alter and add to the questions to suit your own area and church, but limit the number of questions to about five or six or people will lose patience.

vi)   Talk through the best ways of approaching people to ask questions. Role play some situations together with 'researchers' and 'members of the public' to gain confidence. People should work in pairs and, if the exercise is to be carried out in a public place, a time limit should be set and one or two people act as supervisors and check points. Equip people with proper clip boards and question papers so that they look as if they mean business (see Chapter 13 'Cooking Methods' A–Z: Questionaires).

Bible reading
Jesus challenging authority – Luke 20. 1–8 and 45–47.

Prayer
For people in authority and who have power. Pray for current situations where difficult decisions have to be made.

---

b) Switch on (2) (45 minutes) (SSG)

Preparation/equipment needed
This session is based on the completed questionnaires from Switch on (1). Have a flip chart or large paper ready.

Meat of the Session
i)   First let people share their experiences in conducting the survey. It will be surprising if there aren't some funny incidents to talk about!

ii)   Now go through the questions asked one at a time, writing up the responses. Any surprises?

iii) How do the views of the public compare with our own thoughts? By way of follow-up, do we want to share any of the findings with, say, our church through the magazine or even with the local press?

Bible study
Talk about the power that people had when they were filled with the Holy Spirit. And how Jesus left the future of his church in the hands of a few men and women. Read about the miracles that started at Pentecost in Acts 2. 1–13.

Pray that we may use the powers we have carefully and for the good of all. Pray for the guidance and power of the Holy Spirit in our lives.

---

c) The corridors of power (60 minutes) (SSG)

Preparation needed
This session will need to be planned well in advance as it is based on inviting one or two people who influence decisions and have the ability to wield power to meet with the group. You could invite your local MP or a local councillor. Or a head teacher, industrial or commercial boss or trades union official – not all at the same time, of course!

Meat of the Session

i)   Talk with the group about the idea of inviting one or two local people who have some power. Who would they suggest? Do we know of Christians in positions of power? If we can get someone to come to meet us, should we open the meeting to other people in the church community?

ii) Assuming an invitation has been accepted, spend some time in advance of the session preparing for it. Is the visitor going to be asked to speak (if so, what time limit do we suggest?) or do we ask some members of the group to set up an interview and plan questions in advance? What issues is the person or persons involved with at present that affect our lives? How have they got to the position they now hold?

iii) Let the person or persons being invited know of the ways the group has been exploring the subject of power.

iv) If the visitor is a stranger, send clear travel directions. All visitors should be offered travel expenses. Arrange for a couple of group members to be hosts for the visitor(s) to make them feel at home and to offer refreshments.

v)   It is as well to keep quite a strict time limit on the 'formal' part of a session of this kind, probably no more than an hour. Although people may still want to go on talking with the visitors after the main session has concluded.

vi) Allow for a brief time at the end of the session to consider any follow-up – perhaps a visit to a Council Meeting or helping to lobby support for a particular project.

Prayer and praise

Discuss what is appropriate for this kind of session and who should prepare for it.

d) Creative power

Preparation/equipment needed

A subject such as power gives lots of scope for the use of creative sessions where we express ideas with our bodies as much as with our mouths. An outline is given for some creative workshops that, with some space, could be offered as a special session or could be tackled one at a time.

Art

Using paint, marker pens, clay, junk, etc., produce pictures, sculptures, mobiles, collages, etc., that portray power in its many forms.

Pop power

The meaning and effect of pop music and cultures.

Drama and movement

Interpret aspects of power through movement, mime sketches, etc.

The power of the press

Spend time looking at newspapers, magazines, TV clips and sections of radio broadcasts to think about the influence of the press and other media on our lives (see also Chapter 18 'Ready-to-serve Meals – Hold the Front Page').

THEME – CONSEQUENCES

Sessions showing how, in all aspects of life, actions inevitably lead to outcomes that may not always be of our own choosing, and almost certainly affect the lives of other people. A Christian needs to be especially aware of the consequences of what s/he says and does.

a) 'Casualty department' (60 minutes) (SSG)

Preparation/equipment needed

One consequence/instruction card for each person present (see 'Meat of the Session'). Three or more 'casualties of society' role players who have been well briefed before-hand. The full group will be dividing into as many groups as there are 'casualties' so, if you are likely to have, say, thirty or more people, go for four or more role players. A small group could stay together and meet in turn with two or three casualty role players.

Meat of the Session

i)   Everyone receives a card asking them to consider, on their own, the consequences of a particular action. Examples (one on each card):
      What are the likely consequences if:
      – You lose your job?
      – You drive a car without insurance?
      – You give money to Oxfam?
      – You lose your temper with a friend?
      – You smile at a stranger?

      On the back of each card is a further instruction that leads (a) to small group discussion or (b) an action that contradicts an instruction someone else has received.
      Example of (a):
      Join with two or three other people to discuss the consequences of the situation given on this card.
      Example of (b):
      Tidy away or stack all the chairs in the room. (Someone else has an instruction to put chairs out!) (see Chapter 15 – game 19 'Pandemonium'.)

ii)   After no more than ten minutes the enabler should stop all activities (and the chaos!) and give an opportunity to share what has happened.

iii) Three or more 'casualties of society', (preferably appropriately dressed) now introduce themselves briefly to the full group. Examples: a homeless person, a single parent, a long-term unemployed person, an ex-prisoner.

iv)   Divide into as many groups as there are casualties (or see note above about small groups). Each group is told it will be visited in turn by two of the casualty role players who will be looking for help with their problems. Groups are given a few minutes before the visitors arrive to consider the kind of questions they might ask and their attitude to the casualty.

v)   After the groups have met their casualties, allow time, with the role players speaking out of role, for open discussion on the way the counselling was handled.

Bible study and prayer

Read together, discuss and pray around Paul's instructions in his letter to the Romans 12. 9–21.

Follow-up

What should be the consequences of our session? Who are the casualties in our own neighbourhood? Are there ways we can help them?

---

b) Body shop (45 minutes) (SSG)

Preparation/equipment needed

Prepare sets of card, which will hang from a string loop around people's necks. One card is needed for each person taking part. Produce five cards for each team of five people, one card with a simple drawing of a foot, the next card a hand, the next a mouth, the next an ear and the fifth card an eye. Also needed is a glass of water for each team and scarves, etc., to blindfold four out of five members in each team.

Meat of the Session

i)   Divide into groups containing five people. Label each person in the group with the pre-prepared cards, so that each team of five represents one 'body':

    1 Eyes
    2 Hands   )
    3 Ears   ) *Numbers 2–5 are blindfolded*
    4 Feet   )
    5 Mouth   )

ii)   The enabler explains that each body, working together, has to complete a simple task. However, the following rules apply:
- Only the eyes can see. The other parts of the body will be blindfolded.
- Only the ears receive the initial instruction and whisper this to the mouth, the only part of the body able to talk.
- The body can only move if carried by the feet.
- Only the hands can pick up or move anything.

iii) The ears receive the whispered instruction that the body has to carry a glass of water for a pre-determined distance at the end of which the mouth has to drink the water. The ears now whisper this instruction to the mouth who tells it to the whole body.

iv)   Teams now set off together. At the end the enabler helps the group to discuss the exercise, what happened and why.

Bible study

In the light of the fun and confusion of the body exercise discuss 1 Corinthians 12. 12–26 and consider its meaning in terms of the Church and the world.

Pray for the broken Body of Christ, his Church, focusing on local inter-church relationships and contacts.

Praise

Sing 'Bind us together, Lord'.

Follow-up

How can we help heal Christ's broken body locally? Can there be more contact with local young Christians from other denominations?

c) 'A vacancy exists...' (45 minutes) (SSG)

Preparation/equipment needed

People will be working in small groups and a set of 'A Christian is...' papers (see 'Meat of the Session') is needed for each group. Paper and marker pens are needed for the second 'job description' exercise.

Meat of the Session

i) The enabler asks people to go into small groups and, so far as possible, to sit in a neat circle having a space in the centre. The enabler explains that we are going to think about how to describe a person who is a Christian. Each group is given a set of papers with one statement on each. Each statement is the answer someone may give to the question, 'What is a Christian?' Sample statements:

A Someone who goes to church
B Someone who leads a good life
C Someone who tries to help other people
D Someone who is always talking about God
E Someone who gives money to good causes
F Someone who believes in God
G Someone who believes that Jesus is the son of God
H Someone who believes Jesus is Lord
I Someone who has given her/his life to Christ.

Add a few blank sheets of paper to the set.

ii) Each member of each group is asked to have ready an object with which they can vote for their preference – this can be a comb, a coin, a handkerchief, etc.

iii) One member of the group puts each statement in the centre of the group in turn. Asking the group 'Is a Christian ... (sheet A) ... someone who goes to church?' Opinions are expressed about this by each member of the group placing their voting object in a place that represents their feelings. If they totally agree with the statement they put their comb, or whatever they are using, right on the sheet of paper with its statement. If they disagree totally they place their vote near their feet on the outside of the circle. Variations in agreement are symbolized by placing votes between these two extremes. (For a different method see Chapter 13 'Cooking Methods' A–Z: Measuring strength of feeling.)

iv) Voting and discussion continue as each statement is placed in the centre of the group in turn and voting objects are re-positioned.

v) The enabler encourages groups to write their own additional statements if they consider none of the ones in the set say what they want them to say.

vi) Encourage sharing of views between groups when all have finished voting on the set.

Bible study

Think about the people Jesus chose as his disciples. Was there anything special about them? (See Mark 1. 14–20, Mark 2. 13–17 and Mark 3. 13–19.)

Prayer

Use a time of silence to meditate on the Christian life and the commitment of each person in the group. Say a prayer together that reminds us of our responsibilities as Christians, using, perhaps, this ancient one by Ignatius Loyola (1491–1556).

Teach us, good Lord, to serve thee as thou deservest;
to give and not to count the cost;
to fight and not to heed the wounds;
to toil and not to seek for rest;
to labour and not to ask for any reward,
save that of knowing that we do thy will;
through Christ our Lord. Amen.

d) Consequences Special – All back to front! (Whole day) (SSG)

TUCK IN!

'To begin to understand the gospel of Jesus Christ, one must first learn to stand on ones head.'

G.K. Chesterton

This is a special activity that needs to have the best part of a day allocated to it to work effectively. It could be part of a residential event, such as a youth or family weekend or camp. Or you could use a Saturday or Bank Holiday, giving the opportunity to turn it into a money-raising event for a charity or for youth group funds by having parts of the day sponsored.

In summary, the whole day is back to front! Here are some ideas for you to choose from and add to:

- Start in the morning with dinner (evening meal) – pudding first and ending with the starter.
- Everyone taking part must come wearing their clothes back to front. All movement must be backwards.
- All eating should be done with knives and forks the reverse way round to the way they are usually held.
- Make a clock or have an old one that can be turned backwards to mark the passage of time throughout the day. (It will be best if watches are removed.)
- Play games where all movements are done backwards.

- Watch a video backwards.
- Read a well known story (a fairy tale is probably easiest), or make a play from one but start at the end.
- Before finishing with breakfast, think about how Jesus turned so many ideas on their head: he told people to love their enemies; he challenged some of the religious leaders of his time; he chose ordinary, common people to be his closest friends; he spoke with people others despised and treated as outcasts. And he defied death.

THEME – BUILDING
Sessions that include the literal aspects of building, relating this to building friendships and also exploring how we can build each other up and the barriers of prejudice and hate that people build between each other.

a) 'Shelter' (One hour minimum)

Preparation/equipment needed

This session needs to be planned well in advance for three reasons. Firstly, space is needed for the activity: either a large hall, or several smaller rooms, although it is probably best if the whole session can take place outside in a field or, with permission, in a park. Secondly, a range of simple building materials and a small tent have to be collected together and some items of food. Thirdly, if it is intended to use the parable suggested for the closing worship this is best prepared in advance by a small group. If you use the idea suggested for prayer, small strips of paper will be needed and sellotape.

Meat of the Session

i) Divide people into small groups (four or five people at most) and give each small group a different kind of building material. The groups should be as widely separated as possible. One group might receive a few old chairs and sheet of polythene; another group some large cardboard boxes; another a small frame tent from which one part of the frame is missing or for which there are too few tent pegs – and so on. Additionally, each building group receives some items of food that together make up a full meal. Therefore one group could have some sausages, another bread, another items to make tea, another a camping stove but no matches, another a box of matches, etc. Now, to the enabler, the plot is obvious!

ii) Having established the groups and given them their building materials and food, they are told that the objective is to build a shelter and prepare a meal. (Note to enabler: It does not say just for their own group.) The group has half an hour to do this. After the first five minutes they may talk to other groups but this can only be done by one contact person from each group until fifteen minutes of the thirty allowed has passed when there may be full contact between groups.

iii) The enabler should allow a brief time for any questions and then tell the teams they can start building. Announce when five minutes have passed and give a warning as each five minutes passes, until thirty has been reached. Stop the activity at this point whatever stage it is at. Have teams realized that everything is there to shelter everyone adequately? And to provide everyone with a full meal? How long did it take to start co-operating, etc? Now encourage the teams to carry on and complete the task and eat the food.

iv) Conclude the session as the food is enjoyed with one or more of these ideas:

a) Read and think about the miracle of the feeding of the five thousand (John 6. 1–14). Has a miracle happened here today?

b) Does this exercise give us any answers to the problems of a divided and hungry world? If so, is the problem too big for us to have any influence? (If the conversation becomes despairing, give reminders of how all great movements and ideas have started from one or two people. It was just a handful of people who worked hard enough and spoke loud enough, for example, that led our giant super-market chains to develop environmentally friendly products and packaging.)

c) Have a group, who have rehearsed in advance, present the parable given below.

d) For prayers, hand round narrow strips of paper so that everyone has one. For speed, it is best if each strip is self-adhesive (like a paper chain) or small pieces of sticky tape are cut in advance. Invite everyone to write on their paper strip a brief prayer or just the name of a person or situation needing prayer. When this has been done, link all the strips together to make one long chain, ensuring the writing is on the outside of each link. Now let the chain be moved round the group slowly and in silence (or whilst quiet music plays) as people read the prayers.

THE PARABLE OF THE CHOPSTICKS

In Korea there is a legend about a native warrior who died and went to heaven. 'Before I enter,' he said to the gatekeeper, 'I would like you to take me on a tour of hell.' The gatekeeper found a guide to take the warrior to hell. When he got there he was astonished to see a great table piled high with the choicest foods. But the people in hell were starving. The warrior turned to his guide and raised his eyebrows.

'It's this way,' the guide explained. 'Everybody who comes here is given a pair of chopsticks five feet long, and is required to hold them at the end to eat. But you just can't eat with chopsticks five feet long if you hold them at the end. Look at them. They miss their mouths every time, see?'

The visitor agreed that this was hell indeed and asked to be taken back to heaven post-haste. In heaven, to his surprise, he saw a similar room, with a similar table laden with very choice foods. But the people were happy: they looked radiantly happy. The visitor turned to the guide. 'No chopsticks, I suppose?' he said.

'Oh yes,' said the guide. 'They have the same chopsticks, the same length, and they must be held at the end just as in hell. But you see, these people have learned that if a man feeds his neighbour, his neighbour will feed him also.'

John P. Hogan, Here and There

(*From* Words for Worship, *Christopher Campling and Michael Davis, Edward Arnold 1969*)

b) 'Heads you win....?' (30–45 mins) (SSG)

Preparation/equipment needed

Paper bags large enough to go right over a person's head. Ask at a large DIY store, some of which have just the right shape bag. Alternatively, make head sized cylinders from old wall paper. Everyone taking part needs a bag or cylinder on the outside of which has been pasted a picture (from a magazine or newspaper) of an obvious 'type' or of a famous person. Additionally some bags could have just a descriptive word on the 'face' side – Flirt / Swot/ Idiot, etc.

Meat of the Session

i)   Starting in small groups, everyone receives a bag to put over their head without seeing what face or word it carries. When it is on their head they very carefully puncture eye holes in the right place so they can see out.

ii) Conversation takes place in the group where they react to the personality type shown on the head masks of others and, at the same time, try to guess what their own assumed personality is.

iii) When the enabler judges this has gone on for long enough, the masks are removed and prejudices shared. Who did we like? Why? Not like? Why?

Bible study

Read and discuss together one or two passages that tell how Jesus treated people. For example:

Matthew 21. 28–32 The two sons
Luke 19. 1–10 Zacchaeus
Luke 14. 7–14 Humility.

Pray for people who feel outcasts because of their looks or personality. Is there anyone known to the group who needs particular support and is longing to be accepted and loved?

Follow-up

The next session complements this one.

c) 'Honour your partners' (30 minutes) (SSG)

NOTE: This session is best used in a group where the members know each other well, or towards the end of a residential weekend or camp (see also note at the end of this session).

Preparation/equipment needed

A small group to prepare in advance a drama based on the parable of the three servants or talents (Matthew 25. 14–30 or Luke 19. 11–27). Enough small pieces of card are required so that each person has two. Thread string through each card so that it can hang round people's necks.

Meat of the Session

i)   The drama group present their version of the parable of the three servants to the whole group.

ii) People are asked to find a partner, preferably someone they know quite well. Together they work on a list of their personal talents and gifts, listing everything they can think of and prompting each other. This list is transferred to the first piece of card listing their talents under the heading 'I CAN' – (sing, write letters, cook a good curry, talk to strangers easily – and so on). Each person in the partnership hangs their card round their neck on their front.

iii)   Now ask partners to join up in sixes or eights. Read and discuss together the words in Ephesians 4. 29–32. Spend some time, too, looking at each others 'I can' cards and if necessary suggest talents people have forgotten or did not realize they had.

iv)   The enabler now gives everyone the second card to hang down their back so that they cannot see it. This card has the heading 'YOU ARE....'. Firstly in the present groups people write something that is helpful, positive, loving, affirmative below the 'You are' heading. When the small group has done this, people mingle with others and add to their cards.

Praise

If appropriate, in a close, cuddly huddle sing a song such as 'Let there be love shared among us ...'

Follow-up

Have talents been discovered in the group that were not known about? Can these be used? Does anyone in the local church or community need the thanks of the group? It would be a lovely surprise for them to receive a card signed by everyone in the group.

RESIDENTIAL EXTRA!

Add to the loving and sharing of this session by inviting partners, early in a residential weekend or at a day event, to give their partner as a token of esteem some small personal belonging that will be kept in trust until the end of this session.

To avoid embarrassment from loss or damage, suggest that valuable items should not be handed over.

THEME – CHOICE

Sessions demonstrating how we face an enormous range of choices all the time. The sessions help young people to weigh up their views and form opinions on a whole range of ideas and issues. And one session provides an opportunity for looking deeply at commitment to Christ and his Church.

a) The choice is yours (30–45 minutes) (SSG)

Preparation/equipment needed

There are four methods to chose from for this session. Each one is easily arranged and is explained in the 'Meat of the Session'.

NOTE: It has been found that this session can be used as a jumping-off point for a series of sessions on some of the issues raised. This 'taster' helps to indicate the interest and awareness of members of the group in matters of importance, some of which it could be decided to follow up in more detail at a later date. Enablers should keep this possibility in mind.

Meat of the Session

i)   If the total number of people involved is no more than about twelve, the whole of this session can be seen through with everyone together. Above twelve people it will be best to split into groups.

ii)   Give everyone a piece of A4 size paper and have marker pens available. Ask people to fold their paper into roughly three equal parts down its length and write on the three words as in the diagram.

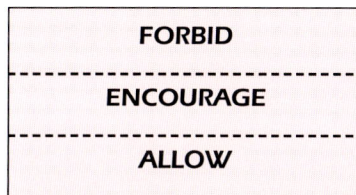

```
┌─────────────────────────┐
│        FORBID           │
├ ─ ─ ─ ─ ─ ─ ─ ─ ─ ─ ─ ─ ┤
│       ENCOURAGE         │
├ ─ ─ ─ ─ ─ ─ ─ ─ ─ ─ ─ ─ ┤
│        ALLOW            │
└─────────────────────────┘
```

iii) The enabler then presents the group/s with a series of topics, one at a time. Some examples of the kind of important and controversial topics that could be used are:
- Sunday trading
- The Royal Family
- Private education
- Religion in schools
- Capital punishment
- Mixed race marriages

iv)   The enabler writes up on a flipchart or has ready prepared on a sheet of paper the first topic, say SUNDAY TRADING. People are invited, at first without speaking, to make their view known about whether shops being open on Sunday is a good thing or not. Would they 'FORBID', 'ENCOURAGE' or 'ALLOW'? Each person is asked to fold their paper to display the word that best expresses their feelings about this matter and show their choice to the rest of the group. The enabler now encourages the group to talk briefly about why they have chosen to vote in the way they have done. (As suggested above, the enabler should make a mental note of the topics that arouse most interest with a view to suggesting that more time could be spent on them at a later date.)

v) At what is felt to be the right time, the enabler introduces a second topic, and so on for as much time as is available.

Alternative methods for this session
1 Instead of using words to introduce the topics use pictures from magazines or newspapers. For instance the enabler could just display a picture of the royal family or of a DIY store that is open on Sunday.

2 Start the session as described in iv), above but with some topics ask people to move to a corner or part of the room that is now the 'Forbid' corner, the 'Encourage' corner or the 'Allow' corner. Then ask the group of like-minded people in each corner to share their views with each other. The enabler could also bring groups of people with different views together at some stage to discuss their opinions.

3 Again, start the session as described above but with some topics ask people to leave their voting paper behind and come and stand in a line to demonstrate their opinion. This allows for shades of opinion not so easily shared with the paper vote. Designate one side of the room 'Forbid' and the opposite side 'Encourage', 'Allow' being the middle ground.

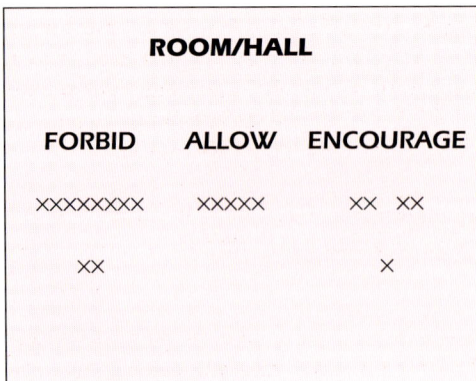

```
┌─────────────────────────────────┐
│        ROOM/HALL                │
│                                 │
│                                 │
│  FORBID    ALLOW   ENCOURAGE    │
│                                 │
│  XXXXXXXX   XXXXX     XX  XX     │
│                                 │
│     XX                  X       │
│                                 │
│                                 │
└─────────────────────────────────┘
```

The instruction is to stand nearest the point in the room that best represents your feelings about the topic. Allow sharing with near neighbours and those who hold opposite views.

Worship
After what might have been strong and even heated debate about important issues, use this time to reflect on what has happened. Thank God for the free will he has given us whilst at the same time trying to understand what God is saying to us about some of the great topics of our time. Read Romans 12. 1–2.

b) 'Super value! Best buy!' (45–60 minutes)(SSG)

Preparation/equipment needed

Prepare a set of small signs that each carry one of the following words:

Friends	Love
Good looks	Lots of money
Sense of humour	Skill at sport
Skill at music	Intelligence
A job	Good clothes
Luck	Good health
Faith in God	

Make an equal number of 'price tickets' showing a range of prices from, say, £1–£100. Also have a 'Best Buy' card. Brief someone in advance to be a market stall-holder who can put over the sales patter and banter.

Secondly, you will need a copy written out for all to see, or have copies of the 'Snowball Discussion' example (see Chapter 13 'Cooking Methods' A–Z).

Meat of the Session

i)   Go for surprise at the start of the session by having the ready-briefed market stall-holder set up a table and place his/her 'words' on it (Friends, Good looks, Sense of humour, etc.) S/he then adds the 'prices' to the words stressing what bargains they are. Ensure all this is quick, noisy and punchy.

ii) The enabler interviews and has a brief argument with the stall-holder about some of his/her prices – 'Good health is worth more than £25…' etc. The enabler invites everyone to swop the prices round if necessary, or, using spare price tags, adding new prices of their own. Let this happen until people get the point that most of these things are price-less. Valuable, but not in monetary terms. Discuss which are the most important 'values' on the stall. Which could we not live without?

iv) Move into the 'Snowball' Bible study given on page 45. After the foursomes have completed their discussion summarize the ideas that have emerged.

Prayer

Pray for those who have no material possessions and who are hungry and homeless. And for those who have great wealth. And for ourselves that we may use what we have well and wisely.

Talking point

It has been estimated that those young people now who are in paid employment for about forty years until retirement will easily earn a million pounds during their working life!

c) 'This is MY life' (45–60 minutes) (SSG)

Preparation/equipment needed

Small collection of items that could have been found in someone's pocket or hand-bag: a comb, some money, a dated till receipt, a photograph of a loved one, a dated bus or train ticket, etc. Secondly, a small booklet of eight pages of plain paper made up for everyone or, if time and funds permit, prepared as the sample given in Meat of the Session – 'This is MY Life'.

Meat of the Session

i) The enabler explains that s/he wants the group to do some detective work. Sadly, a man has been found wandering in the town/village who has lost his memory. He has no identification on him, just these few items (these are displayed). Can we help the police to decide who this person might be: his interests, his personality? The enabler tells people they can examine the property if they want and try to build up a profile.

ii) Do we carry round things that help people to know something about us if, and God forbid, we were to become a missing person?

iii) The enabler introduces the idea that we are going to star in our own 'This is Your Life'. The blank or ready prepared booklets are distributed. People are asked to get into small groups of three or four people.

iv) At a steady pace the enabler takes people through each page of the 'This is MY Life' booklet, asking for sections to be filled in, drawings to be done, etc. (see opposite). Encourage sharing of stories in the small groups but the enabler should try to keep people working at the same pace, moving on to the next stage together.

v) The challenge comes with pages 6 and 7. What are we going to make of our life? Who's in control? What help is needed with decisions? Where can it be found?

Bible study and Prayers

Read about the 'would-be' followers of Jesus in Luke 9. 57–62. Suggest that, having heard each other's story in their small groups, people pray quietly or silently for each other in those groups.

Follow-up

There may be some things for a youth worker to pick up with individuals who have been challenged by this session. The next session could also be used as follow-up.

THIS IS MY LIFE

Session (c) – Sample booklet

4

coming up to 10

WHAT CAN YOU REMEMBER OF...
friends ... or pets ... or playthings

school ... or the family growing up?
school ... or the family growing up?

8

3

3 months old

A FAMILY GROUP
what it looked
like then...

plan view

THIS WAS HOME...
picture or description

7

THE END

IS IT ALSO THE BEGINNING?

"Well," says God "I gave
you 'x' number of years. Tell me,
what did you do with them?"

2

I'm born!

WHEN?
WHERE?

This is what I think I looked like...

What kind of weather...?
Things I've been told about my arrival...

6

My future

*Thought...
TODAY is the first day
of the rest of my life

WHAT WILL BE THE CHAPTER HEADING?

WHO decides what comes next?
Does God come into my reckoning?

1

This is My Life!

ME, NOW

The story of...

5

TODAY

pictures (or words) to show
the things I do most often

d) Challenge to choose (60 minutes) (SSG)

Preparation/equipment needed

Do not go into this session lightly. It may need the help of extra people to act as enablers for small groups. Group enablers should meet beforehand to pray and prepare for the sessions. Allow time for individual discussion and follow-up.

In advance prepare separate slips of paper each bearing one of the Bible references given in the Meat of the Session. Also have written up for all to see, or available for distribution, the details of the Challenge to Choose groups as given below. Have a flip chart available for feed back from i) below.

Meat of the Session

i)   The enabler distributes the twelve Bible references listed below. (If there are fewer than twelve people, keep some of the slips in reserve. If more than twelve, get people to work together on the same reference.) The enabler explains that we are going to look at the human nature and experience of Jesus. Together we will try to put together a profile of him. Read your reference and then write up on the flip chart one word that tells about what Jesus experienced as a man. Can you think of other aspects of his humanity that have not been listed? The word in brackets after the reference is for the guidance of the enabler only and should not be included on the pre-prepared slips.

Luke 2. 7	(Birth)
Luke 2. 52	(Growth)
Mark 6. 3	(Family life and/or job)
John 2. 2	(Happiness)
John 11. 35	(Sorrow)
Luke 4. 2	(Hunger)
John 19. 28	(Thirst)
John 2. 15	(Anger)
Matt 4. 1	(Temptation)
Mark 15. 19	(Suffering)
Mark 15. 13	(Rejection)
Matt 22. 15	(Opposition)

ii) Throughout his life, the enabler explains, Jesus had choices to make and he often prayed to his Father for help and strength (see Mark 14. 32–41 where Jesus prays for his burden to be lifted in the garden of Gethsemane).

iii) The enabler says that in this session there is the opportunity to think and talk deeply about the challenge that Jesus puts to us all to follow him. People may be ready to do this today or just want to talk further about it. Four groups are on offer, plus one or two people available to talk with individuals.

iv) Display or hand out the following, allowing time for people to choose and avoiding any kind of pressure. Suggest a time limit of, say, forty-five minutes but make it possible for groups to meet for a longer or shorter time and to finish with prayer in their own group.

CHALLENGE TO CHOOSE
During this session you can share your thoughts, questions and doubts in a group of your choosing. Select a group that comes nearest to your own thinking:

a) **I am a Christian already** – but I would like advice on how I can progress in the Faith
b) **I have doubts and questions** about the Christian way of life, but I would like to talk about them.
c) **I have decided to follow Christ** – I need help to come to terms with this decision.
d) **At present, Christ (or the Church, or religion) mean nothing to me** – but my mind is not closed and I would like to talk things over with someone.

In addition to the groups, youth workers will be available to meet people for a personal chat if you would prefer this.

Follow-up
Group enablers should meet at the end of the session to consider what follow-up is appropriate both for individuals and the whole group.

e) 'May Day! May Day!' (45–60 minutes)

(This session would probably not work very well with a group of fewer than twenty people in total.)

Preparation/equipment needed
This is an extremely effective and reasonably simple to arrange simulation game and role play. The enabler needs to brief in advance two or three people to be 'cabin crew' as the game takes place in an aircraft. If the crew can rig themselves out in stewards' type uniforms so much the better. You will also need the equipment to play a video* as an 'in flight' movie. Also five rucksacks or back packs that will count as parachutes. 'Boarding passes' for all passengers, each of which has the name of a famous person on it. Added reality will come if you can have an amplified sound effect of an aircraft in flight and the facility to have the pilot's voice saying 'May Day' through the loudspeaker system.

*See note in Chapter 7 'The Place Setting – What You Need', about the use of videos.

Meat of the Session
i)   In advance prepare the room with seats in pairs with a centre aisle to represent the inside of a passenger plane. Try to prevent people from coming into the room until you are ready to start the game. Prop the video-player and monitor at the front of the cabin, reasonably high up for all to see.

ii) When ready, start the video and aircraft noise (if available) and have the cabin crew ready to welcome people on board and show them to their seats. Each passenger is given a Boarding pass as they arrive bearing the name of a well-known living person. (This could include a few well known local people.)

iii) When everyone is seated let them just watch the video for a few minutes whilst the cabin crew serve drinks, bring round magazines and demonstrate safety procedures.

iv) Suddenly the video is switched off and the voice of a pilot is heard saying 'May Day! May Day! We regret this aircraft has developed serious technical trouble and, as we are a long way from a safe landing place, will have to be crash landed on the most suitable terrain we can get to. This aircraft is only fitted with five parachutes for passengers. People should inform the cabin crew if they have a special right to use one of the parachutes. We estimate the aircraft will be at a safe height for jumping for about twenty more minutes. Please stay calm and help each other to decide who should earn the right to a parachute.'

v) The cabin crew now step in and invite people to suggest who should have a parachute. The enabler, through the pilot's tannoy, should give five minutes countdown to twenty minutes. At fifteen minutes the cabin crew should decide, from what they have heard, which five people earn the right to jump. Then let them simulate opening a door and jumping!

vi) Ask people to come out of role and decide for themselves whether the plane crashes and all other passengers are killed, or the pilot makes a terrifying but safe crash landing. Or any other ending to the story!

Bible study

At the end read 1 Corinthians 1. 26–31 about the people God chooses to do his work.

Note: Be sensitive about the use of this simulation game if anyone in the group has been in any way affected by an air accident.

THEME – COMMUNICATIONS
Sessions to encourage good communications, to look at how we are influenced by messages, signs and symbols, and to think about how God communicates with us and we with him.

a) 'Get the picture?' (45–60 minutes) (SSG)

Preparation/equipment needed

A small piece of paper for each person that can be rolled into a narrow tube and secured with sellotape. A wide selection of pictures (see Chapter 13 'Cooking Methods' A–Z: Pictures).

Meat of the Session

i)   Concentrating on the impact that pictures can have on us, use one or more of the ideas given in Chapter 13 'Cooking Methods' 'Pictures', referred to above. Try 'Picture Rummy' and 'Revelation'!

ii)   Conclude by asking people to roll their piece of paper into a tube through which they can look. Make the diameter of the tube about 1 centimetre. Encourage people to move around the room, hall and outside if it is daylight using the restricted view provided by their tube to look closely at the detail of objects – wood grain, dust, a small section of a picture, the skin on a hand or face, a leaf, the bark of a tree, etc.

Worship

Use the Pictorial Prayers' idea in the same section of Chapter 13.

Additionally, whilst people are peering through their tubes, have someone read slowly one of the Psalms (or a part of one) that glory in God's creation – Psalm 8, 19 (verses 1–6), 104 and 148.

Follow-up

Invite people to think about the impact that pictures have on their lives. Do TV pictures manipulate us by attempting to change our mood? Are pictures used to tease, prejudice, excite and anger us in popular newspapers? Ask people to bring examples of emotive, shocking, educative, challenging pictures taken from newspapers to share at a later session.

b) Hotline to heaven? (Timing flexible) (SSG)

Preparation/equipment needed

This is a practical and adaptable session exploring the meaning and symbolism of worship, and the ways we talk with and listen to God. You could spend an hour on the topic, a day or a weekend! Depending on the decision made, you will need access to a church so that you can walk round it when it is empty. Preferably you should also be able to visit a church of a different denomination where you will be able to share in an act of worship and have a tour of the church building.

Meat of the Session

A range of ideas from which you can pick 'n' mix:

i)   Ask the group to try to define what is meant by worship. What is its purpose? This is how former Archbishop William Temple put it:

> 'Worship is the submission of all our nature to God. It is the quickening of conscience by his holiness; the nourishment of mind with his truth; the purifying of the imagination by his beauty; the opening of the heart to his love; the surrender of will to his purpose – and all of this gathered up in adoration, the most selfless emotion of which our nature is capable and therefore the chief remedy of that self-centredness which is our original sin and the source of our actual sin.' *'Readings in St. John's Gospel' published by MacMillan.*

Can the group come up with a better, more understandable explanation?

ii) Using a grading method (*see Chapter 13 'Cooking Methods' A–Z: Measuring Strength of Feeling*) think about what are the most important 'component' parts of worship. Are any essential, in that, worship cannot happen without them?
Check list (*to which you may want to add*):
Prayers
Bible readings
Other readings
Hymns/Songs
Other music
Offertory
Notices
Sermon
Silence
Holy Communion/Eucharist

iii) Visit your own church building when it is empty to examine the way it is designed and the symbols that are in it. Does the shape of the building help people to worship? Does everyone understand the meaning of the various symbols and the use of the different pieces of church furniture – font, flowers, pulpit, lectern, etc?

iv) Draw up plans for a church that it is felt would provide the right atmosphere and surroundings for meaningful worship.

v)   Visit with permission the church of a different denomination from the one to which the group belongs. Try to go to one about which the group feels they know very little. Ask if the group can attend an act of worship and if someone can guide them round the church when it is empty and answer questions about the building and the worship that has been shared. Enquire also about the total life of the church, its other meetings, community work, national structure, etc.

vi) By arrangement visit an ancient church or cathedral. Learn something of its history and its present mission. Think and pray together within its walls, remembering how Christians for perhaps hundreds of years have worshipped in this church. It will have seen people at the times of their greatest happiness and despair. Use this House of God to listen to his message to us for today.

Follow-up

Use the discoveries you have made about worship to improve the quality of the group's times of worship.

c) 'Are you receiving me?' (45–60 minutes) (SSG)

Preparation/equipment needed

Collect together advertisements of many different kinds from newspapers and magazines and videotape some TV commercials lasting about five minutes in total. Video player and monitor required. A candle is required for the prayer time.

Meat of the Session

i) The enabler asks if, when we look at advertisements and commercials, we ask ourselves questions about them. Do we feel we are being got at? Conned? Entertained? Informed?

ii) Look at the newspaper and magazine advertisements critically. Do they have any value or are they only there to make money? Could we do without advertising?

iii) Look at the TV commercials. Some people say they are better than the programmes! Can we honestly say we are not influenced by them?

iv) Divide into small groups of three or four people and try out one or both of these exercises:

- Draft out a newspaper style advertisement encouraging people to come to church.

- Prepare a 30-second (exactly) TV style commercial to recruit disciples for Jesus of Nazareth.

v) Allow each group to present their creations and make an award for the best.

Bible study

Read the parable of the sower in Mark 4. 1–20. How receptive are we to the word of God?

Prayer

Have someone read slowly from John 1. 1–9. It will be most effective if this passage is read whilst the room is in darkness until verse 4 is reached when a candle is lit and placed in the centre of the group.

d) SPECIAL – 'How's your image?' (30–45 minutes) (SSG)

The group could use this theme as an opportunity to look at its own image, think about the way it 'promotes' itself and advertises special events, etc. The discussion could be extended to look at the image of the local church as it is seen by those who attend and those who pass by.

Some suggestions:
- If the group has a notice board, is it well kept and interesting? If not, what can be done to improve it?
- What kind of image does the group show to a) other young people who are not part of it? b) the local church members? c) the local community? Do we need to take steps to improve any of these images?
- As a Christian youth group, what kind of image is projected? Holier than thou? Stuffy? Outgoing and welcoming? etc. What kind of Christian image would we like people to see?

Follow-up

So what are you going to do about your image?

Read how Jesus condemned hypocrisy in Matthew 23. 13–28 but noting especially verses 27 and 28.

THEME – CHANGE

a) 'Their world, our world' (45–60 minutes or much longer) (SSG)

Preparation/equipment needed

This can be a brief session or, if it arouses the interest of the group, become a much longer and more ambitious project. Details are given for a session lasting about an hour. Hints are given as to how you can expand the material. Some brief facts are given below about dramatic changes in the way our world has changed in comparatively recent times. In readiness for the session, people could be asked to do some research at a reference library to add other facts. Information about trends and changes in the local community would add interest.

The session could be extended by inviting in to the group one or two elderly people to talk about the changes they have seen during their life-time. Or, with permission, recordings could be made in a home for elderly people asking them to reminisce about school, work, travel, etc. Could you find a centenarian to interview?

At the other end of the scale, ask young children to give their views on how they see their world into the future. Their dreams and visions.

THEIR WORLD, OUR WORLD FACT SHEET
(For you to add to and develop)

In 1851 **the population of England and Wales** was 17,927,000

In 1951 it was 43,754,000

In 1981 it was 49,155,000

In 1991 it was 51,100,000

(As a matter of interest, a census has been taken every ten years in this country since 1801, apart from 1941.)

The average expectation of life in Britain in 1840 was 29 years.

In 1870 it was 35 years

In 1958 it was 66 years

Today, for a baby girl it is slightly more than 72 years and for a baby boy, it is about 70 years.

Meat of the Session

i)   Share and discuss the facts above plus any others that have been collected.

ii)   Listen to recordings of memories from the past from senior citizens or, if you have invited an elderly friend to join you, listen to his or her stories from childhood onwards. Discuss which of the changes are the most important in influencing our lives for better or for worse.

iii) Divide into small groups to discuss how people will need to equip themselves to face up to the future – to cope with education, employment/non-employment, health, relationships, etc. As this is a big agenda, each small group could look at a different topic and then report back. Which issues prove to be of the most interest and/or concern?

Bible study
   Read and meditate on Luke 12. 22–31 in the light of the conversations you have shared.

Prayer
   Pray for people who are particularly affected by change – the elderly, the very young, the homeless, unemployed, etc.

Follow-up
   As was suggested at the beginning of this session, this topic has many possibilities for development. Your group may want to see if there are planned changes in your local community that threaten vulnerable groups of people or individuals. If so, are there ways we can offer our help and support? Play one of the simulation games in Chapter 18, 'The Planning Game', for example.

b) 'All the time in the world' (45–60 minutes) (SSG)

Preparation/equipment needed
   Collect together a wide ranging set of pictures and posters that are challenging and meaningful (see Chapter 13 'Cooking Methods' A–Z: Pictures). Ask members of the group to bring along to the session favourite pictures and posters from their own bedroom walls! Even for a small group of people you should aim to have a choice of about twenty pictures and posters. For each picture/poster you will need a piece of paper on which comments can be written.

Meat of the Session
i)   Give everyone a piece of paper and ask them to draw on it two concentric circles, as shown below, to look like a large Polo mint!

ii)   Ignoring the inner circle, ask them to divide up the outer part into sections showing roughly how they use their time on an average 'working' or 'school' day.

(Circumference of circle represents twenty-four hours)

iii)   Encourage comparisons. Do any unusual uses of time emerge?

iv)   The centre circle represents the 'core' of our lives – our driving force. Think of a few famous people and consider how their day might be different from our own:
   • The Prime Minister – His/her day revolving round visitors, political considerations, Parliament, etc.
   • A great athlete – His/her programme must be centred round training for a big race or match, affecting eating, sleeping, exercise, etc.

v)   The enabler asks if people can put a word or phrase in the centre circle of their diagram that describes the core of their lives – their driving force. Share ideas.

vi) The enabler reminds everyone we have only a limited amount of life time. This should drive us towards asking ourselves what the really important things in life are.

vii) Now spread out round the room the pictures and posters that have been collected together. Try to ensure that there is clear space round each picture and that there is a piece of plain paper by each one.

viii) The enabler now invites people to take an unhurried look at the pictures and posters and to decide if any of them says something that they feel is important. After looking round all the pictures they can add comments of full agreement, or even disagreement on the pieces of paper.

ix) After a thorough viewing of the display the enabler asks people to 'adopt', if they wish, one picture or poster they consider says something very important and would like to make part of their lives.

x)   Those people who don't feel able to go this far with the displayed material could use another piece of paper to make a simple poster expressing their 'most important thing'.

xi) The session ends with general discussion on the choices that have been expressed. Refer back to the 'time' diagrams made at the start of the session. Does anyone want to revise the 'driving force' or 'core' section?

Prayer
Pray for each other, the ideas that have been shared, and the help and courage needed to change our lives so that God is clearly at the centre of our lives – our core, our driving force.

Follow-up
Some passionate ideas may be expressed in this session. Do people need help to talk through their concerns or more time to share their views?

c) 'Their church, our church' (45–60 minutes or longer) (SSG)

This session runs on similar lines to a) above, but focuses this time on the local church. It is easy to knock the church, so aim to make it a positive and encouraging, if challenging, session. It is suggested that the material could be extended to involve the whole church community.

Preparation/equipment needed
Create a 'Their church, our church' fact sheet with the help of the minister, long-standing church members and church officials.

Suggested headings:
- Number of church members over a period of, say, ten years. Increasing or decreasing?
- Size of community/town served by the church – population changes. Increasing or decreasing?
- Any other facts that affect the life of the church now that are different from a few years ago (ecumenical arrangements, unemployment, unsuitable premises, money problems, etc.).

Arrange for a team from the youth group to conduct a random survey* among church members (perhaps after a service) and also of other users of the church – members of weekday organizations (for adults and younger people). The survey is to ask people to share, very briefly what they would like to see changed in the church and what visions they have for the future of the church. It would help considerably the effectiveness of such a survey if people are given notice of the questions and how the answers are going to be used. With permission, this could be done through the church magazine and/or a notice during a service (see also Chapter 13 'Cooking Methods' A–Z: Questionnaires).

* Some church officials and members may see young people involved in this activity as improper and threatening. Talk about the idea of the session and the positive opportunities for change and growth it could provide, with the minister and other lay officials. Seek their backing. Could it become a co-operative venture with consultations, reports and recommendations involving the whole church, but initiated by the youth group?

Meat of the Session

Depending upon whether this is going to be a one-off session for the youth group or a project involving the wider church community, you will need to consider a number of options from the following suggestions and to adjust these to meet the circumstances of the group and church.

i)   Share and discuss the facts gathered on the 'Their church, our church' sheet. What do they reveal? Any surprises?

ii)   List the findings from the survey on change and visions conducted among church members. Do any ideas and thoughts emerge strongly? How do they compare with the ideas of the youth group?

iii) Which ideas for change emerge as priorities? Do they have general acceptance in the church community? How are they best discussed further with a view to taking action? Where will democratic decisions be made on any recommendations for change? Are all the facts available and clear for sound decisions to be made? If not, what further information is required? Who is to gather it?

iv)   Is the committee structure of the local church (and its wider democratic network, if necessary) fully understood? If not, can it be explained to the youth group so that it can be used effectively and without misunderstanding or division occurring?

v)   Are the visions that have been shared realistic? How can they be turned into reality?

vi)   Should a well-planned one day or weekend consultation be arranged for the whole church family to pray for, think about and discuss the present mission of the church in this community?

vii) Have people from other churches in our area got stories to share of planning for change and making dreams come true? Can we meet and learn from them?

Worship, Prayer, Bible Study

This will need to be a vital and integral part of this project at all stages depending upon how far you are progressing with it. If the whole church is to be involved, a Bible study series on change and the church could be followed through. Read and discuss the meaning of the poem below. Just one verse from the Bible may help to keep things in perspective as you consider this theme: 'Jesus Christ is the same yesterday, today, and for ever' (The letter to the Hebrews 13. 8.)

In search of a round table

It will take some sawing,
  to be a round table,
  some redefining,
  and redesigning.

Changing a narrow-long church
  can be painful
  for people and tables.

But so was the cross
  a painful table.
It means: giving,
  and saying YES.

And from such death comes life, from such dying comes rising,
  and the continued search for a round table church.

And what would a round table church mean?

It would mean no thrones,
  for but one ruler is there,
  and he was a footwasher,
  at a table, in fact.

He was a healer of hearts
  and a giver of disturbing peace.
Some of us have lost track of his footsteps.
But the times and the tables ARE changing and rearranging.
What will happen to narrow-long ministers,

when they confront a round table people,
after years of working up the table (as in 'up the ladder')
only to discover
that the table has turned round?

They must be loved into roundness, where APART is spelled A PART
and where the call is to a gathering.
For God has called a people,
not THEM and US.

THEM and US are unable to gather round,
for at a round table there are no sides.
And all are invited
to wholeness and to food.

But wishing and hoping
will not get us there –
daily dying and rising will (and some sawing).

At one time our narrow-long churches
were built that way to resemble the cross,
but it does no good
for buildings to do so,
if lives do not.
Round tabling means:
no preferred seating,
no first and last,
no better, and no corners.

Round tabling means:
being WITH,
A PART OF,
TOGETHER, and ONE.

It means room for the spirit,
and for gifts,
and for disturbing profound peace for all.

We are called to be church, a people,
and if God calls, we are bound to follow,
all the while being harmless as doves
and wily as serpents
in search of and in the presence of
the Kingdom
that is God's and not ours.
Amen.

Chuck Lathrop, USA (Appalachian Documentation, Washington)

Chapter 17

TAKE AWAYS

Youth Weekends, other times away and treats

'Go on, give yourself a break. Let's have a take away for a change. Where shall it be – the exotic Chinese, the mysterious Indian or the pasta and spices of the Italian pizza parlour?'

'When can we go again?' That's one of the most common reactions to taking a youth group away for a weekend, a day, to a camp or perhaps to a big event like Greenbelt or Spring Harvest.

It's the kind of experience that many young people remember for a very long time and it can sometimes be a life-changing one: 'It was at that youth weekend three years ago that I really came to know Jesus'.

The value of young people and youth workers going away together is rarely disputed. Residential weekends and other similar events give opportunities:

- For people to get to know each other much better
- To see each other, young people and adults, in different roles and situations from usual
- To relax and have fun together
- To explore a subject or theme at much greater depth than can usually be achieved at short weekly meetings
- To try out new skills and ideas
- To face excitement and challenge
- To be away from home and on neutral territory
- To help build confidence and trust in each other
- To try out participation skills
- To experience community life and responsibilities
- To relate worship more closely to the programme and experiences being lived through.

This can only have a bonus effect on participation, responsibility and relationships at ordinary weekly meetings.

TUCK IN!

'Enlarge the limits of your home,
spread wide the curtains of your tent;
let out its ropes to the full
and drive the pegs home;
for you shall break out of your confines right and left.'

Isaiah 54. 2–3.

WHAT'S IT ALL FOR?

It is said that an absent-minded author had to telephone his wife from a railway station to say 'I'm here, but where am I supposed to be going?'

As had been said before (see Chapter 1 'Preparing for the Feast – Is it any excuse for a Party?') it is vital to decide on the reason why something is to be done. An aim is needed with clear objectives against which success can be measured. A youth weekend away may sound like a good idea, but why? What for? At whom is it aimed? What do we hope to achieve? It is strongly recommended that these questions are asked and answered, within the context of the youth group's total programme, before all the detailed planning is begun for taking the group away.

WHAT KIND OF 'TAKE AWAY'?

The ten-stage check list given later in this chapter is to help if you are planning any one of the following types of take-away experiences:

1 AN AWAY DAY A day-out in the country, at a theme park, to a special event, concert, etc. You will need to check out all steps except possibly number 2.

2 A CATERED-FOR WEEKEND at a residential centre* where a charge is made for full board and use of the centre facilities – conference rooms, sports hall, grounds, etc. Such a weekend usually takes place from an evening meal on Friday until Sunday lunch, leaving the centre in the early afternoon. Very convenient, but the most expensive way of organizing a weekend away.

3 SELF-CATERING WEEKEND at a residential centre. These centres are often more basic in their facilities and smaller than the centres described in 2. Usually the group has the whole centre for its exclusive use and is responsible for providing and preparing food and cleaning up before leaving. Considerable saving in cost on number 2 but there is often less time for programmed activities because of the cooking and household duties to be done.

4 SELF-CATERING WEEKEND in a church or similar premises. Many youth groups make arrangements to use a church hall and other rooms in another town or village. Often this can be done very cheaply, for the cost of a realistic donation. The snags are that it will almost certainly mean sleeping on the floor, and kitchen and toilet facilities may be fairly basic. Careful negotiations will need to be undertaken with the officers of the host church to check whether all rooms are available all the time, to be aware of security and fire regulations and especially how Services of Worship and other activities on Sunday morning will affect the visitors (see 'Sleeping on Church Premises' guidelines below).

5 CAMPING Probably the cheapest form of take away but the one needing the most careful planning to ensure safety, health and security. Check out all ten steps thoroughly.

6 PRE-ARRANGED EVENT such as to Greenbelt, Spring Harvest, adventure/activities holiday, etc. This kind of 'take-away' only lets the youth groups' planning committee off Step 4, the programme, which is being arranged for you. Check out all other steps and read carefully all instructions sent out by the event organizers. Remember that responsibility for the young people still rests with the youth workers who are taking the local group.

(*Information about residential centres can be obtained from denominational youth departments or local youth offices. See Chapter 22 'Store Cupboard'.)

SLEEPING ON CHURCH PREMISES

These important guidelines apply to number 4 above. They were prepared for the guidance of Methodist groups by the Methodist Church Property Division (April 1992) but they apply equally to all church premises:

1   Only ground floor accommodation is considered suitable for sleeping accommodation.

2   There should be at least two separate routes leading from the sleeping accommodation and out of the building. A room with two doors leading into a corridor from which the only exit could be impeded with smoke and fire would not be considered acceptable.

3   External doors should be left unlocked. If for security purposes this is impracticable, the fastening should be a simple tower bolt type. Exit doors should be checked for ease of opening.

4   Exit routes and doors should be clearly indicated.

5   In order to minimize the spread of smoke and fire should an outbreak occur, all doors should be kept closed, particularly during the night hours.

6   Portable heating appliances should be sited in positions in which they would not impede exit doors and routes should they catch fire. They should be turned off during sleeping hours.

7   An outbreak of fire often causes a power failure. It is therefore necessary for supervisory staff to have handlamps.

8   Smoking should be forbidden in the sleeping accommodation.

9   A nominal roll of occupants should be prepared and hung just within the main exit door. Occupants should be instructed to meet at a pre-determined assembly point in the event of an outbreak of fire and a roll call should be taken.

10   Anyone discovering a fire should raise the alarm by shouting 'Fire'.

11   The supervisory staff should be aware of the nearest telephone. The Fire Service should be called to all fires using the 999 facility.

12   Cars and other vehicles should not be parked where they obstruct exit routes or access for fire appliances.

13   Supervisory staff should be familiar with the location of and the operation of the fire-fighting equipment. Fire-fighting should only be carried out when it is obvious that it is safe to do so.

THE TEN STEPS TO 'TAKE AWAY'

STEP 1 – PLANNING GROUP
Set up a planning group of four or five people, young people and youth workers, who will take responsibility for all aspects of the Take Away event.

If you are hiring a residential centre, the first meeting of the planning group will need to be at least twelve months before the event, to allow time for the centre to be booked. Many centres make reservations up to two or three years ahead.

Agenda for first meeting:
1 Review the aim of the event:
    a) Purpose?
    b) Who is it for?
    c) What age range?
    d) How many?

2 What kind of residential centre?
Fully catered? Self-catering? Church hall? Camp?

3 Who will check what centre/ churches are available on the dates we require?

4 What is our upper limit for the charge for the weekend?

5 Begin to devise a budget:
    a) Costs of centre
    b) Food (if self-catering)
    c) Travel costs
    d) Expenses for putting on the programme
    e) Other expenses.

6 Do we need money-raising efforts in advance to help subsidize the cost? Could we get any grants from the local education authority or through the church?

7 Style of programme for the weekend – first thoughts:
Theme, recreation, audio visual aids, speakers, etc.

8 Allocating duties based on decisions made:
It may be helpful to appoint from the group one person to contact the Conference centre or church, one to begin to draft ideas for a programme, someone who will handle bookings and money matters and a caterer if self-catering.

9 Date of next meeting (by which time a centre/church will have been provisionally booked and a visit made by the whole planning group, or one or two representatives, to check it out).

STEP 2 – THE CENTRE, CHURCH OR CAMP SITE
Things to check before confirming booking:
Size (number of rooms, beds, size of camp site, etc.)
Accessibility for transport and for disabled
Any restrictions on use (Centre/site rules and regulations)

Cost of hire: (If full board are there any extras to be found?)
Charging structure:
    Deposit needed? If so when?
    Final payment due?
    Dates for final numbers attending?
    Is there a cancellation charge?
    Will we be sharing with any other groups?
If self-catering:
    Are there any local food suppliers? (Cash & Carry card available?)
    How do we gain access?
    Is there a telephone nearby?

STEP 3 – CENTRE, CHURCH OR SITE VISIT

Ask for full guided tour. Explain the type of group you are, the number you are likely to bring, the sort of programme you will be having, any special requirements (access for disabled, etc.).

Check – phone, first aid, doctor, hospital, etc., any House rules, audio visual aids available, any insurance requirements, etc.

After the visit, ask:

Does the centre, etc., meet most or all your requirements, and if not do you need to try somewhere else?

STEP 4 – THE PROGRAMME

This should be designed to meet the aim you have prepared for the weekend.

Prepare a framework, based around meal times, that provides for sessions on a chosen theme or subject; some time for fun and relaxation; worship, etc. (You could use many of the ideas in this book!)

Does the size and shape of the rooms available restrict any activities? Is there a minimum and maximum number of people that would make the programme difficult to manage?

Are there any visual aids, equipment, extra staff, speaker, etc., that need to be booked in advance?

Allocate responsibilities for the action still to be taken.

Ensure that all booking arrangements with a centre, camp site, etc., are confirmed in writing. Similarly with transport arrangements.

STEP 5 – PUBLICITY (*2–3 months before the event*)

Descriptive leaflet and booking form to those at whom the event is aimed and for parents/guardians. It will need to include:

    Date, time of departure from base and return time, details of centre/site; title for the weekend, preliminary programme details, cost and payment arrangements, closing date for bookings, deposit and final payment. Details of any equipment that will need to be taken (especially if camping).

STEP 6 – TRAVEL

How do we travel – hired coach or mini-bus? Self-drive mini-bus or cars? Train, etc.

Are any advance booking/cost estimates to be done now?

Are there any EC regulations/insurance restrictions affecting self-drive vehicles that need to be checked on?

STEP 7 – PLANNING GROUP COUNTDOWN LIST TO THE EVENT

Meet four to six weeks before the weekend to check up on:
- Numbers booked – sufficient? Enough adult youth workers? If not, what action is needed?
- Any final checks with centre/site? Is everything confirmed in writing?
- Is the budget being kept to?
- All aspects of the programme – are they in hand?
- Is equipment, games, worship resources, etc., being assembled to take with us?
- Catering team all OK – if self-catering?
- Have we gone through every detail?
- Any problems still to be resolved – if so how and by whom?

STEP 8 – BRIEFING MEETING

Two or three weeks before the event hold a short briefing meeting for all those attending the event. Remember that for some people it may be their first time away from home and there will be anxieties to be dealt with.

Have ready for the meeting a copy for everyone of:
- Departure times and places with a phone number to contact if anyone is delayed
- Outline programme for the weekend
- Address of the centre/church and phone number to be left at home in case of emergency
- List of everything that has to be taken by participants – special clothing, camping equipment, sleeping bag, Bible, musical instruments, etc.
- Medical form to be completed and returned before the event (give a clear date for this and chase up any not received. It's too important to leave to chance.) Sample on page 114.
- If it is felt necessary and appropriate list any house rules or guidelines for the centre you are going to. Make it clear who is responsible for the group whilst they are away (see Chapter 8 concerning legal responsibility). Emphasize that bringing or using of alcohol, solvents, illegal drugs and tobacco are not acceptable. (This could be varied if there is a designated smoking area.) Make it clear that, after an agreed time, people must remain in the rooms allocated to them and that sexual activity is not permitted at the weekend.

Be ready to answer questions and discuss all aspects of the weekend at this stage. It will save problems at the weekend itself. If necessary arrange to meet separately with any people who seem to be dissenting from any aspect of the weekend's programme.

STEP 9 – THE WEEKEND

If at all possible, arrange for some of or all the planning group to arrive at the centre/site early to make final preparations and to be able to welcome people when they arrive, show to rooms, etc. Ensure, where appropriate, that the centre management is fully-up-to date on the programme and numbers attending (these details should have been sent in advance, two or three weeks beforehand if possible).

Make people aware of fire regulations, having a fire drill if necessary.

Underline the importance of the person in charge knowing where everyone is over the weekend in case of an emergency. Have an accurate nominal role displayed in a prominent position with copies kept by members of the planning group. Devise some system of signing out people for permitted absences so that there is no confusion or uncertainty.

Go ahead with your planned programme and have a great time!

STEP 10 – FOLLOW-UP

An important part of the programme near to the end is to give people the opportunity to evaluate the weekend (*for some methods of doing this see Chapter 20 'Afters'*).

The comments made should be reviewed by a follow-up meeting of the planning group alongside their own assessment of the event. Was the aim met?

Individuals may also need following-up to offer support and counselling following any important experiences that have affected them during the weekend. This should be treated as a matter of urgency.

You may also want to consider as a group an actual follow-up session. This should take place not more than three weeks after you return or the effect will be lost. If you decide to have one, make it purposeful, taking the whole group forward in their relationships and thinking from the weekend together. A 're-union' as such can be a bit of an anti-climax unless it is well planned. In making arrangements for such a follow-up session bear in mind those members of the group who were unable to attend the weekend. Will they feel excluded? How can they be included in the next stage of the group's growth after the Take Away?

OTHER TREATS!

Special treats, special days out. We all like something to look forward to. And every so often it's a boost to the youth group programme to do something special together. There will be a bit more organizing to do and probably money to collect and travel arrangements to be made but it will all help to make an increasingly rich, varied and worthwhile programme. Just a few ideas:

- Go to the theatre or cinema together
- A night at the ice rink, roller skating, ten pin bowling or swimming
- Support a concert by Christian artists
- Take part in an area, District or Diocese youth event run by your denomination or ecumenically (see address list in Chapter 22 'Store Cupboard')
- Have a day out at a theme park, at the seaside or in the country
- Hire a boat or boats on a river or canal for a day.

SAMPLE HEALTH/EMERGENCY FORM
— Confidential —

We need to be clear about parental consent and medical needs. To help the organizers and the applicant, could you please complete the following details:

Name of participant (please print) _____

d.o.b _____ Address _____

_____ Postcode _____

Event to be attended, with dates _____ _____

Name, address and telephone number of person to be contacted (parent/guardian if you are under 18) in case of emergency during the event:

_____

_____

Telephone (day) _____ (evening) _____

Is there any specific medical condition of which we should be aware? (e.g. asthma, allergies, bedwetting, migraine, fits or any other illness or disability?) You may be in an unusual environment, and may be more susceptible.

If so, please give details _____

Are you receiving any medical treatment at present? YES/NO_____

If YES, give details _____

Have you ever had a tetanus injection? YES/NO _____

Please give date of last one if known _____

Name and address of own doctor _____

_____

Is there anything else that would be helpful for the organisers to know in planning and running the event which would enable you to participate more fully?

_____

If you will be under 18 at the time of the event, please ask your parent or guardian to sign the following:

I will inform you if _____ comes into contact with any infectious illness (e.g. German measles, etc.) during the 3 weeks prior to the event. If _____handles his/her own asthma or diabetes I will make sure there is sufficient medication.

I give permission for Paracetamol to be used, if needed.

Signed _____ Date _____

For full reassurance, please talk to the organiser by telephone.

Chapter 18

READY-TO-SERVE MEALS

Simulation games

'Just look at the list of ingredients in this tin of baked beans! It says they're salt and sugar reduced – but they seem to have thrown a whole heap of other things in instead. And all those "E" numbers – it makes you wonder what you're really eating these days. Do we have to put up with all these "additives"! All I want is a few beans to put on toast!'

Many people are suspicious of simulation games (see Chapter 13 'Cooking Methods' – An A–Z of Group Discussion and Development Methods). They think they're gimmicky, difficult to manage, too elaborate for most youth groups and too contrived to be useful. Well, yes, if simulation games are not well thought through and prepared they can end in chaos. If the group taking part is not well briefed the whole point of the game can be lost and there can be real frustration. And if sufficient time is not given for debriefing and talking through just what has happened, the enabler may end up with a group of confused and possibly angry people.

BUT, if good advance preparation is done, the purpose of the game is fully understood and ample time is given for playing and evaluating the experience – **then**, a simulation game is a fascinating, absorbing, challenging method of involving people that can lead to deep and meaningful discussion. **Certainly well worth a try.**

SIMULATION is like putting yourself in someone else's shoes.

American Indians have a saying – To really understand me you must walk for a mile in my moccasins.

'HOLD THE FRONT PAGE'

A newspaper simulation exercise (Playing time – Not less than two hours) (SSG)

Preparation/equipment needed
- At least one copy of every national daily newspaper for the day on which the exercise is to be carried out.
- A 'dummy' newspaper layout of four pages, at least tabloid size, marked up with columns and, preferably, with a common heading to suit the name of the town or group – 'The Blankshire Bulletin', for example.
- Marker pens, paste, scissors, rulers, white paper.
- A radio to be able to listen to a current news summary (use radio rather than television, as the bulletins on the radio are usually much briefer).
- Additional news stories taken from recent newspapers and magazines that give good news of people and events. These are fed to the news teams during stage 2.

- Invite two or three people to come to the session to be interviewed or to share a good news story. You may be able to persuade a local celebrity, athlete, the mayor or MP to help the group in this way for a few minutes, but to stay and see the end result.

Instructions for players (*Break into groups of not more than six people**)
You are a member of a group of journalists with the job of preparing a four-page newspaper.

Many people complain that newspapers don't really show what the world is like. It is said they sensationalize stories, print only bad news, distort the truth and allow what they write to be influenced by the politics of the newspaper proprietor.

So here is a golden opportunity to put across what the world is really like, if you don't think the newspapers you read do a very good job.

There will be three stages to the simulation game.

Stage 1 (*about 30 minutes*)
The enabler will tell you when to move to stage 2.

Meet as a team and get to know each other, if necessary.

Decide if you are going to work together as a group all the time or appoint people to particular jobs, for example:

The Editor	– responsible for the overall content and style
Sub Editor	– responsible for editing the material and the layout of the paper
2/3 Reporters	– rewriting material supplied and gathering stories.

You will be supplied with several of today's morning papers so that you have the major news of the day, plus an opportunity to listen to the latest radio news. There will also be a batch of general news stories for you to look at.

During Stage 1 you should have an editorial conference to decide the main news stories of the day and your line of approach to them.

Stage 2 (*about 1 hour*)
The enabler will remind you of how much time you have left and, by arrangement, extend it if necessary.

Using the 'master' sheet provided, write and paste up your four-page newspaper. It has to be on the streets in an hour.

During this time you may receive additional agency tapes with news and you may have invitations to attend press conferences. So save yourselves time and space to handle late news.

Stage 3 (*about 30 minutes*)
Share the completed newspaper and discuss the contents with other groups who have also been producing 'rival' publications.

*Small groups can work together and produce one newspaper.

HELP! PAT'S ILL!

An 'In' Tray exercise and Simulation Game *(Playing time – about 90 mins)* (SSG)

Most people who work in office jobs have an 'In' tray and an 'Out' tray. It's into the 'In' tray that new messages and letters go. A full 'In' tray can mean a lot of work and possibly quite a few problems.

An 'In' tray exercise is one in which the people involved are presented with a range of messages, etc., and sort out the priority that should be given to each message and how it should be handled.

'Help! Pat's ill!' gives an insight into making priorities and taking action on them. The game starts with an 'In' tray exercise and ends with a role play of a decision-making committee (see Chapter 13 'Cooking Methods' A–Z: Role Play).

Preparation/equipment needed

Everyone taking part needs a copy of your group's own version of *A: Briefing Paper* and *B: Sample Messages*, of which specimens are given on the following pages. Each group also needs a sheet on which they can write messages. *C: Action this day!* gives an example.

In addition to the enabler, two or three other people will be needed to form a control group. This group replies on the 'Action this Day' sheets to queries from each member of the Church Youth Committee.

Summary of game

1   Establish a small control group who need to meet beforehand with the Enabler to ensure the process for the game is understood. Prepare enough papers for all participants.

2   At the start of the game hand out copies of the Briefing Paper on which roles from the people on the Church Youth Committee have already been allocated (either to small groups or individuals).

3   Hand out the papers and messages from Pat's 'In' tray.

4   Talk through the briefing paper and answer any queries. Emphasize that communication with the control group can only be in writing. The control group will reply in writing on the same sheet.

5   Start the game, during which the papers from Pat's 'In' tray are prioritized. Allow about thirty minutes.

6   Call together the 'Committee' (preferably sitting round a table with observers looking on from outside). Instruct the Chairperson to form an agenda for the meeting from the priorities suggested by the Committee members. Members of the Committee should take on the role suggested against their name.

7   The enabler should assume that about twenty to thirty minutes will be long enough for the role playing of the committee but should be ready to step in and stop the meeting earlier if it is running out of steam or extend the time slightly. But do not let the conversations drag.

8   Try to ensure the Committee has made clear decisions and resolved who will take actions.

9   Allow time when the role play is finished for debriefing. What has been learned? In hind-sight would we have done anything differently? Involve the observers in comments and discussion.

A : Briefing Paper

'HELP! PAT'S ILL!'

Pat, the youth leader of the 30-strong youth group for 13 17 year olds has been taken suddenly ill. It is a serious illness and Pat is likely to be out of action for several months.

The time is the present. The minister has called an emergency meeting of the Church Youth Committee for (insert a realistic time), to discuss the situation.

You have just received copies of the main papers and messages from Pat's 'In' tray, sent on by her family.

The minister has asked you to look at the papers and decide what action, if any, should be taken on each one.

The youth group meets next Sunday evening and then again on the following Friday. The minister asks 'who will be responsible for the club in the immediate future and until Pat is fit? Should we close it down?'

In preparation for the Church Youth Committee you have about thirty minutes to look at the papers provided. The 'control group' will be able to answer 'telephone calls' if necessary. You should appoint one person from your group to act as group contact.

Those attending the Church Youth Committee will be:

1 The lay chairperson – John Faulks
2 The minister – Paul Astor
3 Senior church steward – Cecil Reed
4 Church treasurer – Pamela Small
5 Church youth committee secretary – Violet Ogden
6 Youth member aged 14 – Katy Brown
7 Youth member aged 18 – Vince Small
8 Scout group leader – Duncan Black
9 Junior church leader – Linda Bayliss

Your small group (or individuals if you are, in total, only a small group) will be looking at the papers and preparing for the committee in the role of the _____

One of your group will attend the committee in this role.

Through your group contact, you may consult with other members of the Committee during the thirty minutes if you wish.

B: **Sample Messages**

Adapt style, dates and times to make them realistic to your own youth group's situation.

— SAMPLE LETTER ONE —

SPORTY JOE'S
The Extown Sports Shop

STATEMENT (Current date)

Acct No 3724 (A date about 6 months ago)

Amount £46. 34

F I N A L   D E M A N D

Despite our previous reminders our records show that
this account has still not been paid.
    Unless the account is paid in cash within seven
days we shall be reporting this debt to our
solicitors and instructing them to take the necessary
legal action to recover the money.

Yours faithfully

J.Smith

To the Nonsuch Youth Group
Extown

— SAMPLE LETTER TWO —

(Current date)

Dear Pat

Sorry I can't go to the shops for Mr Bailey next
Monday as I'm going for an interview. Can you find
another club member to do it?

Love

Jill

P.S. I usually get his Sunday paper for him (The
People) and will be travelling north that day.

— SAMPLE LETTER THREE —

(Current date)

Dear Pat

I'm sorry that I have to write to you again on behalf
of the Property Committee to complain about the
condition the kitchen had been left in after a Club
meeting.

If there are any further complaints we shall have to
report the matter to the Church Council to see what
action should be taken.

I hope you can sort this matter out as we do not want
to appear to be always complaining about the Youth
Club.

All good wishes
Yours sincerely

George

— SAMPLE LETTER FOUR —

(Current date)

Dear Pat

Sorry but due to a family problem I won't be able to
come on 10th. Sorry to let you down. I'll hope to
come some other time.

Best wishes

Bill

— SAMPLE LETTER FIVE —

(Current date)

PRIVATE AND CONFIDENTIAL

Dear Pat

Forgive me bothering you but I am hoping you can help
me about a problem I am having with Karen.

Since she met up with Simon at the Club she has
changed a lot - for the worse. She has started to
stay out late. Often I can't get her to tell me where
she is going and I'm worried sick. The other night
she had obviously been drinking, and I'm sure her
school work is starting to suffer.

Now I'm on my own and without Trevor I find it very
difficult to control her and feel I'm nagging her all
the time.

Can you help because I'm getting desperate. Can you
see if you can reason with her? Any help will be
appreciated. I hope you understand.

Love to you both.

Sheila

— SAMPLE LETTER SIX —

```
OUTLINE PROGRAMME
(Use current dates and topical events)

5/3 Discussion: Is Mothering Sunday worth keeping?
(Penny introducing)

10/3 Bill Tabert bringing climbing equipment for
abseiling demos.

12/3 ?? Passion Sunday!  ? Kris Holdsworth calling

17/3 St Patrick's Day Ceilidh (? Paddy's Band)

19/3 Visit from St. Nicks. Y F.

Easter Day Dawn Hike and Service
```

— SAMPLE LETTER SEVEN —

```
                                        4 Church St
                                          Saturday

To the Youth Leader

If I find the youths walking along my garden wall on
Friday nights again I will call the Police and have
them close the club down. I have already complained
to Mr Astor and he said he would do something.

A.E.Eight
```

(Add other letters to give a current and local flavour, including an application form for an event that the youth group members are hoping to go to, but where the closing date is in a day or two.)

C: Action this day!

ACTION THIS DAY

Memo to Control:

From Group:
re. letter:

Reply

From Control:

THE PLANNING GAME

(*Allow up to 3 hours for this game, preferably divided into two sessions with a break between.*)

This game will not work effectively with fewer than twenty-five people plus the enabler and a planning department of up to six people. The game is probably best played in the setting of a residential weekend or as part of a full day's programme.

Summary of game

Participants become members of a fictional community called Eastport, a section of Bridgetown, which is faced with a planning application from a local factory. The proposed extension to the factory will affect different sections of the community in different ways. In up to eleven small groups, plus two concerned individuals, players have about an hour to prepare a case, for, against, or neutral, to put to a public enquiry which forms the second part of the game.

The enabler meets with a volunteer group of up to six people who form the central group or planning department. They brief themselves on the management of the game and arrange for the preparation of the Briefing Sheets, etc. (see papers A–C).

Have a short (fifteen minutes) briefing session for players when Briefing Sheet A and the two maps are handed out and questions answered. At this stage participants do not know which 'role' they will play. Allow reading time.

Now hand out Briefing Sheet B, 'The Rules of the Planning Game' on which the roles people will undertake have been marked – For example:
    'You are a member of Group 1 "Private House Residents (St Ronan's Estate)"'.
Give time for groups to form and to establish a base for themselves. Tell them they have one hour to prepare for the public enquiry.

Give each group a supply of Sheet C – the enquiry and reply sheet. Emphasize that enquiries must be in writing. Replies in writing from the planning department will be brought back to the group.

Establish the planning department in a place well separated from the other 'citizens' of Eastport.

The enabler should give time countdowns during the last fifteen minutes of the hour, extending the time a little if groups ask for it. But time pressure helps the realism of the game.

The enabler stops the game and assumes that the public enquiry will take place in (name a room or space) in 20–30 minutes. (Time for a coffee break!) Each group should have a spokesperson ready to speak.

Have a room or space set out formally with a table at one end and chairs facing it in rows. There should be chairs behind the table for the planning group members and the enabler or an independent 'Person from the Ministry'.

The enabler or an extra independent person now takes on the role of the person from the Ministry (Department of the Environment). The person should preferably dress formally in a suit and carry a brief case.

The public enquiry is opened in a very formal manner, each group being invited to put its case and allowing comments from other members of the public. Members of the planning department are invited to comment, if appropriate.

After about thirty minutes or when all contributions have been made and arguments heard, the person conducting the enquiry closes it and says s/he will withdraw for a few minutes (not more than five) to consider his/her verdict, based on the comments made.

S/he comes back and announces the result of the enquiry, that is, whether the factory extension is to be built or not.

THE GAME IS NOW OVER and the enabler and everyone else is asked to come out of role. (Stand up, shake yourself vigorously, shake other people's hands, hug them, etc!)

The enabler helps the group to debrief (see Chapter 13 'Cooking Methods' A–Z: Debriefing and Affirming) and to examine what has been learned.

Briefing sheet A plus two maps of a section of Bridgetown

THE PLANNING GAME

BRIDGETOWN, set on a river estuary, is a town with a population of 125,000 people. Eastport, the section of the town shown on the map, is mainly a working class area (population 4,500) which has grown up since the 1920s around a small dock. Leafield Council Estate was completed in 1979. Lea Meadow Industrial Estate has developed steadily since 1985 and all sites are now taken.

Phoenix Chemicals Limited, situated on the south bank of the river near the wharves, is a progressive private company started ten years ago from scratch by two young chemists and an accountant.

The product they manufacture, methalynic acid, is used in a variety of products but principally furniture polish, the fire-proofing of plastics and industrial metal cleaners. The main market for Phoenix Chemicals is a local polish factory and customers in the Midlands. The product is transported in special road tankers used for corrosive liquids. Methalynic acid is produced from oil and is brought in sea tankers to the nearby wharves.

The present Phoenix Chemicals staff is 85, of which 10 are administrative workers. The 75 factory workers are almost all men, half of them skilled.

The greater demand for methalynic acid, through moving into new markets, including export, now means expansion for Phoenix chemicals and they wish to extend their factory on to waste land alongside their present factory, reclaiming a small amount of marsh land which at present is a breeding ground for a species of red-throated duck.

© *Michael Jebson*, Tuck In. *Briefing sheet may be photocopied. CHP 1996*

THE PLANNING GAME – A Simulation Exercise
Eastport area of Bridgetown
(Section enclosed by dotted lines is reproduced opposite in larger scale)

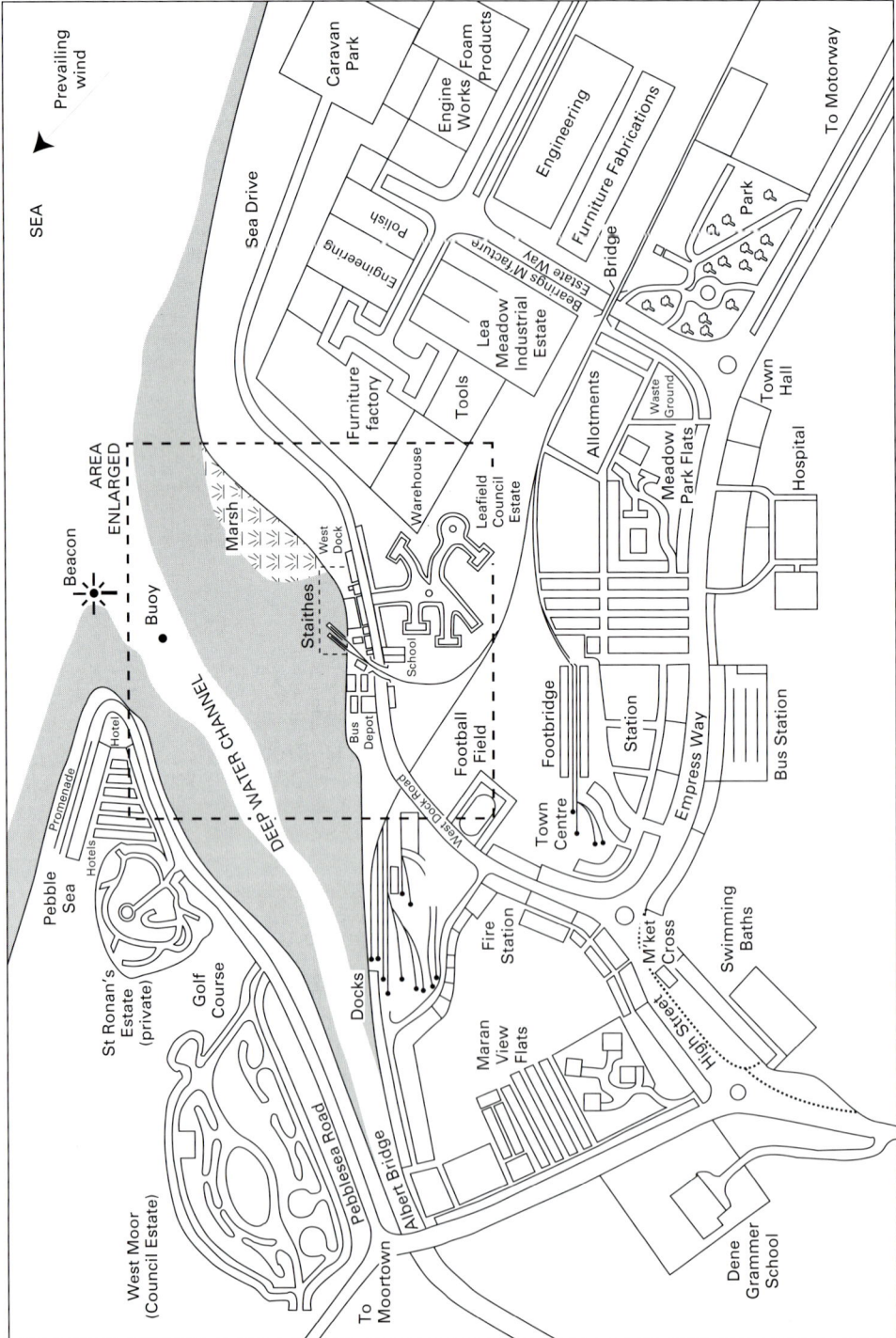

SEA

Prevailing wind

Caravan Park

Engine Works

Foam Products

Engineering

Furniture Fabrications

To Motorway

Sea Drive

Engineering

Polish

Bearings Mfacture

Estate Way

Bridge

Park

Lea Meadow Industrial Estate

Town Hall

Furniture factory

Tools

Warehouse

Allotments

Waste Ground

Meadow Park Flats

Hospital

AREA ENLARGED

Marsh

West Dock

Leafield Council Estate

Beacon

Buoy

Staithes

School

DEEP WATER CHANNEL

Bus Depot

Football Field

Footbridge

Station

Bus Station

Empress Way

Hotel

Promenade

Hotels

Pebble Sea

Town Centre

Fire Station

M'ket Cross

Swimming Baths

High Street

St Ronan's Estate (private)

Golf Course

Docks

Maran View Flats

West Dock Road

Albert Bridge

Pebblesea Road

West Moor (Council Estate)

To Moortown

Dene Grammer School

THE PLANNING GAME – A Simulation Exercise
Enlarged section of Eastport area of Bridgetown

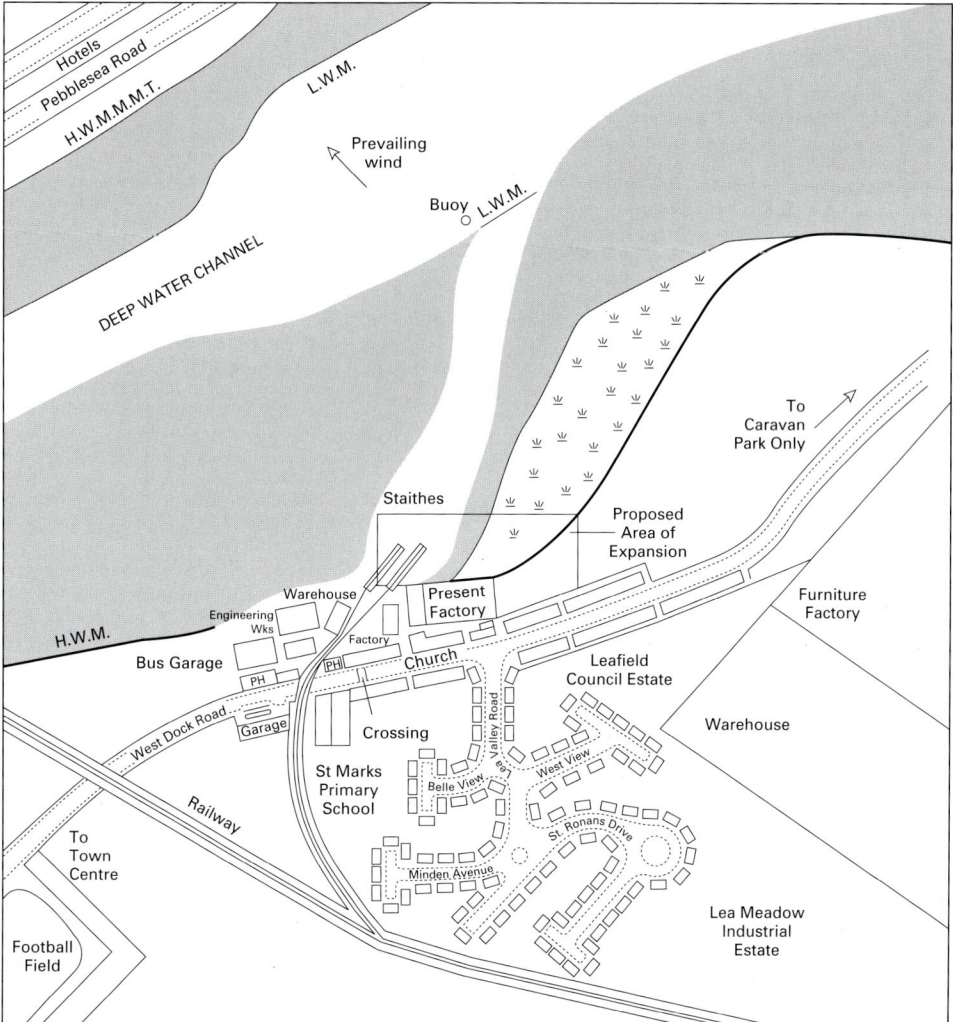

L.W.M. = *Low Water Mark*
H.W.M. = *High Water Mark*
© *Michael Jebson*, Tuck In. *Map may be photocopied. CHP 1996*

<u>**N O T I C E   O F   P U B L I C   M E E T I N G**</u>

We, the undersigned, on behalf of Phoenix Chemicals Limited, have applied for planning permission to extend our present factory at Eastport, Bridgetown. Detailed maps are attached to this application and the Bridgetown Planning Department will answer queries from authorized groups.

A Public Enquiry to consider the plans will be held as announced on public notices.

Signed:

Ian C Ingham B.Sc., Charles E Medd
Directors

Colin A S Hands A.C.I.S.
Company Secretary

Briefing sheet B

Rules of the Planning Game

Only representatives of the following groups may approach the Planning Department with enquiries:

Private house residents (St Ronan's Estate)
'Preserve Our Nature Group' (PONG)
Head, governors and Parents Association of St. Mark's Primary School
Directors of proposed small boat marina to be built near Beacon Point on the north shore
Local Publicans Association
Local Shopkeepers Association
Terrace house owner occupiers
Bridgetown District Omnibus Company
Phoenix Chemicals Limited
Ebenezer Chapel (non-denominational mission) – Church Council representatives
Local Chamber of Trade
Interested individuals: (able to operate independently of groups and having direct access to the planning department)
Local councillor
Member of Parliament for Bridgetown (National Chairman of PONG)

Each group may appoint one contact to act as liaison with the planning department and between the groups. He or she will be issued with an identifying badge.

© *Michael Jebson*, Tuck In. *This sheet may be photocopied. CHP 1996*

Groups may, by majority agreement of the members concerned, hold joint meetings. All communications with the planning department must be in writing.

Groups are to elect one spokesperson to represent them in the public meeting before the meeting is opened to public questions.

Advisors to the Public Enquiry: (who make up the planning department)
Fire chief
Town planner
Town chief executive
Harbour master
Chief constable
Architect to Phoenix Chemicals.

Briefing sheet C Enquiry and Reply Sheet

YOU ARE A MEMBER OF GROUP _____

PLANNING GAME MEMO

To the Planning Department:

From:

REPLY

From the Planning Department:

© *Michael Jebson,* Tuck In. *Form may be photocopied. CHP 1996*

Parable and Truth

A Hebrew story

A rabbi, famed for his learning and his wit, once was asked by his students why he so often illustrated a truth by telling a story.

'That I can best explain through a story' he said, 'a parable about Parable itself. There was a time when Truth went among men unadorned, as naked as his name. And whoever saw Truth turned away, in fear or in shame, and gave him no welcome. So Truth wandered through the lands of the earth, rebuffed and unwanted.

'One day, most disconsolate, he met Parable, strolling along happily in fine and many-coloured garb. "Truth, why do you seem so sad?" asked Parable cheerfully.

'"Because I am so old and ugly that all men avoid me," replied Truth.

'"Nonsense," laughed Parable. 'That is not why men avoid you. Here – borrow some of my clothes, and see what happens."

'So Truth donned some of Parable's lovely garments – and lo, everywhere he went, he was welcomed.' The rabbi smiled.

'For the truth is that men cannot face Truth naked; they much prefer him disguised.'

HOLOCAUST *

A simulation game that we hope and pray never becomes a reality.

* This is an updated version of the same simulation game prepared by the author and originally published by the Methodist Church Overseas Division.

Time required – at least three hours, with a break.

This game could be played by a small group of twelve to fifteen people, plus the 'government' control group, but it is more realistic if thirty+ people are involved. It has been played successfully by a group numbering over seventy people.

This game has been prepared for use only on residential weekends, or day events, where there can be adequate preparation and debriefing time. It is not recommended for use with young people aged under fifteen years.

The purpose of the game...
...is to put people into a position where
- their every move is subject to the attitudes of others
- where they have to question many of their own values
- where, in imagination, they will have to face a very much simpler life-style than they are probably used to
- where discussion on the meaning and purpose of life is given a new interest and edge because of the dramatic simulated situation.

The setting of the game
Groups meet in group rooms or spaces, preferably out of sight and earshot of each other. The meeting places are designated as radiation-proof shelters for use after a nuclear attack. Each shelter has a label on it stating that no more than 'x' people (depending upon the total size of the group) may enter each shelter.

Method of playing
After a brief introduction about the devastating effect on civilization of a nuclear war, the leader points out that there would still be some survivors. How would they cope in the close confines of a radiation-proof shelter in the first dangerous weeks? Then how would they start to pick up the pieces of normal life again? What kind of a community would they plan and build?

Hand out the SURVIVOR'S SHEET Form A and talk through it to make sure it is understood. The game then starts at the sounding of a pre-arranged 'Three Minute Warning' signal. A plan of where the radiation-proof shelters are located is shown in advance.

The young people may choose to go to any shelter they wish but must not exceed the number for which the shelter has been built – as shown on the label by it.

For each shelter of twelve to fifteen people, four people will have been given roles to play (see sheet B) in advance. Everyone else 'plays' themselves. The role players should be allowed into the shelters just before the warning signal to start. In advance of the game it is suggested that people are asked to be dressed in outdoor clothes.

It will probably be best if the police sergeant is played by an adult leader (one for each shelter) who will be well briefed in advance.

Without taking on too dominant a leadership position, the policeman will encourage the group to organize themselves for a lengthy stay and help them to consider such questions as:

- How will people arrange the shelter for sleeping?
- How will health standards be maintained?
- Who will prepare meals?
- Who will maintain the electricity supply?
- Which members of the group need most consideration?
- Will the group try to contact other survivors?
- How will the group occupy their time?

Each shelter will have a small box labelled 'radiation-proof hatch' into which messages to the government can be placed for collection by a special patrolman who may not speak to the group and preferably stay out of sight.

Control of the game
A team of three or four people (depending upon the number of shelters) will act as the government, staying concealed from the groups throughout the course of the game.

They can communicate with shelters in writing or by 'radio' using public announcements recorded on cassette tape which are taken to shelters by the patrol man and played to the survivors.

Progress of the game
Part 1 of the game should run for about an hour and start by the survivors completing the Government Form (C). Soon after the shelter has been occupied the following radio announcement is made:

> 'You are survivors in an area of high devastation. No buildings remain intact. We believe that within a radius of five miles from this shelter there are one hundred other people known to be alive. The Government will do its best to pass on written messages to other shelters. The Government advise that it will probably be necessary to remain in the shelter for eight weeks and you should prepare yourselves for this length of stay.' (This is longer than the estimated food and electricity supply.)

After an hour a coffee break can be taken but the shelters should have this separately to avoid survivors meeting those from other shelters or the control team.

Part 2 starts with an announcement that it is one week later. Then the following official message is given to each shelter:
> 'The Government is advised by its radiation experts that it should be possible to leave your shelter in seven weeks time. New temporary accommodation will then be available and limited extra food supplies.
> 'The Government wishes to know which services survivors consider it is essential to start to build a new community in this area. What talents and skills can the survivors offer to help when work is able to begin?'

Other messages and announcements can be given to the shelters as seem appropriate to the running of the game and depending upon the degree of involvement of the young people.

If the game seems not to be working for any reason the control group should stop it.

Under normal circumstances, at least half-an-hour should be given at the end of part 2 to discussion on what has happened in the group, the decisions they have taken, their feelings about each other, etc.

This debriefing can be done by one of the 'neutral' control group joining the survivors to help them examine their attitudes in the game.

Finally, everyone involved in the game comes together to enable learning points to be listed based on the ideas shown in the 'Purpose of the game' at the beginning of these notes. If necessary, time should be made for more discussion on important points.

Briefing sheets and additional papers for the enabler

Sheet A (Three sides)

Survivor's Notes, plan of radiation shelter, and list of Provisions/Equipment, for which one copy is needed for each participant.

Sheet B

Instructions to role players.

Sheet C

Government Form. One copy to be placed in each shelter at the beginning of the game.

Sheet D

Possible Handout to answer questions about effects of the holocaust.

Sheet E

Shelter debriefing questions.

A: Survivor's Notes (one copy for each participant)

Congratulations! You are a survivor!

This game asks us to pretend there has been a nuclear attack. You have escaped the devastation caused by the bomb by getting into a government-provided radiation-proof shelter, a plan of which is attached, together with a list of supplies and equipment.

Depending upon how you and your fellow survivors play the game – you could all be winners, or all be losers!

The purpose of the game is to help us think about why we do certain things and behave in particular ways. Holocaust may make us change our mind about some of the ideas we hold.

The time is the present

When you arrive in the shelter some people will already be there. Find out who they are. Throughout the game you are yourself. Do not take on a 'role'. React as you think you would normally react to the information you receive and the experiences you undergo.

In the shelter you will find a form which the government require you to fill in within one hour and return to them through the radiation-proof hatch provided. This form is to enable the government to know how many people have survived.

You may ask the government for information at any time by putting written messages in the hatch. These messages will be collected regularly by a specially protected patrol-man. The government may also require you to supply other information from time to time and will probably be in touch with you by radio.

Plan view of radiation shelter
(Dimensions are the same as the room or space you meet in)

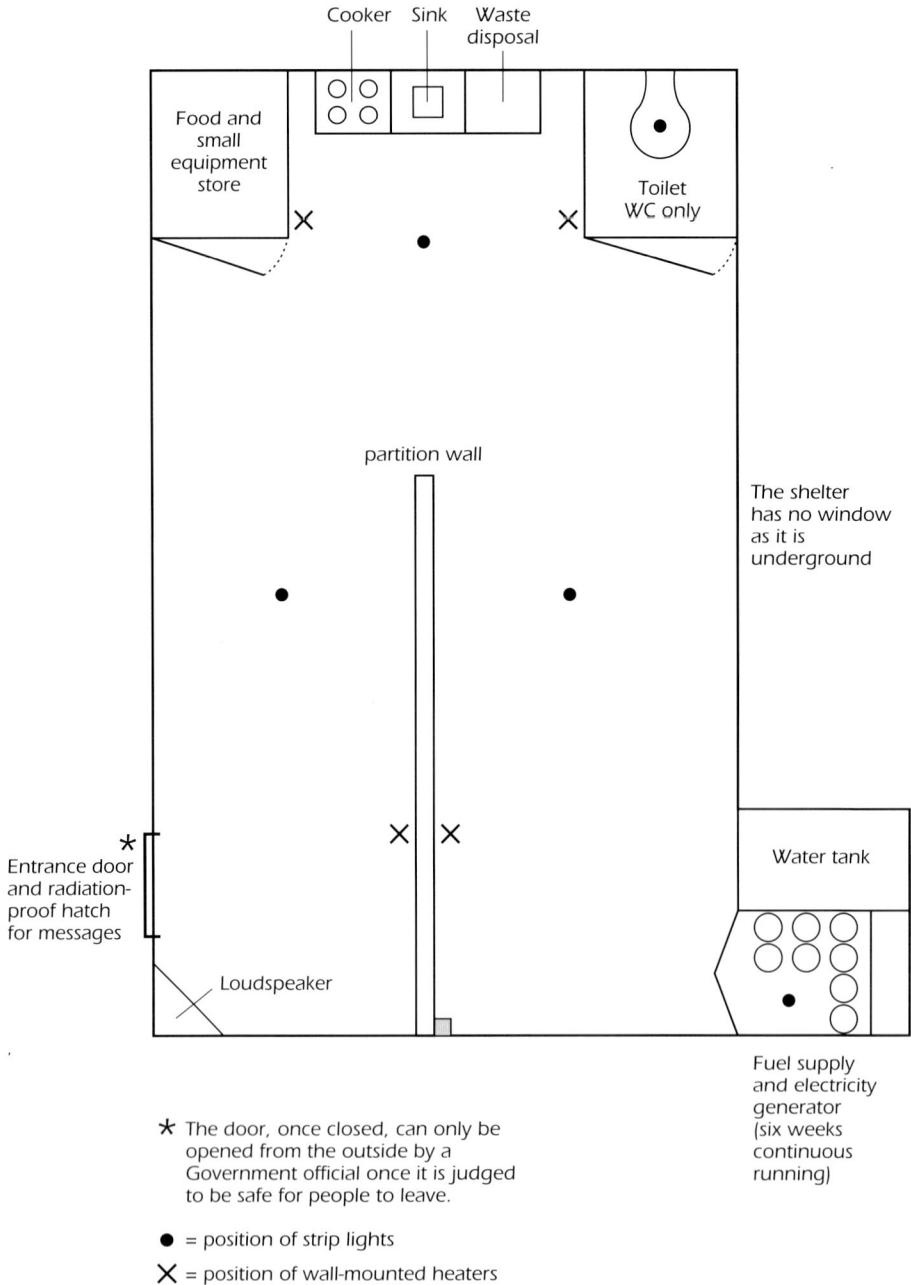

Cooker   Sink   Waste disposal

Food and small equipment store

Toilet WC only

partition wall

The shelter has no window as it is underground

* Entrance door and radiation-proof hatch for messages

Water tank

Loudspeaker

Fuel supply and electricity generator (six weeks continuous running)

* The door, once closed, can only be opened from the outside by a Government official once it is judged to be safe for people to leave.

● = position of strip lights

✗ = position of wall-mounted heaters

© Michael Jebson, Tuck In. *This diagram may be photocopied.* CHP 1996

List of provisions provided

Forty 'Day Packs' made up as two meals each day for each survivor. These include instant soups, fruit juice, desserts, dried meat, fish and vegetables. Also tins of meat and fruit.

400 tea bags, 20kgs of sugar, powdered milk sufficient to make 400 pints of milk.

7lb tin of coffee.

Water for both drinking and washing allows for one bucket each day for eight weeks.

Equipment provided:
1 folding wooden chair per person
2 folding tables each seating up to eight people
2 blankets per person
1 air bed per person
2 hand towels per person
1 plate, bowl, knife, fork, spoon, and mug per person
40 toilet rolls
40 boxes of 'man-size' tissues
1 plastic bowl, 1 plastic bucket
3 kitchen knives, 3 kitchen spoons, 3 glass bowls
6 saucepans, 1 tin opener
Quantity of paper and pencils
Simple first aid kit
500 12" x 12" plastic bags

B: Instructions to role players (for distribution to individual role-players)

YOU ARE MADELINE SUTCLIFFE aged 23. Your husband, David, was at work (as a bank cashier in the nearest large town) when the nuclear attack came, so he is not with you. You are carrying your ten month old baby, Richard, who is having teething trouble.

YOU ARE GEORGE DAVISON aged 67, a retired railway engineer. Your wife died nine months ago after a long struggle with cancer. Your married daughter lives in a small village about ten miles away. You have recently gone very deaf and your hearing aid seems to be very little help.

YOU ARE TIM WRIGHT, an unemployed teacher, one year out of college. You have been living with Amanda Fotherhurst, who is Afro-Caribbean in origin, for two years in her two-roomed flat.

YOU ARE AMANDA FOTHERHURST, an unemployed teacher one year out of college. You rent a two-roomed flat and for two years Tim Wright has been living with you. You are of Afro-Caribbean origin.

YOU ARE POLICE SERGEANT, JOHN HURST, aged 35. You are married with two children. Your wife was working part time at a local supermarket when the nuclear attack came.

YOU ARE PATRICK O'HARA, aged 59, local Roman Catholic priest.

YOU ARE JIM SMART aged 36. You are confined to a wheelchair following an attack of polio in your childhood. You are paralysed from the waist down. You work as a piano tuner.

YOU ARE MIRIAM BEECH aged 49. You are a housewife and the mother of two grown-up children. Your husband is at work as manager of a large supermarket. You suffer from claustrophobia – a dread of enclosed places.

C: Government form (One copy to be placed in each shelter at the beginning of the game)

H M GOVERNMENT

Form C

IMPORTANT

This form must be filled in by occupants of this radiation-proof shelter within one hour of entry and returned to the government through the hatch provided in the shelter. Failure to do so could lead to a lack of full services being provided to the occupants at a later date.

List of occupants

SURNAME	FIRST NAMES	AGE	OCCUPATION (if any)

On the other side of this form list personal belongings carried and clothing worn by occupants at the time of arrival in the shelter. List <u>all</u> items.

Also list the names and ages of next of kin, friends and neighbours who you antici-pate may have reached shelter before the nuclear attack.

D: Government Information Paper

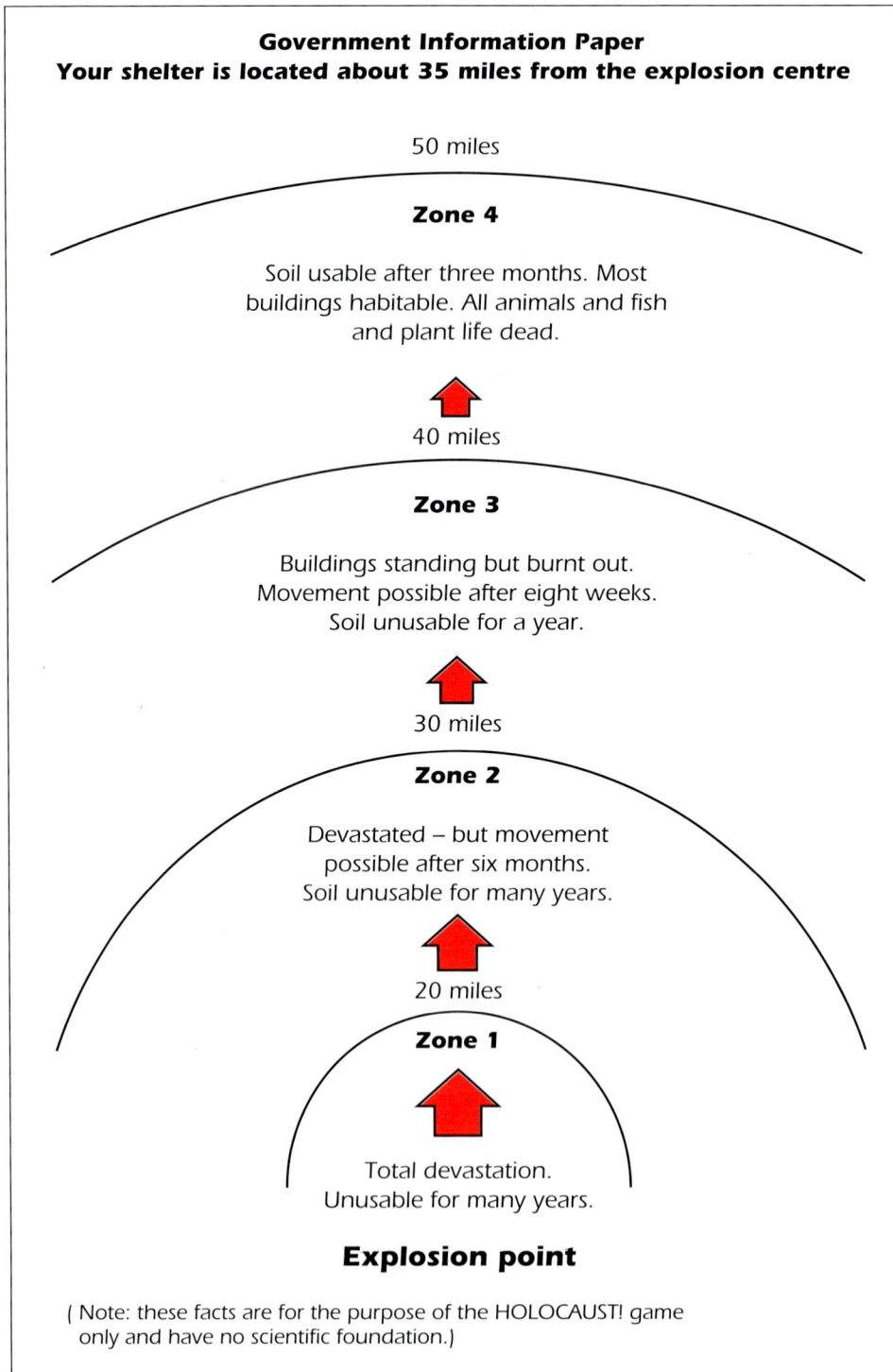

Government Information Paper
Your shelter is located about 35 miles from the explosion centre

50 miles

Zone 4

Soil usable after three months. Most
buildings habitable. All animals and fish
and plant life dead.

40 miles

Zone 3

Buildings standing but burnt out.
Movement possible after eight weeks.
Soil unusable for a year.

30 miles

Zone 2

Devastated – but movement
possible after six months.
Soil unusable for many years.

20 miles

Zone 1

Total devastation.
Unusable for many years.

Explosion point

(Note: these facts are for the purpose of the HOLOCAUST! game
only and have no scientific foundation.)

© *Michael Jebson,* Tuck In. *This diagram may be photocopied. CHP 1996*

E: Shelter de-briefing questions

(This briefing to take place in the 'shelter' before the full group re-assemble to share their visions of a new world.)

IDEAS ONLY!!
Expand as you think fit!

How did you get along as a group? Be honest?

Did someone clearly take charge? If so, was their leadership challenged?

Would you really have coped living together for eight weeks? What problems would there have been?

When food is rationed and normal comforts and freedom of movement are taken away what become the important things in life?

Can the group make a short list of things they have learnt from the experience of being together in this way?

Check out that the group has something to share with the other shelter groups about what they consider to be the life-style, essential services and skills needed to build a new community from the ruins of the old.

* There is a further simulation game (*see Chapter 16 'Main Course' Choice theme, Session (e) 'May Day! May Day!'*)

Chapter 19

SEASONING

A feast of dates

Something to celebrate or remember right through the year.

Give the youth group a present of a special diary. Ask someone to look after and keep up to date a book listing birthdays, anniversaries and other special dates. Make sure the diary is brought to every meeting of the group.

Record in the book:
- The birthdays of all group members
- Special anniversaries of people connected with the group
- Anniversaries of Baptism and entry into the church at Confirmation
- Be aware and sensitive about sad anniversaries. For example, a day when the death of a close relative or friend is remembered. Do not gloss over sadness or tragedy but face up to it as a group. Talk and pray about the meaning and purpose of life and what Christians believe about life after death. Discuss how, as individuals and as a group, we can support and help people we know who have been bereaved, remembering that grief can continue long after the funeral.
- High points and low points in people's lives can also be part of the life of the group. Remember not only those who have achieved success in some area of their life, but also those who have failed (or feel they have failed).
- Celebrate sporting and other achievements but also find things to praise and celebrate for those people who always get poor marks or who seem to miss out on the 'glittering prize'.

TUCK IN!

TIME'S PACES – *on a clock in Chester Cathedral*

When as a child I laughed and wept,
> Time crept.

When as a youth I waxed more bold,
> Time strolled.

When I became a full-grown man,
> Time ran.

When older still I daily grew,
> Time flew.

Soon I shall find, in passing on,
> Time gone.

O Christ! Wilt Thou have saved me then?
> Amen.

How to use 'Seasoning'
Hundreds of ideas going right through thr year

In this section you will find the germ of an idea against many dates, set out month by month, with a special section for Lent, Easter and Pentecost.

Sometimes just a brief reference is given in the calendar about a notable event or the birthday of a special person. Members of the groups will need to do some research to bring out the full value of some of these red letter days.

On other dates more information is given, together with ideas for activities that will provide you with material for a programme that could fill a whole group session.

Some dates are left blank. As they happen, or when you come across them, add details of special anniversaries and events on these days to keep the calendar up to date.

Look for more details in encyclopedias and other reference books. School, college and public libraries will be able to help and some of the organizations listed in Chapter 22 'Store Cupboard'.

Using a calendar like this provides you with a varied range of ideas and topics right through the year – and for many years to come.

In addition to this calendar, you could use a church lectionary, an annual cycle of Bible readings used by many churches week by week. Some Christian education and worship guides, such as the ecumenical *Partners in Learning* (published annually in June by the National Christian Education Council, 1020 Bristol Road, Selly Oak, Birmingham B29 6LB and the Methodist Church Division of Education and Youth, 2 Chester House, Pages Lane, Muswell Hill, London N10 1PR) closely follow the lectionary readings. This ensures that all the great Christian themes are regularly explored and that full use is made of the festivals that mark the high points in the Church's year.

JANUARY
Dedicated by the Romans to Janus, the god with two faces: one looked forward and one backward over the year that had gone. People are sometimes described as being Janus-faced meaning they are hypocritical, facing both ways at once.

1   New Year's Day – a public holiday! The day for making new year resolutions. We resolve to do something that, perhaps, we ought to have done before. Or we resolve to do something better. On January 1 a lot of people promise themselves they will keep a diary but often break that promise after a few days. Is this the experience of the group?
    • Make some new year resolutions for your youth group. List them so that everyone can be reminded of them. Check back on the list every so often to see if the group is keeping its resolutions. If not, why not? Are they too difficult? Should they be reviewed? Are they making any difference?
    • The Naming of Jesus (see Luke 2. 21). The church celebrates this event on this day. Do some research about the name of Jesus. What does it mean? What other names did people call him? Look up some of the names Jesus called himself. See, for example, John 6. 35 and John 8. 12.

    Jimmy Savile presented the first edition of BBC's 'Top of the Pops', 1964.
    • Has this programme now had its day?

    Britain became a member of the European Community, 1973.
    • What advantages can you see in our membership?

2   See 'How to use Seasoning' on previous page about how to use blank dates.

3   Margaret Thatcher, became the 20th century's longest serving British Prime Minister in 1988, as well as being the first woman to hold the appointment. She took up office on May 4 1979 and resigned on November 22, 1990.

    THE FIRST SUNDAY IN JANUARY is traditionally used by the Methodist Church, and an increasing number of other denominations, for a service to 'renew their covenant with God'. The Covenant Service was originated by John Wesley in the middle of the 18th century.

4   Louis Braille born 1809. This blind Frenchman is famous for inventing the system of writing and reading, based on touch, and still used throughout the world.
    • Do you know someone who is visually handicapped and uses Braille? If so, ask if they would be willing to meet the group and explain how the system is used.
    • Contact a local organization working with the blind and see if they need any help.
    • Read and discuss some of the experiences Jesus had with blind people. For example: Luke 18. 35–43.

5   Twelfth Night or Epiphany Eve (see January 6 about the meaning of Epiphany). A day linked to many ancient customs, often changing from area to area of the

country. Traditionally it is the day to take down the Christmas decorations, marking the end of the Christmas festivities. In the old days it was a time of great merry-making. Sometimes a cake was made in which one bean was hidden. The finder of the bean when the cake was cut was crowned with a paper crown which had been used to decorate the cake. The Bean Queen or King was to be obeyed for the rest of the day!

- 'If I ruled the world ...' says the old song. Become Bean Queens and Kings with ultimate power! How would you sort out your youth group? ... the country? ... the world?

6   The Feast of the Epiphany
Epiphany, a Greek word meaning 'manifestation' or 'showing clearly'. This is the Christian festival, twelve days after Christmas, when we remember how the baby Jesus was 'shown forth' to the Magi (or Three Kings or Wise Men).

- Only Matthew records this incident (see Matthew 2. 1–12). Read it together and think about it without all the embroidery that this story has attracted. What gifts do you think modern wise men and women would bring to Jesus?
- Sing the carols 'In the bleak mid winter' and 'Wise men seeking Jesus'.
- List the gifts/talents people have in the group. Think of the powerful effect these would have if they were offered to Jesus.

7   The Orthodox Christian Churches, now well represented in many of our towns and cities, celebrate Christmas on this day. This is because, many centuries ago, there was a rift between the two great Churches of the time, the Eastern and the Western, over the introduction of a new calendar. The Eastern Churches (orthodox) chose to remain with the old Julian calendar (dating from Julius Caesar in 46BC), whilst the Western Church moved to, and remains on, the Gregorian year, introduced in 1582 by Pope Gregory XIII.

- See if you can make contact with an Orthodox Church and learn something about their beliefs, worship and Christmas customs. You will almost certainly find an Orthodox Church where there are people of Greek or Russian origin or people from other eastern European countries.

8   Lord Robert Baden Powell died, 1941. British army commander, hero of the Boer war and founder of the Scout Movement (see also October 27).

Stephen Hawking born, 1942. World renowned as a physicist, Dr Hawking, who is confined to a wheel chair with Motor Neurone disease, was appointed Professor of Physics at Cambridge in 1977 at the age of 36. He can only communicate through a computer but wrote A Brief History of Time, a best seller for several years, selling millions of copies.

- What can Dr Hawking teach us about our approach to disabled people? (see also September 6).

9   BBC broadcast first Desert Island Discs programme, 1942.

- You could invite a local celebrity to make their own choice of eight pieces of music and share them with you, not forgetting the traditional choice of one book (excluding the Bible and the complete works of Shakespeare, which are already on the island!) and a luxury item to have with them on the mythical island.

10   First meeting of the General Assembly of the United Nations, 1946, in Westminster Central Hall, London (see also June 26 and October 23).

THE SECOND SUNDAY AFTER EPIPHANY is observed by some churches as Vocations Sunday and is linked with the call of the Disciples.
• Read, for example, John 1. 35–51.

11

12

13   George Fox, founder of the Quakers (properly called the Religious Society of Friends), died, 1691. There is a quotation from him at the end of Chapter 9, page 24.

14   The 1952 Nobel Peace Prize winner, Dr Albert Schweitzer, was born, 1875. He gave up a brilliant career (medical doctor, theologian, musician, philosopher) at the age of 31 to establish and live in a leper hospital in Africa. He died at the age of 90 and was buried at the hospital in Lambarene in French Equatorial Africa, now Gabon, on September 4, 1965. He once wrote, 'Here, Lord, is my life. I place it on the altar today. Use it as you will'.
(See also the last Sunday in January – World Leprosy Day.)

15   American civil rights activist, Rev Martin Luther King, Jnr born, 1929 (see also April 4).
• Research his remarkable life story. In the USA this date is now observed as Martin Luther King Day.

16   The Gulf War began, 1990, 'Operation Desert Storm'.

17   BBC TV breakfast programmes began, 1983, followed on February 1 by ITV.
• What kind of effect do morning TV and radio programmes have on the family life of the youth group members? Stimulate conversation or stifle it? Do they give little more than background noise and 'wallpaper' pictures or are they really watched and listened to?

18   Environmentalist David Bellamy born, 1933.
• Who can do the best impression of him?
• Then be serious and ask which environmental issues most concern the group. What can be done about them?

18–25
THE OCTAVE OF PRAYER FOR CHRISTIAN UNITY. An annual festival of eight days, observed by many churches. It concludes on the day the Conversion of St Paul is celebrated. Look out for local events and services your group could attend.

19

20 Miles Coverdale, a monk and bishop, died 1569. His was the first translation of the Bible to be printed in English.
- Give thanks to God for all those people down the ages who have used their skill and learning, and sometimes paid with their lives, so that we have free access to the Word of God in so many readable versions (see also March 16, October 6 and Bible Sunday, the first in December).

Terry Waite taken hostage, 1987 (see also November 18).

Bill Clinton took up office as the President of the United States of America, 1993 (see also February 4).

21 Supersonic Anglo-French passenger plane Concorde entered service, 1976.

22 Queen Victoria died, 1901.
- The end of the Victorian age. We still talk about Victorian values, Victorian ideas, Victorian hypocrisy. How do you think people will look back and talk about us, the Elizabethans?

23

24 Sir Winston Churchill died, 1965.

LAST SUNDAY OF THE MONTH – World Leprosy Day (see January 14).

25 The Christian church celebrates the Conversion of St Paul.
- Read the story of the man who started by persecuting Christians (Acts 7. 54 to Acts 8. 3) and ended up preaching that Jesus was the Son of God (Acts 9. 1–22) and becoming the inspiration of Christians in his own time and all down the centuries.

26

27 John Logie Baird, the British pioneer of televison, demonstrated his invention for the first time in public, 1926.
- Would the world be a better place if the 'goggle box' had never been invented? (See also August 21.)

28

29

30 Mahatma Gandhi, the man who, through a policy of non-violence, was largely responsible for freeing India from the rule of Britain, was assassinated in 1948. A devout Hindu, he was once asked by the missionary, Stanley Jones, how Christianity could become part of the way of life in India rather than being seen as an 'imported' religion from the West. 'What would you suggest we do to make that possible?' asked Stanley Jones. Gandhi replied: 'I would suggest first that all of you Christians must begin to live like Jesus Christ. Second, I would suggest that you must practise your religion without adulterating it or toning in down. Third, I would suggest that you must put your emphasis on love, for love is the centre and soul of Christianity.'

- Read about his life or borrow the video of the feature film 'Gandhi' (see also February 7 and October 2).

31

FEBRUARY
The name comes from the Latin word 'februo', to purify by sacrifice. The month was observed by the Romans as a time of purification, a ceremony taken up in the Christian calendar on February 2.

1

2   Candlemas – The Feast of Purification – when we remember the presentation of Jesus in the Temple at Jerusalem as a baby (see Luke 2. 22–38). The law required Mary, the mother of Jesus, to go to the Temple for her 'purification' forty days after the birth of Jesus (see Leviticus 12 for details of the law of the time). The old ceremony of Candlemas celebrates Jesus as the light of the world as candles are carried in procession before the eucharist (Holy Communion or Mass).
- You could mark the day with your own candle-lit procession or service remembering with thanks how with Jesus 'the light shines in the darkness, and the darkness has never put it out' (John 1. 5).

3

4   Dietrich Bonhoeffer, the German Lutheran pastor who stood up against the rise of the Nazis and Hitler, was born in 1906. Although he had the opportunity to settle in America in 1939 he returned to Germany 'to share the trials of this time with my people'. He was suspected of involvement in a plot to assassinate Hitler and was arrested in 1942. In a message to a friend just before he was executed by hanging he said, 'This is the end – for me the beginning of life' (see also April 9).

Governor Bill Clinton elected as President of the USA beating George Bush, 1992 (see January 20).

A SUNDAY IN FEBRUARY, the ninth Sunday before Easter, is designated as EDUCATION SUNDAY and observed ecumenically. Watch for local details of special services and other events on this day.

5   First Comic Relief 'Red Nose Day' to aid famine-struck Africa, 1988. Now usually held in early March – watch for details.

6   Accession of Queen Elizabeth II following the death of her father, King George VI, 1952 (see also January 22 and June 2).

Representation of the People Act, 1918, receives Royal Assent giving votes to men aged over 21, and, for the first time, to married women aged over 30.

The opportunity for women to vote came only after many years of determined, sometimes violent, struggle by women, often known as Suffragettes, who were fighting equally strongly felt male opposition. Women were able to use their hard-won voting rights for the first time in the General Election held in December 1918 (see also June 4, November 28 and December 14).

- Do we take seriously enough our democratic right to vote? Have young people who are approaching their 18th birthday made sure that their name is on the Electoral Register? On what basis do we use our vote? Family tradition? – 'Our family always votes Labour'. Or because we 'like' the candidate? Or do we really think through the policies being put forward then make up our mind in this way? Are local elections for councillors as important as those for Members of Parliament?

7   Helder Camara born, 1909. In 1964 he became the Roman Catholic Archbishop of Olinda and Recife, one of the poorest parts of Brazil. Siding with the poorest of the poor, his motives have often been misunderstood. Dom Helder Camara said that he had been influenced in the way he acted by Mahatma Gandhi (see January 30) and talked about the 'violence of the pacifist'. He said, 'When I give food to the poor, they call me a saint. When I ask why the poor have no food, they call me a communist.'

- How far should the Christian go in opposing Government policies that are considered unjust? How should action be taken? Can the Bible help us about the responsibility we should have and the approach we should take to matters of justice for all people? (see also February 17 and March 24 for some other modern 'saints' and martyrs.)

8   Announcement that cigarette advertising is to be banned on television, 1965. To date, a similar ban has not been extended to include newspaper and magazine advertising despite continued evidence of the harmful effects of smoking on the health of both smokers and those who 'passively' breathe in the fumes created.

- Should all cigarette advertising and sponsorship be banned?
- What else can be done to alert people to the dangers of smoking?

9

10

11   Nelson Mandela was released from prison in South Africa, 1990. He had been a prisoner for 26 years during which time he remained the symbol of the anti-apartheid movement in South Africa and around the world (see also May 10).

12   Abraham Lincoln, president of the United States, born 1809. From humble origins in Kentucky and with little schooling, he learned to spell by reading the Bible. Eventually he became a lawyer and was elected to Congress in 1846. He became President in 1861. At his inauguration he spoke out strongly against slavery in the USA and fought for its abolition. A man of deep religious faith, he was renowned for his honesty. He was elected for a second term as President in 1864. The year following, whilst watching a play at a theatre in Washington, he was assassinated.

- He once said: 'A child is a person who is going to carry on what you have started. He is going to sit where you are sitting, and when you are gone, attend

147

to those things which you think are important. You may adopt all the policies you please; but how they are carried out depends on him. He will assume control of your cities, states and nation. He is going to move in and take over your churches, schools, universities and corporations. All your books are going to be judged, praised or condemned by him. The fate of humanity is in his hands.'

13

14 Valentine's day. It seems that any connection between the two saints, both martyrs, who bore the name Valentine and the lovers festival that young people (and many older ones) so much enjoy, is very obscure. So just enjoy the day!
(See Chapter 16 – 'Main Course' Relationships theme, Session (d) 'Love is…')

15 Galileo, the mathematician and astronomer, born in Pisa, Italy, 1564. His discovery that the earth moves round the sun and not vice versa, was seen as heretical by the Church of the day. The Pope sent him before the Inquisition who put him under house arrest for the rest of his days. In October 1992 the present Pope, John Paul II, officially announced that his predecessors had made a mistake and apologized.
  • Do we as Christians have anything to fear now from the discoveries of scientists?
  • Is there any discovery that would shake your faith?

Decimal coinage introduced, 1971. After centuries of their use in everyday life and language, it was goodbye to pounds, shillings and pence, at least in their eccentric form with 240 pence to the pound, twelve pence to the shilling and twenty shillings to the pound. Yet £sd still forms part of, at least, nursery folklore with 'Sing a song of sixpence', and 'Half a pound of tuppenny rice' and many other references to the pre-decimal days.

  • Have a little quiz to see if people know how the old coinage was made up and understand some of the old slang such as 'tanner' for 6d, 'bob' for a 1/-, etc., and how much half-a-crown (2/6), ten shillings (10/-), a guinea, etc are worth now. (You might be able to find some of these old coins in the back of a drawer.)

16

17 The Archbishop of Uganda, the Most Reverend Janani Luwum, died a martyr's death, 1977. He was a victim of the tyrant who ruled Uganda at that time, Idi Amin. Originally a teacher, Janani was ordained into the Anglican church in 1956. He became the Archbishop of the Church of Uganda in 1974. A man of peace and compassion, he was sickened by the killings and 'disappearances' under the Amin regime. On February 11, 1977 with other bishops, he wrote to President Amin objecting to the reign of terror that was taking place. He knew that in writing the letter he was, in effect, signing his own death warrant. He was murdered on the orders of the President. His body was not released in time for his funeral and the congregation met round an empty tomb. Symbolic indeed of the faith of this brave man (see also February 7 and March 24 for some other modern 'saints' and martyrs).

18 Martin Luther died, 1546 (see October 31 for main entry).

19

20 Rev Benjamin Waugh born, 1839, founder of NSPCC. It is sad but true that the National Society for the Prevention of Cruelty to Children, which Waugh founded in 1884, is needed as much today as it was over a century ago.
- Find out about the local and national work of the NSPCC and see if there are ways your youth group can help.
- Consider the words of Jesus in Matthew 18. 1–7.

21 The Duke of Edinburgh Award Scheme for young people announced, 1956.
- Have you any Award holders in the youth group? Can they interest others in the Scheme?

22 Celebrated in the USA as the birthday of a great President, George Washington, the first President on the founding of the Republic. He was born in 1732 and served his first term as President from 1789.

23

THE THIRD SUNDAY IN FEBRUARY is observed in many churches as Unemployment Sunday. Prayers are offered for those affected by unemployment and for those who make decisions in government, industry and commerce that influence the working lives of men and women.

24 The arrest of George Loveless, lay preacher, in 1834. He was one of six farm labourers transported to Australia in 1834 for forming a trade union. They came from the village of Tolpuddle near Dorchester and became known as the Tolpuddle Martyrs. Because of a public outcry they were pardoned two years later.
- Pray for the brave men and women who stood up against unjust practices and exploitation in employment and, through the Trades Union Movement, fought for dignity and fairness for working people.

25 Christopher Wren, the architect of St Paul's Cathedral in London, died at the age of 91, 1723 (see October 20 for main entry).

26

27

28 A Dutch woman, Corrie Ten Boom, was arrested in 1944 from her home in Haarlam because, with her family, she had given shelter to Jews. There are a number of books about and by Corrie, the best known being *The Hiding Place* which tells of how her Christian faith saw her through the most terrible ordeals. After the Second World War she travelled widely telling her story of faith and courage. At one meeting in the German city of Munich she had been speaking about the necessity for forgiveness. As people were leaving the church where the meeting had been held, she found herself face to face with a man who she recognized as one of the German guards who had cruelly treated Corrie and her sister. The man held out his hand and said, 'How grateful I am for your message, Fraulein. To think that he has washed my sins away.' He then told Corrie how he had been a guard at the

Ravensbruck camp but that, since then, he had become a Christian. 'I know that God has forgiven me for the cruel things I did there, but I would like it from your lips as well. Fraulein, will you forgive me?' Remembering the words of Jesus (see below), but after a long pause when she wrestled with her emotions, she shook the man's hand and said, 'I forgive you my brother, with all my heart.'

- Read the parable of the unforgiving servant as told by Jesus and recorded in Matthew 18. 21–35 (see also Mark 11. 25).
- This prayer, written by an unknown prisoner, was found in Ravensbruck concentration camp where it had been left alongside the body of a child:

'O Lord, remember not only the men and women of good will, but also those of ill will. But do not remember all the suffering they have inflicted on us; remember the fruits we have bought, thanks to this suffering – our comradeship, our loyalty, our humility, our courage, our generosity, the greatness of heart which has grown out of all this, and when they come to judgement let all the fruits which we have borne be their forgiveness.'

29   Leap Year Day. Traditionally the day, very much from a bygone age, when a woman could propose to a man.
- Who takes the lead now in 'popping the question'?
- On this 'make weight' day that only happens once in every four years, is it a very special birthday for anyone in the group or church? Make a special party of it!

MARCH
Named by the Romans after their god of war, Mars. It is the month in which the first day of spring occurs, March 21, and generally we feel as if we are moving out of winter with lengthening evenings.

For special days associated with Lent, Easter and Pentecost, see the section between March and April

1   St David's Day. The patron saint of Wales, David was born about AD601. He built many monasteries, the most famous being on the site of what is now St David's Cathedral, Dyfed, right on the extreme west coast of his native land. He became Archbishop of Wales and, when he died, was buried at St David's, one of the great centres of Celtic Christianity.

2   Death of John Wesley, 1791 (see main entry on May 24).

In 1988 on this date Clive Jermain died of cancer of the spine, aged 22. He had been battling with the disease since the age of 17 and originally was given a year to live. But Clive had other plans and, whilst in bed, wrote a play for TV about the disease. His play, 'The Best Years of Your Life', was broadcast and gave Clive the idea of starting a multi-million pound charity appeal, 'Search 88', in aid of cancer care and research. Part of the money raising was through a photographic project devised by Clive and called 'One Day for Life' (see entry on August 14).

3

4

5   William Beveridge, one of the founders of the welfare state, was born 1879.
During 1942, in the dark days of the second world war Lord Beveridge, as he was
to become, chaired a government committee that produced the framework for a
system of social security for all citizens 'from the cradle to the grave'. Although
much amended and discussed, we still benefit from this unique humitarian legislation with which the name of Beveridge will always be associated.
• What do you think of the government's present approach to the health and
welfare of citizens? What changes would you like to see made? (see October 8).

6

THE FIRST FRIDAY IN MARCH is recognized as the Women's World Day of
Prayer. There will be special services in your area.

REFUGEE WEEK, to remember and take action on displaced persons, is observed
in the FIRST OR SECOND WEEK IN MARCH.

7   St Thomas Aquinas, 'the Father of Moral Philosophy', died at the age of about
48, 1274. Italian born of aristocratic parents, he became a Dominican monk and,
through his writings, influenced the thinking of theologians down many centuries.
You will find prayers written by him in many prayer books. Here is one:

Give me, O Lord, a stedfast heart which no unworthy thought can drag down-
wards; an unconquered heart which no tribulation can wear out; an upright
heart which no unworthy purpose can tempt aside. Bestow on me also, O Lord
my God, understanding to know thee, diligence to seek thee, wisdom to find
thee, and a faithfulness that may finally embrace thee; through Jesus Christ our
Lord. Amen.

8

9

THE SECOND MONDAY IN MARCH is observed as Commonwealth Day.
The map of the world used to contain many countries coloured pink to show
that they belonged to the huge British Empire. As countries Britain had once
colonized became independent and self-governing, we changed to having a
British Commonwealth of nearly fifty nations loyal to the Queen. The
Commonwealth includes remote islands such as the Solomons and huge land
masses like Australia.
• Is there still purpose and value in having a British Commonwealth? Should we
celebrate today or ask for forgiveness for the way in which our ancestors
aquired land and countries? (see also November 20).

10 Did you know that all women school teachers had to be single, until this date in
1944 when the Minister for Education said that in future it would be permissible
for them to marry? So that's why they still get called 'Miss'!

11

12 At Bristol Cathedral, the first woman priests were ordained into the Church of England, 1994.

13 16 children and their teacher were killed on this day in 1996 by a lone gunman at a primary school in Dunblane, Scotland.

14

15

16 We remember St Joseph of Arimathea in the Church's calendar today. It was Joseph who offered his own tomb for the burial of Jesus.
- Read the story of this rich follower's gift in Matthew 27. 57–61.

The New English Bible published, 1970. The first of the major translations of modern times, the NEB was an immediate best seller with one million copies going on the first day of publication.
- How many different modern translations of the Bible can your group get together? Do some comparisons, using the different versions, of a well known passage from the Bible. Does any of the wording change the meaning of the passage between different translations? Do you prefer one version of the Bible to all the others? (see also October 6 and Bible Sunday in December)

17 St Patrick's Day – a holiday in Ireland to celebrate the life of the island's patron saint. St Patrick was almost certainly not born in Ireland, but it is known that, at the age of 16, he was kidnapped by pirates and taken to Ireland and sold as a slave. After six years he was able to escape and eventually settled in France where he became a devout Christian. After many years, it is said, he had a dream in which he felt called to return to Ireland as a missionary, despite the bitter memories of his captivity there. He travelled the country, preaching and teaching for many years, eventually becoming a bishop. Many stories and myths surround the life of St Patrick and among the best known is his use of the three-leaved shamrock to illustrate the mystery of the Holy Trinity. He would describe how it had three separate leaves yet they were all part of the same leaf – one in three and three in one. Traditionally the shamrock is now worn on the St Patrick's Day holiday.

18

19 The feast day of St Joseph of Nazareth, the husband of Mary, the mother of Jesus. A carpenter, he taught Jesus the skills of the trade.
- Think your way into the emotions and problems faced by Joseph as you read Matthew 1. 18–24 and in the only recorded story from the childhood of Jesus, in Luke 2. 41–52.

David Livingstone, Scottish doctor, missionary to Africa, explorer and crusader against the slave trade born 1813.

20

21   The first day of Spring.

   Archbishop Thomas Cranmer, who gave the Church of England its first Prayer Book, was burnt at the stake 1556 (see main entry on July 2).

22

23   A Pope met an Archbishop of Canterbury officially for the first time in 400 years, 1966. Pope Paul said to Archbishop Michael Ramsey, 'You rebuild a bridge, which for centuries has lain fallen between the Church of Rome and the Church of Canterbury; a bridge of respect, of esteem and of charity.'
   • How are inter-church relations in your area? How might they be improved and what part can your youth group play in this? Are there some theological differences that are so great between churches that it would be found impossible to work together to spread the Gospel in your community?

24   Oscar Romero, Archbishop of San Salvador was murdered at the high altar of the Cathedral whilst he was saying mass for his dead mother, 1980. The murder was in retaliation for his opposition to violence, injustice and oppression within El Salvador. Shortly before his death he had said prophetically, 'Martyrdom is a grace from God which I do not believe I deserve. But if God accepts the sacrifice of my life, then may my blood be the seed of liberty, and a sign that hope will soon become a reality' (see also February 7 and February 17 for some other modern 'saints' and martyrs).

25   The Feast of the Annunciation or Lady Day. This is when the Church celebrates the announcement to Mary that she would be giving birth to Jesus. The date is exactly nine months before Christmas day.
   • Read how the angel Gabriel came to the young Mary, who was probably still in her teens, with the news – Luke 1. 26–38.
   • It is interesting to reflect that many young people complain that the Church does not take them seriously, yet God trusted the earthly upbringing of his son to a teenager. Is there something the Church can learn from this?

26   The driving test was first introduced and made a requirement, 1934.
   • How many young people in the group are drivers?
   • Is the driving test hard enough? Should drivers retake a test every so often throughout their driving career?
   • Setting aside drivers who have to give up for health reasons, should there be a compulsory retirement age?

27

28

29

30   Elizabeth Pilento, died 1945. A wealthy and well-educated Russian woman, after moving to Paris in 1923 she founded a community of nuns who belonged to the Russian Orthodox Church. Elizabeth became known as Mother Maria. Despite her

privileged upbringing, Mother Maria devoted herself to the poorest people in Paris. When the Germans occupied Paris in the Second World War, Mother Maria and the chaplain of the convent took great risks by befriending persecuted Jews. They were offered a place to hide in the convent and, where possible, helped to escape to safety. Unfortunately, the Gestapo discovered what was happening and Mother Maria was arrested and sent to the concentration camp at Ravensbruck. The chaplain died of starvation in another concentration camp, Buchenwald. But even in the dreadful conditions in which she now found herself, Mother Maria continued to serve those around her. Even the guards called her 'that wonderful Russian nun'. After more than two years in the camp, a new block of buildings was put up which the prisoners were told would be for hot baths. In fact they were gas chambers for the systematic execution of the prisoners. One day as some women were lined up outside the new block a young girl became hysterical, realizing her fate. Mother Maria, who was not part of the group but happened to be near by, went to the girl and comforted her. 'Don't be frightened,' she said to the girl, 'Look, I'll take your turn.' She went into the gas chamber on March 30, 1945. It was Good Friday.

31 LAST WEEKEND IN MARCH, British Summer Time begins at 2am on the Sunday morning when clocks are put forward one hour. (British Summer Time ends on the last weekend of October.)

SPECIAL DAYS ASSOCIATED WITH LENT, EASTER AND PENTECOST
These three special Festivals in the Christian calendar are 'movable feasts', meaning that they do not fall on a fixed date. How the date of Easter is set is complicated and is closely linked to phases of the moon, occurring at the same time of year as the Jewish Passover. Easter is set by discovering when the first full moon is due on or in the 28 days after the first day of spring (the Vernal Equinox) on March 21. Easter Sunday is celebrated on the first Sunday after that full moon. Got it? This means that Easter Day can be celebrated as early as March 22 or as late as April 25. All this was laid down by the Church's Council of Nicea in AD325 and, not surprisingly, there have been repeated suggestions that Easter should become a fixed date! So to find out the date on which the special days listed below are observed, you will need to look in a current diary.

SHROVE TUESDAY – The day before Lent, which begins on Ash Wednesday. It is the last day of feasting before the time of fasting that begins with Lent. Traditionally, pancakes are made as this used to be seen to be a way to use up rich foods such as eggs and butter. The word 'shrove' comes from an old word 'shrive' meaning to confess sins, in this case especially before the solemn festival that is about to begin.
• Have a pancake party but also spend some time thinking about the meaning of Lent and the unfolding story of Easter.

ASH WEDNESDAY – The first day of Lent marking forty weekdays, i.e., excluding Sundays, to Easter and so remembering the forty days of the fasting and temptation of Jesus in the wilderness before he began his three year ministry. In Roman Catholic and some Anglican churches a special service is held when, as an act of penance, the priest makes a cross-shaped mark on each person's forehead using ash made from the burning of last year's Palm crosses.

- See if you can attend as a group an Ash Wednesday service either as participants or, in consultation with the priest, as observers.
- Read about Jesus' time of preparation in Matthew 4. 1–11 or in Luke 4. 1–13.

MOTHERING SUNDAY – The fourth Sunday in Lent, or mid-Lent. Generally a happy festival not originally observed as we do now but seen as a time when Christians visited their 'mother church', or cathedral. Now the focus is usually on thanksgiving to God for our own mothers and most churches hold special services in which children give out flowers. There needs to be special sensitivity to those who, for whatever reason, do not remember their mothers with gratitude, or have lost them through separation or death. We also need to remember women and men who have remained single but long for children of their own and those married couples who have not remained childless from choice.

- It is traditional to eat a Simnel cake on Mothering Sunday and during the time leading up to Easter. (The word probably comes from an old English word derived from the Greek for 'fine flour'.)

PASSION OR JUDICA* SUNDAY – The fifth Sunday in Lent. The day on which we remember the forthcoming sufferings and death of Jesus. The word 'passion' is used here to mean the sufferings of Jesus on the cross and is not to be confused with the more usual meaning which is linked to emotion, anger and sexual feelings.

- Read how Jesus calmly talked of his coming Passion to his frightened disciples and followers as he headed for Jerusalem – Mark 10. 32–34.

PALM SUNDAY – The Sunday before Easter and the day on which we remember the triumphant entry by Jesus into Jerusalem. The story is told in all four Gospels starting with Matthew 21. 1–11. It is probable that they were palm branches the people pulled from roadside trees to throw down in front of Jesus as he rode in on a donkey. The nearest equivalent British tree, and traditionally used in Palm Sunday processions, is pussy willow. It is sometimes called English Palm. Many churches now distribute specially made palm crosses, often imported from Africa. This can make a useful symbol to be kept through the year reminding us of the heart of the Gospel, that Jesus died for us (see also Ash Wednesday, above, and the reference to palm crosses).

HOLY WEEK – The week that leads up to Easter Day and includes MAUNDY THURSDAY and GOOD FRIDAY. Most churches have special services throughout this week, often organized inter-church or ecumenically.

On MAUNDY THURSDAY we remember the special meal, the Last Supper, that Jesus shared with his disciples before he was betrayed and arrested. It is this meal, with its sharing of bread and wine, that forms the pattern for Holy Communion or Eucharist, the central act of worship for the majority of Christian churches. The word 'Maundy' comes from the Latin word for 'command' – *mandatum*. It was at the Last Supper that Jesus commanded his disciples to: 'Do this in remembrance of me.'

---

* Judica comes from the first Latin word used in the Introit to the Mass for this Sunday taken from Psalm 43.

- Read about the events of the first Maundy Thursday and their links with the Jewish Passover festival, in Luke 22. 7–20, but preferably reading the whole chapter.

GOOD FRIDAY – is when we commemorate the crucifixion of Jesus, a most solemn day in the Christian calendar. Special services sometimes take the form of a vigil from noon to 3pm when, according to Mark 15. 33–34, Jesus hung on the cross. The word 'Good' was originally used in the sense that we might use holy, but it could also be said to be a Good day as we believe that Jesus died on the cross for us and that our sins are forgiven.
- Attend a Good Friday service as a group.
- Read Mark 15.
- Many Christians use this as a day of fasting and penance. As a group you might like to confine the food you eat to a strictly limited number of hot cross buns, traditional on Good Friday. (Fasting should only be undertaken after discussion about the reasons for doing it and after ensuring it is safe medically for everyone to take part.)
(See March 30 for a Good Friday story)

EASTER DAY – The greatest and most joyful of all the Christian festivals, when we celebrate the resurrection of Jesus. 'He is risen!' The word Easter seems to have been adopted from a pre-Christian festival held at this time of year and dedicated to a goddess of the spring called Eostre.
- Enjoy this day to the full and all its happy customs. Try to attend a special service, sometimes held outdoors at dawn. Make, give and eat Easter eggs, symbolizing new life.
- Some villages and towns have their own special customs for Easter Day, such as egg (hard boiled!) rolling down hills – whose can travel the farthest, etc.

ASCENSION DAY – This is observed on the fortieth day after Easter, a Thursday. Special services are held to remember the time when, after many appearances following his resurrection, Jesus returned to his Father.
- Read the accounts given in Mark 16. 19–20 and Matthew 28. 16–20, noting especially how the disciples were commissioned to go out and preach the gospel. The same challenge comes to us today (see also Acts 1. 1–11).

PENTECOST OR WHITSUN – The Sunday fifty days after Easter. The great celebration of the coming of the Holy Spirit to the disciples of Jesus, empowering them for the work he had commissioned them to do. The old title of Whitsun comes from the day being known as White Sunday when those being baptized or confirmed into the Church traditionally wore white clothes. Some confusion has arisen since the Bank Holiday was moved away from Whitsunday and is now taken on the last Monday in May, whether or not this happens to coincide with the Christian festival. This means people sometimes talk about the Whitsun holiday which has tended to draw attention away from the actual festival when it has not fallen on the same weekend as the Bank Holiday.
- Join in local Pentecost celebrations such as Whit Walks and processions.
- Read the exciting account of the coming of the Holy Spirit in Acts 2. 1–13.
- As a reminder of the association of the Holy Spirit with the wind, make kites and fly them. Or make small land yachts and see how far they can travel.

- Celebrate the coming of the Holy Spirit being likened to fire by concluding with a Pentecost bonfire and barbecue.

TRINITY SUNDAY – The Sunday after Pentecost. On this day we celebrate the mystery of the one God – Father, Son and Holy Spirit – one in three and three in one. God is like three 'persons' each exercising different functions but acting in perfect harmony.
- Never an easy doctrine to talk about but, as Christians, we should try to get our mind round it. A simple example of something that can be 'three in one' is water. It can be liquid, vapour (steam), and solid (ice).
- See the entry on March 17 for St Patrick who is famous for another way of symbolizing the Trinity.
- Although it is the Church down the centuries that has taught the doctrine of the three-in-one God, the concept is clearly referred to in the commissioning of the disciples mentioned above in the paragraph on Ascension Day (see Matthew 28. 19–20). St Paul emphasizes the different gifts of the triune God when he gives a benediction or blessing at the end of his second letter to the Corinthians 13. 13.

APRIL
From the Latin *aperire* – 'to open'. The month when nature unfolds, buds open and earth comes back to life after winter.

1   All Fools' Day – There is no real explanation as to why this day become the one when people are sent on silly errands and all kinds of pranks are dreamed up. Remember that, by tradition, all tricks must be over by noon: 'Twelve o'clock is past and gone. You're the fool for making me one!'
- The day does give the opportunity for talking about 'harmless' fun. How far can we go? Is it a way of taking revenge? Can a practical joke be hurtful in more ways than one to some people?

2   Adolf Hitler, sometimes described as the most evil man who ever lived, was born in Austria, 1889. His lust for power and the desire to establish a 'master race' led to the Second World War beginning in 1939 and his dreadful policy of trying to 'eliminate' the Jews. His extreme right-wing views have, to the shame of the human race, not been eliminated with only the language changing so that the awful phrase 'ethnic cleansing' has now entered the vocabulary of hate and prejudice.

'SPRING HARVEST' WEEKS take place at this time of the year in different places. These popular weeks offer worship, seminars, fellowship and leisure activities.

3   1978 – The BBC began regular radio broadcasts from the House of Commons. Within days there was concern that Parliament would become a laughing stock as behaviour in the House was likened to a zoo! A government minister said that listeners were disgusted by the 'bellowing, abuse, baying hee-hawing and the rest …

We really must behave,' he said.
- From what you see and hear of the proceedings in the House of Commons and the House of Lords do you like the way the debates are conducted? Do you see democracy being done? How would you like to improve things?

4   1968 – Martin Luther King, Jnr. was assassinated in Memphis, Tennessee, USA (see also January 15).
- Of all the things said by Dr Martin Luther King, he is best remembered for his 'I have a dream' speech, of which a part is given below, but he also said some challenging things directly to Christians, for example:
'The judgement of God is upon the Church as never before. If the Church of today does not recapture the sacrificial spirit of the early Church, it will lose its authentic ring, forfeit the loyalty of millions, and be dismissed as an irrelevant social club with no meaning for the twentieth century. I am meeting young people every day whose disappointment with the Church has risen to outright disgust' (from *Letter from Jail*, Birmingham, Alabama, 1963).
'Any religion that professes to be concerned with the souls of men and is not concerned with the slums that damn them, and the economic conditions that cripple them is a dry as dust religion.'
'I have a dream that my four little children one day will live in a nation where they will not be judged by the colour of their skin but by the content of their character' (a brief extract from Martin Luther King's 'dream' speech).
- Has anything changed since these words were written?
- Create your own 'dream' speech and ask what is needed for it to become a reality.

5   Robert Raikes, founder of the Sunday School movement, died 1811. Raikes was moved by the sight of desperately poor children who, during the week, worked long hours and had no schooling. As he went to church one Sunday he spotted the children running wild in the streets of Gloucester on their one day off. He started Sunday Schools in 1780 where the Bible was not only taught but used as an aid to literacy. Raikes, the owner and editor of the *Gloucester Journal*, used his paper to gain support for his initiative and to publicize the value of Sunday Schools, which spread quickly throughout the land (see also November 4 for another campaigning newspaper editor).
- Setting aside the original purpose of Sunday Schools, what is their value today, by whatever name they are called in churches? Should the religious education of children and young people be separated from that of adults, or should worship and teaching be an all-age and joint activity?

6

7

8

9   Dietrich Bonhoeffer was executed on this day, 1945 (see February 4).

10   William Booth, founder of the Salvation Army was born, 1829. At the age of 13 he became a Methodist but left to set up his own movement that combined evangelism

with practical social service. It was first called the Salvation Army in 1878. The first band was formed in Consett, County Durham in 1879. Music has played a significant part in the image and appeal of the Salvation Army ever since. Now a highly respected branch of the Christian Church world-wide, the 'Sally Army', as it is affectionately known, is as busy as ever it was serving the needy in Christ's name, just as when the young William Booth went out to the poor in London's East End more than a century ago.

• Enquire about the work of the Salvation Army in your area. Where is their work and witness most needed now?

11

12

13 In Dublin in 1742 the first performance of Handel's oratorio, 'Messiah'. German born George Frederick Handel spent most of his working life in England. Whilst in poor health and working in a small room in London, he wrote 'Messiah' in only twenty-four days. It is, without doubt, the best known, most loved and most performed choral work, with hundreds of performances every year in this country alone. It is said that, as he wrote the 'Hallelujah Chorus', he said to his servant who had brought him some food, 'I did think I did see Heaven before me, and the great God himself'. Tears streamed down Handel's face as he spoke (see also April 20).

• Try to attend a performance of 'Messiah' as a group. Some members may be able to offer themselves to sing in a local choir who are performing the oratorio. Alternatively, listen to some parts of a recorded performance and look up the Bible text from which they are taken. Or watch the feature film 'The Great Mr. Handel' (1942) available on Connoisseur Video.

14

15 On her maiden voyage the 'unsinkable' passenger liner, the SS Titanic hit an iceberg in the North Atlantic and sank. It was the worst ever disaster at sea: 1,500 of the 2,340 passengers and crew drowned. The year was 1912.

16 Charlie Chaplin born in London 1889. Considered by many to be the greatest ever comedy actor, he was also a film director who found his way into the infant film industry via the music hall.

• Have a Charlie look-alike competition and laugh at some of his films.
• Watch the feature film 'Chaplin', the story of his life.

17

18 Sometimes called the 'Father of the Protestant Reformation', German-born Martin Luther had to appear before a church court, the Diet of Worms, and the Emperor charged with heresy on this day in 1521 (see main entry October 31).

19

20 George Frederick Handel died, 1759 (see April 13).

21 Her Majesty Queen Elizabeth II born 1926. The Queen also has an 'official birthday', celebrated on the second Saturday of June and marked by the ceremony of the Trooping of the Colour.

22

23 St George's Day – the patron saint of England. A little verse written in 1688 neatly makes the point about how little we know about St George:
>'To save a Maid, St George the Dragon slew
>A pretty tale, if all is told be true
>Most say, there are no Dragons, and 'tis said
>There was no George: pray God there was a Maid!'

- There are certainly more legends than facts about the life of George although it is probable he was a Roman soldier who stood up for his Christian faith and paid the penalty for his beliefs with his own life. But, just for now, believe that he did slay dragons and ask yourselves what modern-day 'dragons' we need to be ready to face with Christian courage.

24 In 1932, before the days of National Parks, there was a planned 'mass trespass' in the Derbyshire Peak District. Climbing Kinder Scout, hundreds of people were seeking the right to be able to walk on moors and mountains, many of which were (and still are) in private ownership. Five men were arrested.
- What rights should the public have to walk in and enjoy the countryside? Land owners are sometimes accused of obstructing footpaths to keep the public out. What right have we to object to this action?

25 The Feast Day of St Mark. This is John Mark, the author of the earliest of the Gospels, named after him. Mark was the son of Mary, a wealthy woman, in whose house in Jerusalem some early Christians used to meet (see Acts 12. 12). There is an intriguing reference to a person, thought to be the young John Mark, in his own Gospel (see Mark 14. 51–52). If it wasn't the author why else would the incident be recorded? When he was one of St Paul's missionary assistants, John Mark does not always seem to have pleased his master. It looks as if he was given the cold-shoulder, for a time at least, as can be read in Acts 15. 37–38. It helps us to remember that those we call Saints still had their human failings.

26 Traditionally the day on which the waters of the Flood began to go down and Noah's ark came to rest.
- Read the story as it is recorded in Genesis 6–9. Discuss the meaning of this ancient story and thank God for the promises he made and which are given in Genesis 9. 8–17.

27 The House of Commons on this day in 1939 agreed that men of 20 years of age (later reduced to 18 years) should be conscripted for military service as the threat of war with Germany increased. 'National Service' continued for young men right up until the 1950s. Single women aged between 20 and 30 were 'called up' from 1941.
- Some adults say it would do young people good to have a spell in the Army. It is said the discipline would do them good. Do you agree?

28

29

30   A fire broke out in 1986 in a nuclear power station at Chernobyl in Russia and led
      to high radiation levels in the surrounding area. Other parts of the world were also
      affected, including places in Britain where polluted sheep in Wales and Cumbria had
      to be destroyed. Chernobyl is probably the world's worst nuclear accident to date.

MAY
Named after Maia, the Roman goddess of increase and growth.

1   For centuries May Day has been a day of celebration. In times past, towns and
      villages enjoyed games and dancing round a May pole and sometimes elected a
      May Queen. More recently May Day has been linked with Socialist rallies and in
      the USA is known as Labor Day. Since 1978, the first Monday in May has been a
      Bank Holiday.

2   Leonardo da Vinci born, 1452. He was the illegitimate son of a nobleman from
      Florence and a country girl. One of the greatest all-round geniuses of all time, he
      was way ahead of his time with many inventions including the parachute and
      submarine. He was a sculptor, architect, musician, engineer, anatomist. As a
      painter he is best known for the 'Mona Lisa' and the 'The Last Supper'.
      • Get some books out of the library that show Leonardo's many inventions,
        drawings and paintings. Marvel at his skill and thank God for the creative gifts
        he gives us.

3   After lengthy conversations between the two churches, the Church of England
      Synod failed in 1972 to reach the majority required to support union with the
      Methodist Church.
      • Despite this decision, in many areas Churches work closely together, with
        many 'shared' churches, such as Anglican/Methodist, United Reformed/
        Methodist and Local Ecumenical Projects involving several denominations.
        What is happening in your community?

4

5   Karl Marx was born in Germany of Jewish parents on this day in 1818. His radi-
      cal and revolutionary views made him unpopular in his own and several other
      countries and he eventually moved to England and settled for the rest of his life in
      London. He used the reading room of the British Museum to write his best
      known work, *Das Kapital*. This advocated a classless, communist society and the
      end of the exploitation of the 'working class' by 'capitalist society'. His philoso-
      phy became known as Marxism and has influenced political thinking ever since.
      On his grave in Highgate cemetary in north London is this inscription from his

own words: 'The philosophers have only interpreted the world in various ways. The point however is to change it.'

6

7

8   Jean Henri Dunant, founder of the Red Cross, was born 1828. He witnessed a dreadful battle in which 40,000 men were killed or wounded. Using volunteers he offered medical aid to those who needed it on both sides, an approach unknown in those days. Eventually, through his influence, sixteen countries signed the Geneva Convention, in 1864. This Convention is still in operation today and ensures that those who provide help to the wounded in wars will themselves be protected. They are identified by the sign of the red cross on a white background – the Swiss flag, Dunant's own country, in reverse. In peace and war the International Red Cross still offer today help where it is most needed, carrying on the work and vision of this Christian man. He was awarded the Nobel Peace Prize in 1901.

9

10   After the first elections in South Africa open to people of all races, Nelson Mandela is inaugurated as President, 1994 (see February 11).
- President Mandela said in Pretoria, following his swearing in as South Africa's first black President:
  'We have triumphed in the effort to implant hope in the breasts of the millions of our people. We enter into a covenant that we shall build the society in which all South Africans, both black and white, will be able to walk tall, without fear in their hearts, assured of their inalienable right to human dignity – a rainbow nation at peace with itself and the world.'

11

12   From a well-to-do background, it was unthought of that a woman like Florence Nightingale, born 1820, should become a nurse. But that is what she believed God wanted her to do and, against the wishes of her family and the social conventions of the time, in 1854 she took a small group of nurses to the war that was raging in the Crimea.

This led to a lifetime of dedication to raising the standards of nursing and introducing proper training. An indication of the esteem with which 'The Lady with the Lamp' was held was that the 'Nightingale Fund', set up at the end of the Crimean war, raised over £45,000, a vast sum at the time. Florence used this money to establish the first training school for nurses at St Thomas's Hospital in London. In 1907 she became the first woman to be awarded the Order of Merit (see also May 14).
- Ask a nurse to describe the work they do. Are there ways in which the local hospital could use the help of volunteers from the youth group? Are there patients to call on who do not often receive visitors?

13

14   Mary Seacole died in 1881. A Jamaican-born nurse, she also worked in the Crimea (see May 12) tending the sick and dying soldiers. She travelled there at her own expense. It was remarkable for the times for a black woman to do this kind of work and to be accepted by British soldiers. 'Mother' Seacole, as she became known, developed her own medicine to treat cholera, and describes in her autobiography, *Wonderful Adventures of Mrs Seacole*, (published by Falling Wall Press, Bristol) how she met her heroine, Florence Nightingale, in the Crimea.
   • Most job advertisements now say 'We are Equal Opportunities Employers'. Is this true, do you think? Do women, black and Asian people and disabled people really have the same opportunities open to them as, for example, white men?

THE THIRD WEEK IN MAY is Christian Aid Week. See what help you can give.

15   At the end of the First World War many children were suffering terribly in the nations defeated by the Allied forces. Their plight touched the heart of a woman, Eglantyne Jebb, and she had handbills printed telling of the needy children. But she fell foul of the censors at the time and was sent to court for circulating the bills without their permission. Eglantyne appeared in court on this day in 1919 and was fined £5. But, as a result of the publicity she received, money came pouring in and led to the founding of the Save the Children Fund. One of the first people to make a donation was the prosecuting counsel in the court!

16   On this day in 1983 wheel clamps were introduced for the first time into parts of central London.
   • Are they a good idea do you think? How would you solve the parking problems of Britain's towns and cities?

17

ANNUAL WEEKENDS AND RALLIES FOR YOUTH ORGANIZATIONS take place at different times of the year, and are well worth attending. The huge London Weekend organized by the Methodist Association of Youth Clubs breaks into its usual exciting activity on the third weekend in May.

18

19

20

21   Elizabeth Fry, the prison reformer, was born, 1780. A Quaker, Elizabeth was horrified by what she saw of the conditions in which women prisoners were kept in Newgate prison in London. Despite the opposition and scepticism of the prison authorities, she set up a school for the children of the prisoners and for young mothers and founded craft workshops. Her efforts restored some dignity to the wretched lives of the prisoners, to whom she made it clear that all she did was in the name of Jesus. Her reforming ideas and methods slowly led to a new approach to the treatment and rehabilitation of people kept in prison.
   • Invite a prison visitor or chaplain to speak to the group (see also the third week in November).

22 1900, the lower age limit for boys working in coal mines in Britain was raised from 12 to 13. Yes, that happened this century!

23

24 In his diary for this day in 1738 John Wesley wrote these words:
> 'I think it was about five this morning that I opened my Testament on the words: 'There are given to us exceeding great and precious promises ...'.Just as I went out, I opened it again on these words: 'Thou art not far from the Kingdom of God.' In the evening I went very unwillingly to a society in Aldersgate Street (in the City of London) where one was reading Luther's 'Preface to the Epistle of the Romans'. About a quarter before nine, while he was describing the change which God works in the heart through faith in Christ, I felt my heart strangely warmed. I felt I did trust in Christ, Christ alone for salvation; and an assurance was given me that he had taken away my sins, even mine, and saved me from the law of sin and death. I then testi-fied openly to all there what I now felt in my heart.'

- This conversion experience for John Wesley set him on his way as a great evan-gelist, travelling all over Britain on horseback and taking the message of the Gospel, especially to ordinary people who were not being reached by the Church of the day.
- Get a small group to research the story of John Wesley and his brother, Charles (see December 18), and tell the story of how Methodism began as a society within the Church of England and grew to be a worldwide movement (see also March 2 and July 24).

25

26 The Feast Day of the first Archbishop of Canterbury, St Augustine. He was sent by the Pope from Rome in AD597, with a group of about forty monks, to evan-gelize England. Because of our reputation as a missionary nation, we need to remind ourselves that the good news of Jesus came to us first, long ago, from overseas and thank God for his messengers down the centuries.

THE LAST WEEKEND IN MAY is Spring Bank Holiday

27

28

29 In 1953 at 11.30 Edmund Hillary from New Zealand and Sherpa Tensing from Nepal were the first people to reach the summit of Everest, at 29,002 feet the highest mountain in the world.

1982 Pope John Paul II became the first Pope to visit Britain for 450 years. Together with the Archbishop of Canterbury, he prayed at the tomb of St Thomas á Becket in Canterbury Cathedral. St Thomas was murdered on the orders of the King, in 1170, for standing up for the rights of the Church (see also March 23 and October 16).

30

31   If you have stayed in a hotel or conference centre you will almost certainly have found in your room a Bible placed there by The Gideons. This international society was begun on this day in 1899 by two American businessmen. The Gideons even made sure there was a Bible on the first manned space flight round the moon and it was from a Gideon Bible that, in sending a message back to earth, the crew of Apollo 8 felt moved to quote the first few verses from Genesis 1: 'In the beginning God created the heaven and the earth ...' (see also July 21).

- If you had the opportunity of sending a message to the world from the Bible, which passage would you choose?

JUNE

The Roman goddess Juno gives her name to this month. She was thought to protect women especially during childbirth.

1   Henry Francis Lyte born 1793 in Ireland. He gave us two well-known hymns, 'Praise my soul the King of Heaven' and 'Abide with me'. Because of the way it has been traditionally sung at the FA Cup Final each year, 'Abide with me' is probably one of the most famous of all hymns. The Rev. Lyte, who at the time he wrote the hymn was living in the fishing port of Brixham, knew that he was dying of consumption when he completed the words in September 1847. He died in November of the same year. 'Abide with me' draws on images of evening and low tide and relates them to both the close of day and also the close of life itself.

- Sing and study the words of 'Abide with me' and read the story of the two disciples who walked with Jesus on Easter Day on the Emmaus road (see Luke 24. 13–35). In the Authorised Version of the Bible the translation of verse 29 is 'Abide with us: for it is towards evening ...' and this passage gave further inspiration to the writer of this hymn.

Frank Whittle, the inventor of the jet engine for aircraft, was born in Coventry on this day in 1907. He first had the idea for jet propulsion, which now provides the power for virtually all today's planes, when he was a student in 1927. But government support was not forthcoming until 1939, with the first test flight in 1941.

2   Coronation of the Queen in Westminster Abbey, 1953 (see also January 22 and February 6).

3   The international 'Earth Summit' on the environment began in 1992 in Rio de Janiero, Brazil.

- Do you see any evidence that governments, as well as ordinary people, are caring for the environment as they should?

4   To draw attention to the campaign for women to have votes, a suffragette, Emily

Davidson, threw herself under the King's horse 'Anmer' as it competed in the Derby at Epsom on this date in 1913. She died from her injuries a few days later (see also February 6 and November 28).

5

6

7

8

9   Elizabeth Garrett Anderson born, 1836. She was the first woman in Britain to qualify as a doctor and surgeon. She established a hospital for women, which bore her name, where women could be treated by women (see also December 17).

This is St Columba of Iona's Day. He came to the remote Scottish island from Northern Ireland and took the message of the Gospel to many parts of Scotland. He died in AD597, but Iona remains a place of pilgrimage to this day. The Iona Community produces exciting and challenging resources for worship.
- Try to obtain some of the Iona worship publications and use them in the youth group (published under the name of 'Wild Goose').

10

11

12   Anne Frank, was born in 1929. On her 13th birthday she was given a diary by her father. A German Jewish family, the Franks moved to the Netherlands in 1933, but when the Germans invaded the Netherlands at the beginning of the Second World War they were, in 1942, forced into hiding, creating a tiny safe place within their home in Amsterdam. During their time in hiding, Anne kept a diary describing her thoughts and experiences as a teenager. Towards the end of the German occupation the Frank's were discovered and sent to concentration camps where Anne died. Her father, Otto, survived and, after the war, published Anne's diary. Both a film and a play have been based on Anne's writings. It is now one of the most famous diaries ever written having been translated into more than fifty languages. The Franks' home in Amsterdam is preserved to show not only how they lived, but to remind visitors of the evil policy of the Nazis that led to the extermination of so many Jews.
- *The Diary of Anne Frank* (published by Longmans) is still obtainable in paper back. Have a copy for members of the group to read.

13

14

15   The Queen's Birthday Honours List, on this date in 1965, announced that the Beatles had, collectively, been awarded the MBE. The four lads from Liverpool, who were probably the best known pop group ever, had been rejected by the Decca recording company in January 1962 as it was felt their music would never

make it into the charts! A year later their first record, 'Please Please Me' was issued and was an instant success.
- Do young people still like to listen to the Beatle's music?

16

17   John Wesley born, 1703 (see May 24).

18   Paul McCartney of the Beatles born 1942 (see June 15 above).

THE THIRD SUNDAY IN JUNE is celebrated as Father's Day.

19

20

21   The longest day of the year – that is, the most daylight, marking the Summer Solstice, the beginning of summer. However, although summer is seen as being from this date until the Autumn Equinox on September 22, Midsummer Day falls on June 24! Explain that if you can!

22   It was announced on this day in 1970 that women would be able to be ordained as Ministers in the Methodist Church. The United Reformed Church and the Baptist Church were already ordaining women (see also March 12 and November 11).

23

24   Midsummer Day (see June 21) and the Feast Day that marks the Nativity (birth) of John the Baptist. John was a cousin of Jesus and was the son of a priest, Zechariah, and his wife, Elizabeth (see Luke 1.57–66). John had his own mission which you can read about in Luke 3. 1–22.
- Jesus was baptized by John (see Matthew 3. 13–17). Talk about the importance and meaning of Baptism within the various traditions of the church. Some churches do not baptize babies, believing in adult baptism. Other churches only baptize babies. Do some research about the importance and meaning of Christian baptism and, perhaps, attend different kinds of Christian initiation ceremonies in denominations other that your own.

25

26   The United Nations founded 1945 when fifty nations signed the World Security Charter. The Prime Minister of South Africa, General Smuts, and one of the most senior politicians present at the ceremony in the United States, said of the Charter: 'It provides for a peace with teeth; for the unity of peace-loving peoples against future aggressors; for a united front amongst the greatest powers, backed by the forces of the smallest powers as well.'
- United Nations forces and monitors operate in many of the world's trouble spots today. Discover where they are at work at the present time and pray for peace to be restored and for communities to be re-built (see also January 10 and October 23).

27

28

29 Samuel Adjai Crowther, became the first black person to be consecrated as a Bishop in the Church of England, 1864. At the age of 12 Samuel had been sold into slavery, but he was rescued and educated in a mission school. He was eventually ordained by the Church Missionary Society and became a Bishop in his own country of Nigeria.
- Do black and Asian Christians hold enough positions of authority within the churches today? Ask a black priest or minister to meet with the youth group to share their views on the church.
- Feast Day of St. Peter. Have a Bible search game, going through the Gospels (and the Acts of the Apostles if you have time) and finding as many references as possible to Simon Peter. (Jesus gave Simon the name Peter, meaning rock.) From the stories you read try to discover what kind of person Peter was.

30

JULY
Named by Mark Anthony in honour of Julius Caesar, who was born in this month.

1 The first Oxfam shop was opened in Oxford 1948 (see also October 5).

The system of '999' emergency calls began 1937.
- Has any member of the group got reason to be thankful for this national emergency system?

2 1489 – Thomas Cranmer was born. The first Protestant Archbishop of Canterbury, he is especially remembered as the person who was responsible for the first version of the Prayer Book used by the Church of England and published in 1549. The present Prayer Book dates from 1662 with several revisions this century. Despite Cranmer's great gift to the Church of a magnificent service book, he was eventually imprisoned, charged with heresy and burnt at the stake on March 21, 1556.
- Look at copies of the 1662 Prayer Book and the more recent Alternative Service Book (1980). Is there still value in using orders of service written in the language of the seventeenth century?

3 Feast Day of St Thomas the Apostle, one of the twelve chosen by Jesus. He is best known as the doubting disciple who was not present when the frightened followers of Jesus, who had locked themselves away on the first Easter Day, were visited by their risen Lord.

- Read in John 20. 24–29 of the encounter between Jesus and Thomas and how Jesus handled Thomas' doubts.
- How do present day Christians cope with doubts about their faith?

4   Thomas Barnardo, born in Ireland 1845. Whilst training as a medical student in London, Thomas was shocked by the conditions in which some children existed in the capital. Later he set up homes for orphaned and destitute children and publicized their need in a very modern manner for the times, by using photographs. The work of Dr Barnardo continues today through the organization bearing his name.

American Independence Day. The Declaration of Independence was passed by Congress on this date in 1776. Part of the Declaration states:

> 'We hold these truths to be self-evident; that all men are created equal; that they are endowed with certain inalienable rights and that these are life, liberty and the pursuit of happiness.'

- How far does present day America measure up to these rights do you think? And, for that matter, Britain, from whom they were becoming independent? (see also December 10.)

5

6

7

8

9   Archbishop of Canterbury, Stephen Langton died 1228. Imagine what the Bible would look like if it was virtually solid text with no helpful chapter and verse divisions. Well, it was like that until Archbishop Langton, took on the mammoth task of putting the Bible into the style with which we are familiar with chapters and verses (see also March 16, October 6 and Bible Sunday in December).

10

11   The famous music by Vangelis from the film 'Chariots of Fire' will always be associated with running. The film is the story of Christian athlete Eric Liddell who, on this day in 1924, won a gold medal at the Paris Olympics for the 400 metres. Eric refused to compete in heats being run on a Sunday for the 100 metre sprint for which he had been entered. At the last minute he was entered for the 400 metre race which he won convincingly. Later, Eric became a missionary in China but was interned in a Japanese prisoner of war camp and died there on February 21, 1943.
- View the film 'Chariots of Fire' which won four Oscars, including Best Film of the Year Award in 1981.

a feast of dates – JUL

12 The man who invented roll film for cameras, George Eastman, born in 1854. We must all be grateful to the person who enabled even the most amateur of photographers to capture precious memories on paper.

13 Moved to action by television pictures of starving people in Ethiopia, Bob Geldof organized the Live Aid concert at Wembley, 1985. It was viewed in 160 countries by about 2 billion people, probably the largest ever TV audience. This followed the Christmas 1984 Band Aid single, 'Do They Know It's Christmas?' involving rock superstars, also brought together by Bob Geldof. Live Aid raised £70 million for relief work.

14

15 Watch out, it's St Swithin's Day and tradition has it that if it rains on this day we're in for a long spell of wet weather:

> St Swithin's Day, if thou dost rain
> Full forty days it will remain
> St Swithin's Day, if thou be fair
> For forty days, twill rain no mair.

St Swithin became Bishop of Winchester in AD852. He flouted custom by asking that, when he died, his body be buried outside the cathedral with the poor. This request was carried out but later, the church authorities built a huge shrine inside the cathedral. It is said that, on the day his bones were moved, July 15th, 971, it rained and continued to do so for forty days. The people thought it was the Saint crying with displeasure. And so a superstition was born!

16

17 Isaac Watts was born in 1674. Young Isaac didn't like the way psalms were sung in church in his day, not unlike many young people now who are critical of the music and hymns in church. But rather than just criticize he set about writing some of the best known of all hymns, such as 'When I survey the wondrous cross' and 'O God, our help in ages past'.
   • Do members of the group have favourite old-style hymns and modern hymns and songs?
   • Write a hymn or chorus together.

18

19

20

21 First moon landing, 1969: At 03.56 BST astronaut Neil Armstrong was the first person to set foot on the moon. As commander of the lunar module from Apollo 11 and watched live on TV around the world, Armstrong said the immortal words as he stepped on the dusty surface: 'That's one small step for a man, one giant leap for mankind' (see also May 31).

- Has space travel and research contributed anything useful to the human race?

22 Feast Day of St Mary Magdalen. There are several Marys mentioned in the New Testament, but this one is thought to have been a woman who, before she met Jesus, had led an immoral life. In Luke 8. 2 it says that Jesus had driven 'seven demons' out of her. Yet it was this Mary who was one of the first people to see Jesus alive after his resurrection (see John 20. 11–18).

23

24 In his famous Journal, John Wesley (see May 24) records this advice from his mother, Susanna, on how to bring up children. As she had nineteen of her own she presumably knew what she was talking about!:

24th July 1732

Dear Son,

According to your desire, I have collected the principal rules I observed in educating my family; and which I now send you.

1 When turned a year old (and some before), they were taught to fear the rod and to cry softly; by which means they escaped abundance of correction; and that most odious noise of the crying of children was rarely heard in the house.
2 It had been observed that cowardice and fear of punishment often led children into lying till they get a custom of it which they cannot leave. To prevent this, a law was made that whoever was charged with a fault of which they were guilty, if they would confess it and promise to amend, should not be beaten.
3 No child should ever be chid or beaten twice for the same fault; and that if they amended, they should never be upbraided with it afterwards.

- What do you think of these Eighteenth century guidelines for parenting? Write your own for today's parents.

25 Feast Day of St James, the brother of St John and a disciple of Jesus. With his brother, James was called from his trade as a fisherman on Lake Galilee (see Matthew 4. 21–22). It is thought that James was the first disciple to be martyred. His death is recorded in Acts 12. 2.

26

27

28 Johann Sebastian Bach died, 1750. The German composer wrote much wonderful music.
   - Listen to some of Bach's music. Better still, see if there are some musicians in the group who could perform some.

29 William Wilberforce, the man through whose determination, legislation was passed abolishing the slave trade, died 1833. William saw his Christian vocation to

a feast of dates – JUL

be in Parliament and he was Member of Parliament for Hull. Eight years after becoming an MP he presented his first Bill to abolish the slave trade throughout the British Dominions. Before he was successful, he had to present the Bill each year between 1788 and 1805 until, finally in 1806, slavery was abolished. However, it was not until the year that Wilberforce died that slaves were finally emancipated.

30 England won the football World Cup in 1966 when they beat West Germany by 4 goals to 2 at Wembley. And since...?

31 Leonard Cheshire VC died, 1992 (see September 7).

AUGUST
Named in honour of Augustus, the first Roman Emperor, who lived from 63 BC to AD14.

1 Lammas, one of the oldest celebrations in the church calendar. It is a festival at the beginning of the harvest. (Harvest Festival comes at the end.) On this day, as far back as the time of King Alfred, people have made a loaf of bread from the first cut corn. The loaf was taken to church and blessed. The word Lammas is probably derived from two old English words 'hlaf' (loaf) and 'mass' (feast).
 • Thank God for bread

2 Pat Seed died 1984. She was told in 1977 that because of cancer, she only had six months to live. In fact she lived a further seven years. She did not waste those 'bonus' years. Her work for cancer research charities earned her the MBE in 1979. Altogether she was instrumental in raising £3,500,000, some of the money being used to buy a computerized body scanner for the Christie hospital in Manchester where Pat's cancer was diagnosed and she was treated.
 • If you were told by a doctor that you only had six months to live, how would you use the time? (see also March 2.)
 • Consider the words of Jesus in Luke 12. 22–31.

3

4

5 Marilyn Monroe committed suicide, 1962. More than thirty years later, as the Fontana Dictionary of Modern Thinkers puts it, 'Her photographs, film performances and legend continue to haunt the popular imagination, and even for writers and artists she remains a challenge to their own imaginations'.
 • Why does Marilyn continue to hold this fascination for people?

6 First atomic bomb dropped 1945. Four square miles of the Japanese city of Hiroshima were devastated by Allied forces. Over 50,000 civilians were killed

and many others received terrible injuries and suffered from the long-term effects of radiation. (Three days later on August 9 an atomic bomb was also used on another Japanese city, Nagasaki) (see also September 7.)

The grim anniversary of the destruction of Hiroshima and the Christian Festival of Transfiguration, which falls on this day (see Mark 9. 2–13) were used in 1981 to launch the World Prayer for Peace, which is as follows:

> Lead me from death to life,
> from falsehood to truth.
> Lead me from despair to hope,
> from fear to trust.
> Lead me from hate to love,
> from war to peace.
> Let peace fill our hearts,
> our world, our universe.
> Peace, peace, peace.

7

8 Described as 'the most audacious crime in British history', the 'Great Train Robbery' occurred on this day in 1963. The robbers got away with £2.6 million from a train they had stopped with a fake signal at Cheddington, Bucks.

9

10

11

12 'The Glorious Twelfth' on which grouse shooting may officially begin.
- Do the members of the group approve of 'field' sports such as grouse, pheasant and hare shooting?
- Why are they called a 'sport'?
- Should fishing be counted as a 'cruel' sport?

13 Social reformer Octavia Hill died 1912. At a time when women were little involved in matters outside their homes, Octavia, from the age of 14 took an interest in the housing conditions of poor people. By the time she was 17 she had obtained and renovated a house in London where homeless people could have at least temporary shelter. Octavia Hill was one of the first women ever to sit on a Royal Commission and one of the founders of the National Trust (see also September 2).
- Are there ways in which your group could help the homeless in your area? Octavia's story shows us that age should not be a barrier to involvement.

14 See entry on March 2 about Clive Jermain. Clive's photographic project, 'One Day for Life' began at midnight on August 14, 1987. People all over Britain were invited to take a photograph on that day of whatever seemed to them to capture the essence of Britain in the pattern of their lives. It was all part of a fund-raising project for cancer charities. The best 350 photographs were published in a best selling book 'One Day for Life' (see also August 2).

- Organize your own town, neighbourhood or church photo competition on an aspect of local life or on a particular day in the year. Entry fees could go to charity and then you could mount an exhibition of the best pictures and charge for entry. Maybe even publish a book?

15

16 Two legends of the world of pop can be remembered (or forgotten if you would prefer to!) on this day – Elvis Presley died on this day in 1977 and Madonna (real name Louise Ciccione) was born in 1958.

17 William Carey born, 1761. His humble background, he was a Northampton shoemaker, meant he had to educate himself, but he still felt called by God to go to India, and went there supported by the newly founded English Baptist Missionary Society. Within five years he had translated the New Testament in the major language of Bengali and portions of Scripture were translated into twenty-four other languages and dialects.

- Is there still a need for people to go as missionaries from this country?
- Does anyone in the group feel called to serve God in this way?
- Should Britain receive missionaries from other countries? (see May 26)

18

19

20

21 The first ever television broadcast was made from Alexandra Palace in north London 1936 (see also January 27).

22

23

24 Feast Day of St Bartholomew. Who? No disrespect, but we know very little about this disciple of Jesus. You'll find him in the list of the chosen Twelve in three of the Gospels (see Matthew 10. 3, for example). The only other mention of Bartholomew is in Acts 1. 13 where, once again, he is listed as being with the other disciples. Not a high profile disciple this one. But we must assume he was a faithful one, always there, to be trusted, shy perhaps, no great theologian, but still a committed follower of Jesus. And that's what matters.

William Wilberforce born 1759 (see main entry July 29).

25

26

27 The world-famous Albanian nun, Mother Teresa of Calcutta, born 1910 (see main entry on October 17).

28

THE LAST WEEKEND IN AUGUST IS A BANK HOLIDAY. The Greenbelt Christian Arts Festival is held on this weekend with music, seminars, drama, art and much more. Plan to take a group.

29

30

31 1994, after twenty-five years, 3169 dead, 38,6080 injured, 10,001 bombings, the IRA announced a 'cessation of military activities', leading to the beginning of a peace process in Ireland.

Guess how long ago it is since Coca Cola was first introduced to Britain. 20 years? 35 years? 50 years? 75 years? All wrong. Coke first came to these shores on this date in 1900. There's a surprise! It had come into existence fourteen years earlier in the USA.

SEPTEMBER
In the old Roman calendar this was the seventh (sept) month, March then being the first month of the year.

1 The German army invaded Poland, 1939, the event that finally led to the Second World War (see September 3). On this day in the same year schemes began for the evacuation of civilians in England and Wales, particularly women and children, who were moved away from areas, such as large cities and towns likely to be at risk from bombing. More than a million people were moved in this way.
  • See if you can find someone in your church or community who was evacuated as a child and ask them to tell you their story of those times over fifty years ago.

2 Final end of the Second World War in 1945 when the Japanese surrendered.

Shelter, the charity dedicated to helping those both homeless and affected by poor housing, was founded 1966.
  • Is there a branch of Shelter near you? Discover the ways this campaigning charity still helps those without a proper place to live and what kind of help and support they need (see also August 13).

3 'This country is now at war with Germany. We are ready.' With these words in the House of Commons on this day in 1939 the Prime Minister, Neville Chamberlain, signalled the start of the Second World War.

4 Albert Schweitzer died 1965 (see January 14).

5

6   Christy Brown died 1981. He suffered from cerebral palsy and, from birth, he was treated as a person of no importance and with nothing to offer to the world. That was until one day he found that he could hold a piece of chalk between his toes and that he could use this to draw. As time went by he learned to type with the toes of one foot, became celebrated as a novelist and, in 1970, brought out his best selling autobiography, *Down All Our Days*.
    • Read the story of King David and the crippled man, Mephibosheth, in the second book of Samuel 9. 1–13.
    • Have a time of confessing how we have underestimated people because of their looks, their disability, their odd manner, their age. Jesus released people from all kinds of cruelties inflicted by disease, poverty and human prejudice. Read and meditate on the story of Jesus and the crippled woman who he made better on the Sabbath (see Luke 13. 10–17, and also January 8).

7   Leonard Cheshire born in Chester 1917. He was a senior officer in the RAF during the Second World War and was, for a time, Commanding Officer of the famous 617 Squadron, the Dambusters. In 1945 he was an official British observer of the dropping of the atomic bomb on the Japanese city of Nagasaki (see August 6). After the war, converted to Roman Catholicism. Leonard Cheshire felt that God had a task for him to do, but he could not discover what it was. Caring for a man dying of cancer led Leonard eventually to found the Cheshire Homes and spend the rest of his life helping the sick and disadvantaged. Today there are about 200 Cheshire homes in Britain and abroad. In 1953 Leonard Cheshire married another famous philanthropist, Sue Ryder (Baroness Ryder of Warsaw). Leonard Cheshire was made Baron Cheshire in 1991 and died on July 31, 1992.
    • Learn more about the remarkable war-time ace bomber pilot who, afterwards gave his life to the relief of suffering, and about the Cheshire and Ryder Homes. There is likely to be one not all that far from you.

8   Celebrated as the Festival of the Blessed Virgin Mary, the mother of Jesus. Traditionally observed as the day of her Nativity, or birth (see also March 25).
    • Read together the key passages from the Bible that concern the task that God gave to this very young woman. For example Luke 1. 26–56.
    • If you do not understand why some branches of the Christian church give special veneration to the Virgin Mary, do some research about it or invite into the group a Roman Catholic who can describe the part that the mother of Jesus plays in their faith.

9

10

11

12   Steve Biko died whilst in police custody, 1977. In his own lifetime he became a symbol of oppression in white dominated South Africa. As a black medical student he helped to found the South African Students' Organization. A believer in 'black consciousness', he urged black South Africans to have pride in themselves and free them-

selves from 'the shackles of servitude'. The government officially banned him in 1973 and so silenced him. His cause was taken up by the white editor of a South African newspaper, Donald Woods, who himself was eventually banned and fled the country.
- See the feature film 'Cry Freedom' based on the book Donald Woods wrote about Steve Biko (see also February 11 and May 10).

13

14 Kidbrooke School, the first Comprehensive School in London, opened in 1954. It was controversial and revolutionary at the time.
- What is the system of schooling in your local authority now?
- What views do the group have on how best to educate children for life?

15

16 102 emigrants set out for a hazardous sea journey from Plymouth, Devon to America in a tiny boat, the 'Mayflower', 1620. Thirty-five of the group were Puritans who were leaving England looking for religious freedom. They founded the colony of Plymouth, New England. Many of these early settlers died during their first winter but they were helped to survive by the native American Indians. The time of Thanksgiving they celebrated at their first harvest in 1621 is still commemorated with a national holiday, Thanksgiving Day, on the fourth Thursday in November in the United States and on the second Monday in October in Canada.
- Thank God in prayer and song that we now have religious freedom in our country and in the USA and Canada.

17

18 The Inner London Education Authority abolished corporal punishment (caning, etc.) in its schools, 1979.
- What is the attitude of the group to physical punishment in school? If we 'spare the rod' do we 'spoil the child'? (see also July 24)

19 A day of celebration for 'chocaholics' – the birthday of George Cadbury in 1839! At the age of 21, with his elder brother, Richard, George inherited the small firm from his sick father. They moved to the outskirts of Birmingham and not only developed their thriving, and now internationally known, chocolate business, but also showed care and concern for their workers. In an age when workers were sometimes wickedly exploited, the Quaker Cadbury brothers built Bournville, a model village for their employees which was way ahead of its time. As Christian employers they saw it as their duty to provide for all the needs of the people who worked for them.
- Pray for employers and the problems they face, especially when times are hard. Do the group know of any more examples of 'good' employers who aim to provide for the full needs of employees?
- Enjoy some chocolate!

20 The nine days from this date to September 28 are observed in the Jewish calendar as the harvest Festival of Tabernacles, a time of great rejoicing.
- If you have a Synagogue near you, see if the Rabbi or some other member of the congregation will share with you something of the importance and customs

of this Harvest Festival which falls at around the same time as most Christian churches thank God for the harvest.

21 Feast Day of St Matthew. A man despised in his time because he was a tax collector but chosen by Jesus to be one of his Disciples and believed to be the writer of the first Gospel.
   • Read of the calling of Matthew by Jesus in Matthew 9. 9–13.

22 The first day of Autumn.

The first ever TV commercial broadcast in Britain went out in 1955 for Gibbs SR toothpaste.
   • Which commercials do the group like most and hate most?
   • Can TV commercials be said to have any purpose and value?

23

24

25

26 William Carlile, who founded the Church Army, died 1942. The Church Army is a uniformed organization within the Church of England. Terry Waite trained as an officer of the Church Army (see November 18).
   • Discover whether there is a Church Army officer working in your area. Invite them to the group to tell you about their work.

27

28 'Good King Wenceslas looked out...' We all know the carol and on this day the Church celebrates the feast of St Wenceslas, the good and reforming king of Bohemia. But his attempts to bring justice to his country made him enemies among those who gained from the slave trade and through bribery and he was assassinated in the year AD929 whilst still a young man.
   • Celebrate a brave man and have an early carol practice by singing the song that records a legend told about this Christian martyr.

29 Feast Day of St Michael and All Angels. St Michael is recorded as being the chief of all the angels in heaven. He is mentioned in some of the visionary books of the Bible: Daniel, Jude and Revelation (see Revelation 12. 7–9 where he is portrayed as battling with Satan).
   • Do people still believe in angels? Where are they to be seen today? There may be a clue in Hebrews 13. 1–2.
   • Is there still a battle going on between good and evil, as symbolized in the story of St Michael? Who's winning?

30 In 1967 BBC radio replaced its Light Programme, Third Programme and Home Service with Radios 1, 2, 3 and 4.
   • Who prefers listening to radio rather than watching TV?
   • Which radio stations and programmes are the most liked and least liked?

OCTOBER
The ancient Roman calendar began in March, so this was the eighth
month, from the Latin 'octo'.

1   The American hamburger chain, McDonalds, opened its first restaurant in south
     London on this date in 1974.
     • Use a large piece of paper divided into two columns and headed Good and Bad
       to start discussion about the things that are liked and disliked about
       McDonalds and other similar fast food restaurants.

2   The Indian nationalist leader Mahatma Gandhi was born 1869 (see January 30
     for main entry).

3   The saint to whom is attributed one of the most famous and best loved prayers,
     St Francis, died 1226:

          Lord make me an instrument of your peace:
          where there is hatred,
          let me sow love;
          where there is injury, pardon;
          where there is doubt, faith;
          where there is despair, hope;
          where there is darkness, light;
          where there is sadness, joy.

          Grant that I may not
          so much seek to be consoled,
          as to console;
          to be understood,
          as to understand;
          to be loved, as to love.

     • Several religious Orders were inspired by the life of St Francis. See if there is a
       member of one of these orders (probably in the Roman Catholic Church or
       Anglican Church) who could share with the group something of the story of St
       Francis and his influence down the centuries.

     • Sing the song based on his prayer 'Make me a channel of your peace ...' which
       is in many hymn and chorus books.

4

5   OXFAM, short for the Oxford Committee for Famine Relief, founded in 1942,
     initially to relieve the plight of the victims of the Nazi invasion of Greece. It is
     now one of the major aid and relief agencies (see also July 1).

The United Reformed Church came into being, 1972, by the combining of the Congregational Church of England and Wales and the Presbyterian Church of England.
- Do you know what the special beliefs and traditions of the URC are? If not, invite someone from the local URC church to tell you.

6   The Archbishop of Canterbury says that the reason why the churches are poorly attended is because of poor preaching and 'outdated clergy'. By the way, this was on this date in 1925 – so what's new! And, more importantly, has anything changed?

William Tyndale, 'the Father of the English Bible', martyred in Brussels, 1536. He had lived the life of an outlaw for many years because of his determination to print copies of his translation of the Bible into English so that it could be used by ordinary people.
- Ask some members of the group to do some research about the extraordinary life and death of William Tyndale, and present it to the group.
- Thank God for those who gave their lives that we might have the Word of God available to us so freely (see also January 20, March 16 and Bible Sunday in December).

7   Desmond Tutu, who became Archbishop of Cape Town, South Africa, in 1986, was born, 1931. He was awarded the Nobel Peace Prize in 1984 for his total but non-violent opposition to aparthied (see also September 12).
- Archbishop Tutu once said: 'I am puzzled which Bible people are reading when they suggest religion and politics don't mix.'

8   At the Conservative Party Conference in Brighton meeting in 1982, the Prime Minister, Margaret Thatcher, told the delegates: 'The National Health Service is safe with us.'
- Was she right? (see also March 5)

9

10

11

12

THE SECOND WEEK OF OCTOBER is observed as Prisoner of Conscience Week. Details from Amnesty International.

13

14   This is the birthday of Harry Webb, born in India in 1940. He's better known as Cliff Richard and was knighted in 1995.

15

THE THIRD FRIDAY IN OCTOBER is observed as World Food Day. Special material for use on or near the day is usually available from the aid agencies such as CAFOD, Christian Aid or Oxfam.

16   A Polish Cardinal, Karol Wojtyla, was elected Pope John Paul II in 1978. He is the first non-Italian Pope for over four hundred years (see also May 29).

17   An inspiration to millions for her total devotion to God and the poorest of the poor, the Albanian born nun, Mother Teresa, was awarded the Nobel Peace Prize on this date in 1979. Her work with her Sisters of Charity is especially centred on the Indian city of Calcutta (see also August 27).
   • On a visit to Britain Mother Teresa said: 'But here in Britain you have a different kind of poverty. A poverty of loneliness and being unwanted, a poverty of spirit. And that is the worst disease in the world today.'

   A prayer of Mother Teresa:
   Make us worthy, Lord,
   To serve our fellow-men
   Throughout the world who live and die
   In poverty or hunger.
   Give them, through our hands
   This day their daily bread,
   And by our understanding love,
   Give peace and joy.

18   Feast Day of St Luke – the author of the third and fullest of the Gospels – and of the Acts of the Apostles. Companion of St Paul on some of his journeys, he is referred to in the Letter to the Colossians 4. 14 as 'our dear doctor', and is recognized as the patron saint of the medical profession.

19

20   Christopher Wren was born in 1632. Best known as the architect of St Paul's Cathedral in London, Sir Christopher was also a mathematician and astronomer. He was commissioned to design a new St Paul's to replace the one destroyed in the Great Fire of London but also drew up the plans for many other churches and buildings in the City. He is buried in St Paul's where his epitaph, translated from the Latin reads: 'If you seek a monument, look around you' (see also February 25).
   • What will be the 'monuments', good and bad, to some famous people living today?
   • How would we like to be remembered?

THE THIRD WEEK IN OCTOBER is observed as One World Week. It was started by the churches as a focus for everyone in the community concerned for people and planet to work together. Special resource and promotional material is available.

21   Alfred Nobel born in Sweden, 1833. An explosives expert and inventor of dynamite, he used the fortune he made to endow the Nobel prizes, the first being awarded in 1901 (see, for example, Mother Teresa on October 17). There are Nobel prizes awarded annually for physics, chemistry, physiology or medicine, literature and peace. In 1969 a sixth prize for economics was added to honour Alfred Nobel.

22

23 Commemorated as United Nations Day. There is probably a branch of the United Nations Association near you. Ask if they can supply you with information and, possibly, a speaker to meet with your group (see also January 10 and June 26).

24

25

26

27 William Smith, founder of the Boys' Brigade, born 1854. The movement started in 1883 and is the oldest of the uniformed youth organizations.
  • What contribution to society do organizations of this kind, especially single-sex ones, make today? Are there members of a uniformed youth organization in the group who will argue strongly in favour of them?

28 John Bunyan, the author or *The Pilgrim's Progress* born 1628. He was the son of poor tinker parents at Elstow, near Bedford. He was imprisoned for his non-conformist religious views for the best part of twelve years in Bedford prison. It was here that he wrote several books including his famous allegory (see also November 18).
  • Ask some of the group to look at *The Pilgrim's Progress* and to bring some extracts for reading at the group. There are up-dated versions of the story which may be helpful. How real is what Bunyan wrote to the Christian life today?

ON THE LAST WEEKEND IN OCTOBER British Summer Time ends at 2am on the Sunday when clocks are put back one hour. Please don't laugh too much at the person who forgets and arrives an hour early for church looking very confused!

29

30

31 All Hallows Eve or Hallowe'en. A pagan festival which many Christians feel is best left alone. Use the day instead for preparations for a celebration for All Saints' Day tomorrow.

  • However, you may want to discuss whether Hallowe'en is just a time for harmless fun (now much commercialized) or should we take seriously those who are worried about its links with occult practices?

German religious reformer Martin Luther nailed to the door of a church in Wittenberg his list of ninety-five 'theses', or points, about the way he thought the church of his time should be, 1517. Later he was called to account for his behaviour before the Holy Roman Emperor and the princes of Germany. He was accused of heresy, his books were burned and he was threatened with excommunication and death. But Luther stood by his beliefs and these words secured him a place in church history:

I cannot and will not renounce anything, for to go against conscience is neither right nor safe. Here I stand, I cannot do otherwise, God help me. Amen.

- Are there issues, ideas or beliefs that your group feel so stongly about that they
could make their own list of 'theses', like Martin Luther? You don't need to go
for as many as ninety-five! When you have compiled your list, you will have to
decide how you are going to share your views. Luther nailed them to a church
door. You might want to send them to an MP or an MEP, or to your local
paper, or a church committee. But, remember, like Luther, you must be prepared to stand by what you have written. His act of defiance led to the
Protestant Reformation. What effect could yours have? (see also February 18.)

NOVEMBER
The ninth month from March in the old Roman calendar. Latin:
novem (nine). Thomas Hood (1799–1845) wrote:
No sun – no moon!
No morn – no noon –
No dawn – no dusk – no proper time of day.
No warmth, no cheerfulness, no healthful ease,
No comfortable feel in any member –
No shade, no shine, no butterflies, no bees,
No fruits, no flowers, no leaves, no birds! –
November!

1 All Saints' Day when we remember all the saints, including those whose names
and deeds have not been recorded for history and our inspiration. St Paul at several points in his letters calls ordinary Christians 'saints' (see Romans 1. 7 – Not
all modern versions use the word saint. The Good News Bible talks about 'his
own people'). But we follow in a great line of Christian people down the ages and
thank God for them (see also April 25).
- Have an All Saints' Day celebration. Tell stories of good Christian people,
ancient and modern, especially of those who have some connection locally or
with your own Christian denomination. There are many books that record the
lives of the saints which you should be able to borrow from a library. Sing
great hymns such as 'For all the saints who from their labours rest'.

2 A London clergyman, Rev Chad Varah, started a simple service for desparate people on this day in 1953. He offered people his phone number so that they had
someone to call and talk to. From this idea has grown the nationwide and highly
respected counselling service known as the Samaritans. There will be a branch
near you. Find out more about them.

3

4 James Montgomery born 1771. In most church hymn books you will find some
hymns by James Montgomery. The Christmas hymn, 'Angels from the realms of
glory' was written by him, for example. Born in Scotland, he settled in Sheffield
where he became a campaigning newspaper owner and editor. He used his paper
to denounce the evils of the slave trade, child labour and many other social ills of

his time (see also April 5 for another campaigning newspaper editor).
- There may not be any hymn-writing newspaper editors today, but how far is it still the job of newspapers to campaign? Look at recent newspapers and try to find good examples of campaigning by the press for truth and justice.

5   All right then, enjoy your bonfire and fireworks, but spare a thought for poor old Guy Fawkes whose failed attempt to blow up King James I and the Houses of Parliament on this day in 1605 has never been forgotten. A Roman Catholic convert, he planned his dirty deed because of his religious zeal and paid for it by being tortured and executed.

A film censor was appointed for the first time in Britain in 1912. He was able to classify films as being either for 'Universal' showing or as 'Not suitable for children'.
- Does the group think that it is important that there is a system of censoring and classifying films? How should TV films and other programmes be regulated? (see also November 29)

The Prime Minister of Israel, Yitzhak Rabin, is assasinated in 1995 by a fellow Israeli who is opposed to the peace agreement signed on 13 December 1993 with the Palestine Liberation Organization.

6

7   Dr Billy Graham, the American evangelist, born 1918. Through his crusades, often relayed by satellite around the world, it is claimed he has preached to more people than any other person in history.

8   Dr Christian Barnard born 1922 in Cape Province, South Africa. He pioneered open heart surgery, initially against much opposition. In 1967 he performed the first heart transplant operation.

On Sunday November 8, 1987 at the Cenotaph in Enniskillen, Northern Ireland, the townspeople gathered for the Remembrance Day service (see 11 below). It never took place. Shortly before 11 am an IRA bomb brought tragedy and disaster. Gordon Wilson, aged 60, and his daughter, Marie, a nurse, were buried in a deluge of rubble. 'I asked her for the fifth time ..."Are you alright? Marie?"... She said, "Daddy, I love you very much"... Those were the last words she spoke to me...I kept shouting, "Marie are you alright?... There was no reply...But I bear no ill will. I bear no grudge. Dirty sort of talk is not going to bring her back to life again. Don't ask me please for a purpose. I don't have a purpose. I don't have an answer. But I know there has to be a plan. If I didn't think that, I would commit suicide. It's part of a greater plan, and God is God. And we shall meet again.' *Gordon Wilson died in 1995.*

9

10 Having been in place since August 1961, on this day in 1989, the Berlin Wall, separating East from West, was breached and dismantling began, opening the way for reunification.

11 Originally known as Armistice Day, the day on which the First World War finished in 1918, the Sunday nearest to this date is now observed as Remembrance Sunday for the dead of both world wars and other conflicts, such as the Falklands war, Northern Ireland and the Gulf war *(see November 8 above)*.
The Church of England Synod approved a procedure for the eventual ordination of women to the priesthood, 1992 (see March 12).

12

13 St Augustine, Bishop of Hippo, born AD354. After what some people would describe as a mis-spent youth, he returned to his Christian faith and became a Father of the Church. He left many beautiful prayers still used today after sixteen hundred years. Look in a prayer book to find one.

14 Prince of Wales, born 1948.

15

16

17

18 Terry Waite was released from being a hostage in Beirut, Lebanon, 1991. On his arrival back in Britain he said: 'I was kept in total and complete isolation for four years. I saw no one and spoke to no one apart from a cursory word with my guards when they brought me food. And one day out of the blue a guard came with a postcard. It was a postcard showing a stained glass window from Bedford showing John Bunyan in jail … I turned the card over and there was a message from someone I didn't know simply saying, "We remember, we shall not forget. We shall continue to pray for you and to work for all people who are detained around the world." That thought sent me back to the marvellous work of agencies like Amnesty International and their letter writing campaigns, and I would never despise those simple actions. Something, somewhere will get through to the people you are concerned about as it got through to me and to my fellows eventually' (see also October 28).
• Write to Amnesty International for details of their letter writing campaign. You could make this a regular activity in your group sessions.

19

20 On this day in 1926 the British Empire was renamed the British Commonwealth (see also the second Monday in March, Commonwealth Day).

21

22 John F Kennedy, President of the United States, was assassinated 1963 by a gunman whilst he was being driven in an open car through Dallas, Texas.
• It is said of this world-shattering event that many people can remember exactly what they were doing when they heard of President Kennedy's death. Are there events in recent history that have had a similar impact on members of the group?

THE THIRD WEEK IN NOVEMBER is usually observed as Prisoners' Week in churches. It was set up to encourage Christians to focus their attention, thoughts and above all prayers on prisoners, ex-prisoners, their families, the victims of crime, prison staff and all those working in this field whether paid or voluntary. (See if you can get a prison visitor or chaplain to come to talk with the group, see also May 21.)

23

THE FOURTH THURSDAY IN NOVEMBER is observed as Thanksgiving Day in the USA (see September 16). If there are some Americans living in your neighbourhood send them greetings on their special day.

24

25 John Flynn, an Australian Presbyterian minister, born in 1880. It was his vision that led to the founding of the Flying Doctor Service, so essential in the remoter parts of Australia.

THE SUNDAY BEFORE ADVENT SUNDAY, which falls at this time of year, is sometimes called 'Stir-up Sunday' partly because it is traditionally the day on which Christmas puddings are made with the whole family having a stir at the mixture. But it also has this name because of the Collect said on this Sunday from the Book of Common Prayer or the Alternative Service Book in the Church of England. This reads: 'Stir up, O Lord, the wills of your faithful people; that richly bearing the fruit of good works, they may by you be richly rewarded; through Jesus Christ our Lord.'

26

27

28 On this day in 1919 American born Viscountess Lady Astor became the first woman MP to sit in the House of Commons (see also February 6 and June 4).

29 Mrs Mary Whitehouse launched the National Viewers' and Listeners' Association in 1965 to tackle 'BBC bad taste and irresponsibility.' She claimed to have half a million people backing her (see November 5).

30 St Andrew's Day. He was the disciple called by Jesus who then brought his brother, Simon, to Jesus. Read about it in John 1. 35–42. The patron saint of Scotland, tradition has it that St Andrew was martyred on an X-shape cross, which has become known as the St Andrew's Cross.
  • How good are we at telling people about Jesus?

DECEMBER
The Latin word for ten, 'decem', gives the root of the name for the last month of our year and the tenth month in the old Roman calendar.

ADVENT – The time in the Christian year when we prepare ourselves for Christmas. The fourth Sunday before Christmas is called Advent Sunday. Advent means 'coming' or, from the Latin '*adventus*', 'arrival'. We look forward to our celebration of the coming of Christ – the first coming – but also remember that Jesus made it very clear he would come again – his second coming (see, for example, Luke 21. 25–33). This difficult doctrine has led to much fear and controversy and to the setting up of countless sects, some of them predicting exact dates for the return of Jesus.
- Ask someone with theological training, and who you know and trust, to help the group to study what the Bible says about the mystery of the second coming.
- Prepare for Christmas, the first coming of Christ. There are some ideas noted on December 19 and 23 (see also December 6).

1   Observed as World Aids Day. Through the World Health Organization, wide publicity is now given to this day to draw attention to this global problem.
- Your group should have the opportunity to decide whether HIV/Aids is an issue they want to discuss together within a Christian setting. Certainly young people need to be knowledgeable about Aids and to work towards overcoming ignorance and prejudice, especially among people of their own age.
- A first step in thinking about the issue could be to obtain some leaflets from health authorities about HIV/Aids. The Methodist Association of Youth Clubs, supported by other Christian youth organizations, has produced an information and discussion leaflet on the subject for young people.

THE SECOND SUNDAY IN ADVENT is observed as Bible Sunday (see January 20, March 16 and October 6 for some stories and ideas to use on this day).

2   At 3.25pm on this date in 1942 something happened in a scientific experiment at the University of Chicago that changed the world. Dr Graham Farmelo of the Science Museum, London, has called it the 'most singular scientific experiment of the century'. A team, led by Italian born Enrico Fermi, who had been working on producing a chain reaction in uranium, succeeded in building a reactor that was to be the prototype for those that have produced plutonium for the atomic bomb and for nuclear power reactors. Their reactor became 'critical' for the first time on December 2, 1942 (see also August 6 and September 7).
- We may say it would have been best if man had never harnessed atomic energy in this way. But we can look on it as a gift from God. The choice is ours as to whether it is used for good or evil. Do some research to find out the good uses of the force first released on this day over fifty years ago.

3

4

5   Mickey Mouse, Pluto, Donald Duck – the creative mind behind these popular cartoon characters, Walt Disney, born in Chicago on this day in 1901.

6   St Nicholas Day. If you were a child living in Belgium, Germany, the Netherlands or several other countries, he would most likely be your favourite saint who you would know, in our anglicized translation, as Santa Claus. On the eve of

December 6 you would be waiting for him to bring you presents. St Nicholas' life is surrounded by legends. In reality he was a fourth century bishop for Myra in Asia Minor. A pagan Roman emperor had him imprisoned and tortured for his faith but, Constantine, a Christian emperor, released him. He is the patron saint of children and sailors.

7   The world famous violinist, Yehudi Menuhin, then aged 14, performed at the Royal Albert Hall in London, 1930.
   • How can great talent be recognized and encouraged? Does our education system make allowances for the exceptionally gifted and help them, whether or not they come from a family that can afford special tuition?

8

9   The first episode of Coronation Street was broadcast on this date in 1960.

   1992, it was announced by Buckingham Palace and the Prime Minister that the Prince of Wales, heir to the throne, and the Princess of Wales were separating.

10   Human Rights Day. 1948 the United Nations proclaimed the Universal Declaration of Human Rights. The Declaration set out what were then agreed to be the basic human rights to which every human should be entitled. These included the right to freedom of conscience, expression and association; freedom from arbitrary arrest and torture or ill-treatment; and the right to a fair and early trial. 'It is essential, if man is not to be compelled to have recourse, as a last resort, to a rebellion against tyranny and oppression, that human rights should be protected by the rule of law.' says the Declaration. In 1990 the UN General Assembly extended these rights to cover children too. Yet, all these years on, in at least half the countries of the world people are locked away for speaking their minds, often after trials that are no more than a sham; and in at least a third of the world's nations, men, women and children are tortured and ill-treated.
   • See November 18 for ways of helping prisoners of conscience.
   • Read the 'manifesto' set out by Jesus at the start of his ministry in Luke 4. 16–21.

11

12   Choosing to show what they believed through good organization and the power of the masses, on this day in 1982, 30,000 women formed a ring round the Greenham Common missile base in Oxfordshire to protest against nuclear weapons.

13

14   Women, (who had to be married and over 30), had their first opportunity to vote in a British general election on this date in 1918 (see also February 6, June 4 and November 28).

15

16

17 Elizabeth Garrett Anderson, the first woman doctor, died 1917 (see June 9).

18 Death penalty abolished in Britain, 1969.
   - It is said that the majority of the general public favour the return of capital punishment. Is there any justification for its use? Does anyone have the right to legally take the life of another person?

Charles Wesley, younger brother of John (see May 24) was born 1707. Is has been written that Methodism 'was born in song' and Charles Wesley certainly contributed to this, writing over 6,500 hymns, many of them of great power and beauty. He had a great gift for using words enabling him to sum up complicated theological ideas in a few words, as he does in these lines from his hymn: 'Let earth and Heaven combine ...':

> Our God contracted to a span,
> Incomprehensibly made man.

   - Have a Charles Wesley hymn sing to celebrate his birthday.

19 *A Christmas Carol*, the famous novel by Charles Dickens, was published 1843. The name of Scrooge, a character in the book, has gone into the English language to represent all things mean and miserly. Not an attitude to be found in your group.

Hopefully, by this time, your group will have made plans for Christmas activities including carol-singing in aid of a charity and, possibly, providing a Christmas meal and some simple entertainment and gifts for local people who might otherwise be on their own over the Christmas holiday. Apart from contacts through your own church, social workers and charities for the elderly and disabled are usually very willing to give the names of people who could be visited in their own homes or invited to a Christmas meal.

20

21 The shortest day of the year – that is, the least daylight!

Pan Am flight 103 was the target of a terrorist bomb and blew up over Lockerbie in Scotland with the loss of 220 lives, 1988.

Converted slave dealer who became a clergyman and hymn writer, John Newton, died 1807. He's best known as the author of the hymn 'Amazing Grace'.

23 Make some time with the group, amid all the preparations for Christmas, to have a quiet look at the Christmas story as it is told in the Bible. Strip it of the layer of sentimentality that may have built up around it for some members of the group and, together, draw out the startling and sometimes shocking truths of the story – an unmarried teenage mother ... a homeless family ... refugees ... that the birth was first announced to simple shepherds on the night shift ... a jealous king killing babies ... and so on (see the early chapters of Matthew and Luke). But chiefly that 'The Word became a human being and, full of grace and truth, lived among us' (John 1. 14).

24 Christmas Eve. One of the best loved carols, 'Silent Night', written by a poor Austrian priest, Joseph Mohr, was first sung in the little church at Oberndorf on Christmas Eve 1818.

25 Christmas Day. Some people will need to be with their families, but others in the group may be able to give some time to the housebound and lonely, as suggested (December 19). It will be very worthwhile and could make your Christmas.

26 The Feast of St Stephen. St Stephen was the first Christian martyr. Read about him in Acts 7. 54–60, noting that Saul, later to become St Paul, was a witness of the death.

27

28 Holy Innocents Day, when the slaughter by King Herod of little boys in an effort to destroy the baby Jesus, is remembered (see Matthew 2. 16–18).

29 Now most of the festivities are over you might like to think back over Christmas and talk about what it has been like. Were the Christmas services meaningful and did the real message of the Festival come through? Did the commercial side of Christmas get to us and tempt us?

30

31 New Year's Eve – reflect on the year that is ending, prepare for the new year to come perhaps by taking part in a traditional Watch Night service either side of midnight. But also, have fun … and a Happy New Year!

Part 3

The Icing on the Cake

Chapter 20

AFTERS

Reporting back and evaluation

It's the end of the meal. Everyone sits back from the serious business of eating and mulls it over.

Evaluation – it's a natural and common-sense reaction to everyday life. Even if only i our own mind, we weigh up what we have done and learn from what has happened whether it was good or not so good.

Equally, evaluation should be a vital and normal part of our youth group programme and our youth work. Earlier chapters in this book emphasize the importance of reflecting on what has happened as a result of the aims that have been set (see especially the Youth Worker Check List in Chapter 8 'Too many cooks? Who's in charge?').

Here we look at some further ways young people can be helped to give feedback on the youth group and its programme.

It is best to introduce any method of evaluation by reminding members of the group of the aims of the group, the programme or the event that is being discussed. Was the aim met?

SOME EVALUATION METHODS
Rounds (see also Chapter 13 'Cooking Methods' A–Z: A Round)
Preferably sitting in a circle or circles, everyone in turn says–

> 'One thing I disliked (about this session/youth group, etc)' …
> 'One thing I liked …'
> 'In three months time I will remember …'

It can help this exercise if there is a rule that no one can comment on what someone else has said until everyone has had their turn. All contributions are counted as of value.

Smiles and frowns
This is, initially, wordless feedback. On a flip chart questions are listed about the group, programme or event and comments are made on these questions by individuals drawing simple faces in circles. These record feelings about the group or activity by showing expressions of, for example, puzzlement or a broad smile or anger or pain. Drawings are shared in pairs before disclosing them to the full group.

Questions on cards
Questions are written on separate cards. Sitting in small groups people take one card in turn and answer the question on it. Others in the group can then add their opinion in open discussion about the question. This method usually helps quiet and shy young people to speak up and express their opinion.

Here are some possible questions:
- What would you miss most if this youth group closed?
- What would you like to change in the way the youth group is organized?
- What do you gain from coming to the youth group?
- How would you describe this youth group to a total stranger?

Link up

Two approaches with a similar outcome. The first method is to provide everyone with strips of paper that can be stuck together to make a paper chain. Sitting in a circle, everyone makes some kind of evaluation (to an agreed question) by writing it on their paper strip. The strips are then linked up to form a paper chain (with the writing on the outside!) and the chain is moved slowly round the circle allowing people to read the comments.

The second method is to substitute luggage-type labels for the strips of paper. Have ready one label per person. Thread them on a piece of string long enough to encircle the group.

Individuals write their comments on the labels which are then moved round the circle on the string for all to read.

For other ideas see Chapter 15 'Cooking Methods' – A–Z, especially:

- brainstorming
- feedback or reporting back
- measuring strength of feeling
- scrap book.

MOST IMPORTANT

In whatever way the evaluation is made, it is the responsibility of the youth workers to see that the views expressed are taken into account in future planning.

Chapter 21

"OUR COMPLIMENTS TO THE CHEF"

– The Craft of Youth Work:
Keep in Training

She's a fully trained nurse you know. (Thinks: I should hope so or I wouldn't let her near me when I'm ill!)

People are often introduced as 'fully trained', although really there is no such person. With every craft, profession, trade or skill there is always something more to learn.

Some people believe anyone can be a youth worker. Of course youth work needs a certain kind of person – loving, caring, sensitive, enthusiastic, imaginative, committed – but however naturally gifted someone is, their talents can still be improved and extended with the right kind of training.

This training is available in several ways but especially for older young people who may be prospective youth workers, and adult youth workers it is on offer through the church's own scheme, *'Spectrum'**.

'Spectrum' is a basic training programme for those involved in Christian youth work. It aims to bring together youth workers with the 13+ age group to develop their skills and increase their confidence. Experienced tutors assist with the course and a certificate is available on satisfactory completion.

The Spectrum Management Group which manages *'Spectrum'* is a co-operative venture of the Christian Churches, organizations and agencies involved in youth work in Britain and Ireland.

Spectrum is a partnership between the following Churches, organizations and agencies:

The Baptist Union of Great Britain
The Boys' Brigade
CAFOD (Catholic Relief and Development Agency)
Church Mission Society
Christian Aid
Council of Churches Britain and Ireland
Council for Sunday Schools and Christian Education in Wales
The Church of England
Episcopal Church of Scotland
Frontier Youth Trust
The Church of Ireland
The Methodist Church
Independent Methodist Connexion of Churches
The Methodist Church in Ireland
National Christian Education Council
New Testament Church of God
Platform for Young Women – Girls' Friendly Society

Presbyterian Church of Wales
Religious Society of Friends (Quakers)
The Roman Catholic Church – England and Wales
The Roman Catholic Church – Ireland
The Salvation Army
The United Reformed Church
The Church in Wales
Youth Action Scotland
Youth for Christ

The 'Spectrum' material is also being used outside church circles by trainers in other voluntary youth organizations and by local education authorities.

The material is published by the National Christian Education Council (NCEC), 1020 Bristol Road, Selly Oak, Burmingham B29 6LB, from whom more details and an order form can be obtained.

The Course
Spectrum is a pack of 12 sessions of training material.

It includes all the material for each session, with extensive notes offering guidance to tutors and providing much additional material including worship ideas; warm-up games; work sheets; role plays, etc.

The sessions are:
- **Youth Work and Youth Workers 1**
  Understanding basic principles and practice of youth work and the worker's contribution – including aims and motivation for youth work and the skills and qualities of a youth worker.

- **Youth Work and Youth Workers 2**
  Understanding the 'values' underpinning work with young people and how different values can affect the style and method of working. Understanding the term 'empowerment of young people'.

- **Development in adolescence**
  Understanding key areas of development which affect the lives of young people during adolescence. Identifying the workers role in this area.

- **Group Work** (Day Workshop)
  Developing group work skills and gaining an understanding of how groups are formed and how people behave with them.

- **Communications**
  Recognizing the process and methods of effective communication both within peer groups and between workers, young people and the local church.

- **Sprituality and Faith Development**
  Developing an awareness of one's own and young people's spirirtuality and faith development.

- **Exploring Leadership**
  Developing an understanding of the concepts and practice of leadership in a wide range of youth work situations. Identifying how Christian principles relate to leadership styles.

- **Pastoral Care**
  Developing appropriate relationships with young people as individuals and in groups – supporting, listening, understanding.

- **Working Relationships**
  Identifying and developing working relationships in the context of youth work.

- **Church, Young People, and the Community**
  Exploring the meaning of community. Considering the Church as a model of community. Understanding how to support and strengthen the links/relationships between the youth group, the church and other community groupings.

- **Management**
  Understanding the areas concerned with management – procedures, preparation and planning, good practice and evaluation.

- **Support for Youth Workers**
  Identifying sources of support. Exploring the benefits of and beginning to develop one's own support networks.

A *'Spectrum'* group may be in operation near you. Contact your own Church's youth officer, your denominational youth department or the Youth Desk at the Council of Churches for Britain and Ireland, Inter-Church House, 35–41 Lower Marsh, London, SE1 7RL or the National Christian Education Council, 1020, Bristol Road, Selly Oak, Birmingham B29 6LB.

Other Youth Work Training Opportunities
One-off courses, training days or weekends through your own church or denomination or:
- The annual Brainstormers weekend
- British Youth for Christ
- Frontier Youth Trust/Scripture Union
- The annual Greenbelt Festival
- Local Education Authority Youth Office
- National Christian Education Council
- Spring Harvest weeks
- Uniformed organizations – Covenanters; Boys' Brigade; Church Lads' Brigade; Girls' Brigade; Girls' Friendly Society (GFS); Guides; Scouts.
- Youth Clubs UK
- YMCA
- YWCA
(see Chapter 22 – 'Store Cupboard' for addresses)

The first edition of 'Spectrum' was published in 1989. A completely revised edition was published in 1996.

Chapter 22

STORE CUPBOARD

Useful addresses

It is not our intention to supply a comprehensive/exhaustive list; we are merely giving you an insight into the wide range of organizations/groups/resources which are available to you.

Contact addresses for Churches, organizations and agencies who are part of the 'Spectrum' partnership (see chapter 21).

The Baptist Union
of Great Britain
PO Box 44,
Baptist House,
129 Broadway,
Didcot,
Oxon OX11 8RT.
Tel. 01235 512077.

Boys' Brigade
Felden Lodge,
Felden,
Hemel Hempstead
HP3 0BL.
Tel. 01442 231681.

Catholic Fund for
Overseas Development
(CAFOD)
Romero Close,
Stockwell Road,
London SW9 9TY.
Tel. 0171 733 7900.

Catholic Youth Services:
(England and Wales)
39 Fitzjohn's Ave.,
London NW3 5JT.
Tel. 0171 435 3596.
(Ireland)
Down & Connor
Youth Council,
68, Berry Street,
Belfast BT1 1FJ.
Tel. 01232 232432.

The Church of England
Church House,
Great Smith Street,
London SW1P 3NZ.
Tel. 0171 222 9011.

Church Mission Society
Partnership House,
157 Waterloo Road,
London SE1 8UU.
Tel. 0171 928 8681.

Christian Aid
PO Box 100,
London SE1 7RT.
Tel. 0171 620 4444.

Council of Churches
for Britain & Ireland
Inter Church House,
35–41 Lower Marsh,
London SE1 7RL.
Tel. 0171 620 4444.

Council for Sunday
Schools and Christian
Education in Wales
Cyngor Ysgolion Sul Ac
Addysg Gristnogol Cymru,
School of Education
U.C.B.,
Deiniol Road,
Bangor,
Gwynedd LL57 2UW.
Tel. 01248 382947.

Frontier Youth Trust
70–74 City Road,
London EC1Y 2BJ.
Tel. 0171 336 7744.

Independent Methodist
Connexion of Churches
Resource Centre,
Fleet Street,
Pemberton,
Wigan,
Lancs. WN5 0DS.
Tel. 01942 223526.

The Church of Ireland
217 Holywood Road
Belfast BT4 2DH.
Tel. 01232 472744.

The Methodist Church
*(England, Scotland
and Wales)*
2 Chester House,
Pages Lane,
Muswell Hill,
London N10 1PR.
Tel. 0181 444 9845.
(Ireland)
Aldersgate House,
University Road,
Belfast BT7 1NA.
Tel. 01232 327191.

National Christian
Education Council
1020 Bristol Road,
Selly Oak,
Birmingham B29 6LB.
Tel. 0121 472 4242.

The New Testament
Church of God
Main House,
Overstone Road,
Overstone,
Northampton NN6 OAD.
Tel. 01604 492671.

Platform for
Young Women
Girls Friendly Society
Townsend House,
126, Queens Gate,
London SW7 5LQ.
Tel. 0171 589 9628.

Presbyterian Church
of Wales – Y Coleg
Bala,
Gwynedd LL23 7RY.
Tel. 01678 520565.

Religious Society of
Friends (Quakers)
Friends House,
173–177 Euston Road,
London NW1 2BJ.
Tel. 0171 387 3601.

The Salvation Army
Youth Department,
William Booth Training
College,
Denmark Hill,
London SE5 8BQ.
Tel. 0171 738 5533.

Scottish Episcopal Church
21 Grosvenor Crescent,
Edinburgh EH12 5EE,
Tel. 0131 225 6357.

United Reformed Church
86 Tavistock Place,
London WC1H 9RT.
Tel. 0171 916 2020.

The Church in Wales
Yr Eglwys Yng Nghymru,
Woodland Place,
Penarth,
South Glamorgan
CF64 2EX.
Tel. 01222 705278.

Youth Action Scotland
Kirk Street
Dunblane
Scotland
SK15 0AG
Tel. 01786 823588.

Youth for Christ
Cleobury Place,
Cleobury Mortimer,
Kidderminster,
Worcs. DY14 8JG.
Tel. 01299 270260.

**Other Useful
Organizations**
*We have provided the
head office telephone
number as it is impossible
to list all area contact
numbers.)*

Activities/ Programmes/
Resources/ Training/
Support:

National Youth Agency
0116 285 6789
Youth Clubs UK
0171 353 2366
Youth Clubs Scotland
0131 554 2561
NABC – Clubs for Young
People
0171 793 0787
0131 555 1729 (Scotland)

Methodist Association
of Youth Clubs
0181 444 9845
United Society for the
Propagation of the Gospel
0171 928 8681
Christian Institute of
Training and Development
0121 472 4242
Youth Hostel Association
01727 855215
Ocean Youth Club
01705 528421
(Sea-going activities)
National Federation of
Young Farmers Clubs
01203 696544
Sports Council:
England – 0171 388 1277
Wales   – 01222 397571
Scotland– 0131 317 7200

**Locally based Church
Youth Officers**
Several denominations have
full-time Youth Officers
working in dioceses, dis-
tricts and regions. They are
there to help you with
training, information and
resources. If you do not
know your church's local
youth officer contact your
denominational headquar-
ters above.

ACKNOWLEDGEMENTS

We are grateful to the authors and publishers who have given permission for extracts and quotations from their works to appear in this book, and apologise to any copyright holder whom we have been unable to trace.

Page:

vi — A Celtic blessing by John Hearn Stubbs (David Higham Associates)

3–4 — Statement of Purpose for the English Youth Service (DfEE – The Department for Education and Employment)

5 — Extract from the Service for the Baptism of Infants, The Methodist Service Book (Methodist Publishing `House 1975)

6 — Extract from 'Bread for Tomorrow – Praying with the World's Poor.' Edited by Janet Morley (SPCK/Christian Aid 1992). Copyright sought.

9 — Extract from 'Safe from Harm' researched and written by David R Smith. (The Home Office 1993. Crown Copyright. Reproduced with the permission of the Controller of HMSO)

10 — Prayer published by the Quaker Peace Service

16 — Celtic Poem. Source unknown

21 — 'A leader is best…' Chinese saying – source unknown

22 — Youth workers' Checklist. Adapted from 'Face to Face with Young People' (Methodist Church Division of Education and Youth 1984)

24 — 'The Parable of the Eagle' from 'Aggrey of Africa' by Edwin W Smith (SCM Press 1929)

26 — 'Take time to think…' from 'At All Times and in All Places' by Myra Blyth and Tony Jasper (Marshall Pickering 1986)

32 — 'Keeping Discussion Going' from 'Talking about Talking' (Youth Clubs UK 1986)

51–67 — Chapter 15– Starters. Acknowledgements printed on page 53

69 — 'Accept Surprises…' from 'A Thousand Reasons for Living' by Dom Helder Camara (Darton Longman and Todd 1987)

86 — 'The Parable of the Chopsticks' from 'Words for Worship' by Christopher Campling and Michael Davis (Edward Arnold 1969)

98 — 'Worship is…' Extract from Archbishop William Temple 'Readings in St John's Gospel' (MacMillan)

105–106
'In search of a roundtable' by Chuck Larthrop (Appalachian Documentation, Washington, DC)

109
'Guidelines for sleeping on church premises' prepared by the Methodist Church Property Division 1992

114
Sample Health/Emergency Form (Quaker Home Service – Children and Young People's Section 1996)

130
Parable and Truth – A Hebrew Story. Source unknown

140
'Time's Paces' poem on a clock in Chester Cathedral

140–190
Chapter 19 Seasoning. The following publications have been invaluable in the preparation of this chapter:

'A Pocket Calendar of Saints and People to Remember' by Brother Kenneth (Mowbray 1981)
'Mary Batchelor's Everyday Book' (Lion 1984)
'A Book of Special Days' compiled by Jan Reynolds (Lion 1987)
'Seasons of the Spirit' Readings selected by George Every, Richard Harries and Kallistos Ware (SPCK/Triangle 1990)
'Dates and Meanings of Religious and Other Festivals' by John Walshe (Foulsham 1989)
'The Perpetual Almanack of Folklore' by Charles Kightly (Thames and Hudson 1987)
'We always put a candle in the window' by Marjorie Freeman (National Society/Church House Publishing 1989)
'Harrap's Book of British Dates' by Rodney Castleden (Harrap 1991)
'Chronicle of the 20th Century' (Longmans 1989)
'Chambers Biographical Dictionary' 1990

194–195
Chapter 21. Information concerning 'Spectrum' (revised edition 1996) supplied by the publisher, The National Christian Education Council

200
Final Blessing – source unknown

TUCK IN!

May the road rise to meet you
May the wind be always at your back,
May the sun shine warm upon your face,
the rains fall softly upon your fields,
And, until we meet again, may God hold you in the palm of his hand

Traditional Irish Blessing